OUT OF OUR MINDS

OUT OF OUR MINDS

The Power of Being Creative

THIRD EDITION

SIR KEN ROBINSON, PHD

CAPSTONE

This edition first published 2017
© 2017 Sir Ken Robinson
First edition published 2001, revised and updated edition published 2011
all by John Wiley & Sons, Ltd

Registered office
John Wiley & Sons Ltd, The Atrium, Southern Gate, Chichester, West Sussex, PO19
8SQ, United Kingdom

For details of our global editorial offices, for customer services and for information
about how to apply for permission to reuse the copyright material in this book please
see our website at www.wiley.com.

Wiley publishes in a variety of print and electronic formats and by print-on-demand.
Some material included with standard print versions of this book may not be
included in e-books or in print-on-demand. If this book refers to media such as a
CD or DVD that is not included in the version you purchased, you may download
this material at http://booksupport.wiley.com. For more information about Wiley
products, visit www.wiley.com.

Designations used by companies to distinguish their products are often claimed as
trademarks. All brand names and product names used in this book are trade names,
service marks, trademarks or registered trademarks of their respective owners. The
publisher is not associated with any product or vendor mentioned in this book.

Library of Congress Cataloging-in-Publication Data is available

A catalogue record for this book is available from the British Library.

ISBN 978-0-857-08741-6 (hbk) ISBN 978-0-857-08755-3 (ebk)
ISBN 978-0-857-08744-7 (ebk)

Cover Design: Wiley
Cover Image: © Wiktoria Matynia / Shutterstock

Set in 11/14 Plantin Std Regular by Aptara Inc., New Delhi, India
Printed in the United States of America

10 9 8 7 6 5 4 3 2

For Terry, who makes everything possible.

IN PRAISE OF OUT OF OUR MINDS (1ST EDITION)

"Out of Our Minds *explains why being creative in today's world is a vital necessity. This is a book not to be missed. Read and rejoice.*"
Ken Blanchard, co-author, *The One Minute Manager* and *The Secret*

"*If ever there was a time when creativity was necessary for the survival and growth of any organization, it is now. This book, more than any other I know, provides important insights on how leaders can evoke and sustain those creative juices.*"
Warren Bennis, Distinguished Professor of Business, University of Southern California; Thomas S. Murphy Distinguished Research Fellow, Harvard Business School, best-selling author, *Geeks and Geezers*

"*This really is a remarkable book. It does for human resources what Rachel Carson's* Silent Spring *did for the environment. It makes you wonder why we insist on sustaining an education that is narrow, partial, entirely inappropriate for the 21st century and deeply destructive of human potential when human beings have so much latent creative ability to offer. A brilliant analysis.*"
Wally Olins, Founder, Wolff-Olins

"*The best analysis I've seen of the disjunction between the kinds of intelligence that we have traditionally honored in schools and the kinds of creativity that we need today in our organizations and our society. I learned a lot.*"
Howard Gardner, A. Hobbs Professor in Cognition and Education, Harvard Graduate School of Education; bestselling author, *Frames of Mind*

"*Books about creativity are not always creative. Ken Robinson's is a welcome exception: a set of wide-ranging, provocative and useful reflections for anyone concerned with bringing new ideas to fruition in business, academia, or the arts.*"
Mihaly Csikszentmihalyi, C.S. and D.J. Davidson, Professor of Psychology, Claremont Graduate University; Director, Quality of Life Research Center; best-selling author, *FLOW*

"If you would like to start to unlock the inherent creativity that exists in every human being (including you), then start ... by reading this book!"

Simon Woodroffe, Founder Yo Sushi

"Ken Robinson's is an original and creative mind. I can think of no better spokesperson on creativity. His views are as much directed to learning institutions as they are to industry. Out of Our Minds *is a genuine challenge to complacency."*

Ruth Spellman, Chief Executive,
Investors in People, UK

"I definitely want to meet Ken Robinson. I have a great affinity with the ideas he proposes. His writing is witty, sometimes caustic, and he supports his arguments with evidence and research. Robinson points us towards a future where young people must be enabled to unleash their creativity and deal with change through a different and better education system. As someone who gains a living from management development, this is all too evident to me. Robinson makes powerful arguments for change. I recommend that you read this book, take part in the debate and become part of the paradigm."

People Management

"For a book called Out of Our Minds, *Ken Robinson's illuminated assault on the current state of academic education is actually a very sane read. The current obsession is not only failing businesses but also our children. Robinson is right on the money."*

Arts Professional

*"*Out of Our Minds *has a powerful agenda – how to solve the appalling lack of skills in a world demanding ever more brainpower. This is a thoughtful book that does not dodge such cruel paradoxes of our time as the fact that standards of living get higher while the quality of life declines: a truly mind-opening analysis of why we don't get the best out of people in a time of punishing change."*

Director Magazine

"This is a deeply significant work in this area – I am really impressed with the historical perspectives and breadth of insights drawn from the arts, sciences, psychology and many other fields. It is an immensely powerful statement of the current educational situation and highlights very powerfully the need for transformed thinking from top to bottom."

Creative-Management

"Out of Our Minds *calls for radical changes in the way we think about intelligence, education and human resources, in order to meet the extraordinary challenges of living and working in the 21st century. This book will make compulsive reading for anyone who shares an interest in the future of creativity, education and training.*"

Center for Creative Communities

"*Sometimes a writer has an uncanny knack of sharply focusing something, which up until then you had not seen in all its simplicity and brilliance. This book does that but at the next moment it makes connections never before imagined ... Even the most obstinately prosaic and safe thinkers will be tempted out of their box by Ken Robinson's ideas, theories and speculations. What's more, he writes as he speaks, in a way that, magnetically and compulsively, is simply irresistible.*"

Professor Tim Brighouse

"*There are certain books that manage to be authoritative, entertaining and thought-provoking and are also well written and richly exemplified. Few authors are able to fashion this attractive mixture. Alvin Toffler and Charles Handy can craft it. I add Ken Robinson's absorbing account of creativity to my personal list of gems. Creativity is one of those topics that excites some and enrages others. For Ken Robinson it is a universal talent that all people have, often without realizing it. Society in general and education in particular, can squash the imagination and rock self-confidence. I was sorry to reach the end of the text, as it had maintained its momentum throughout. The reading may finish, but the thinking goes on, just as you would expect from a book on this intriguing subject.*"

Professor Ted Wragg

CONTENTS

ACKNOWLEDGMENTS

THIS IS THE THIRD EDITION of *Out of Our Minds*. I'm especially grateful to Annie Knight at Wiley for suggesting a new edition. The plain fact is that without her gentle encouragement I would probably not have thought of doing it – and I'm very pleased I did. I'm grateful too to the whole production team at Wiley, and particularly to Tessa Allen, for their care and expertise in bringing this edition to the world in such a beautiful form. Thanks are due as always to my literary agent, Peter Miller, the Literary Lion, for his passionate and constant support of my work. I must also thank Brendan Barns, founder of the London Business Forum and my first speaking agent, who was responsible, with my wife and partner Terry, for making me write the original edition of this book against an improbable deadline and with a steely determination to make sure I did. At this distance, I can say I'm grateful to them both for holding their ground while I ground away at it over the long, hot summer of 2000. I wasn't so grateful at the time! My deepest thanks are due as always to Terry, who I celebrate at the front of the book and in everything we do together. She's an inspiration to me and to so many others.

ABOUT THE AUTHOR

SIR KEN ROBINSON, PHD is an internationally recognized leader in the development of creativity, innovation and human resources. He works with governments, education systems, international agencies, global corporations and some of the world's leading cultural organizations to unlock the creative energy of people and organizations. He has led national and international projects on creative and cultural education in the UK, Europe, Asia and the United States. The embodiment of the prestigious TED Conference and its commitment to spreading new ideas, his 2006 talk, "Do Schools Kill Creativity?" has been viewed online over 46 million times and seen by an estimated 400 million people in 160 countries.

For 12 years he was professor of arts education at the University of Warwick in the UK and is now professor emeritus. He led a national commission on creativity, education and the economy for the UK Government. *All Our Futures: Creativity, Culture and Education* (The Robinson Report) was published to wide acclaim. He was the central figure in developing a strategy for creative and economic development as part of the Peace Process in Northern Ireland, working with the ministers for training, education enterprise and culture. He was one of four international advisors to the Singapore Government for its strategy to become the creative hub of Southeast Asia, and the guiding force in Oklahoma's statewide strategy to cultivate creativity and innovation in culture, commerce and education.

He was named as one of *Time/Fortune/*CNN's "Principal Voices". He was acclaimed by *Fast Company* magazine as one of "the world's elite thinkers on creativity and innovation" and was ranked in the Thinkers50 list of the world's top business thinkers. He has received honorary degrees from ten universities in Europe and the United States. He has been honored with the Athena Award of the Rhode Island School of Design; the Peabody Medal for contributions to the arts and culture in the United States; the Benjamin Franklin Medal of the Royal Society of Arts for outstanding contributions to cultural relations between the United Kingdom and the United States; the Gordon Parks Award for Outstanding Contributions to Creativity and Education; City of New York YMCA, Arts and Letters Award for Outstanding Leadership; the LEGO Prize for Extraordinary Contributions on Behalf of Children and Young People; and the Sir Arthur C. Clarke Foundation Imagination Award. He speaks to audiences throughout the world on the creative challenges facing business and education in the new global economies. In 2003, he received a knighthood from Queen Elizabeth II for his services to the arts.

Sir Ken was born in Liverpool, UK. He is married to Thérèse (Lady) Robinson. They have two children, James and Kate.

Also by Sir Ken Robinson: *The Element: How Finding Your Passion Changes Everything* (Penguin/Viking, 2009) is a *New York Times* bestseller. It has been translated into 23 languages and has sold over a million copies worldwide. *Finding Your Element: How to Discover Your Talents and Passions and Transform Your Life* (Viking, 2013) is also a *New York Times* bestseller. *Creative Schools: The Grassroots Revolution That's Transforming Education* (Viking, 2015) tackles the critical issue of how to transform the world's troubled educational systems and is now available in 15 languages.

PREFACE TO THE THIRD EDITION

I WROTE THE ORIGINAL EDITION of *Out of Our Minds* during 2000. A second, fully revised edition was published in 2011. What you have in your hands now is the third edition, which has been thoroughly revised again. Why another new edition?

The main reason I wrote this book in the first place is that the pace and nature of change demand that we think differently about ourselves, about education and about how we run our businesses and institutions. On almost every front, the pace of change has become ever more frantic and the issues at the heart of this book have become more pressing. This new edition is my own attempt to keep pace with these changes.

The second reason is that the arguments I put forward here have become more – not less – urgent, and this edition presents them more sharply. The more complex the world becomes, the more creative we need to be to meet its challenges. Yet many people wonder if they have any creative abilities at all. *Out of Our Minds* is about why creativity matters so much, why people think they are not creative, how we arrived at this point and what we can do about it. My aims in this book are to help individuals to understand the depth of their creative abilities and why they might have doubted them; to encourage organizations to believe in their powers of innovation and to create the conditions where they will flourish; and to promote a creative revolution in education.

I said in the original introduction that I had called the book *Out of Our Minds* for three reasons. I still have three reasons and here they are. First, human intelligence is profoundly and uniquely creative. We live in a world that's shaped by the ideas, beliefs and values of human imagination and culture. The human world is created out of our minds as much as from the natural environment. Thinking and feeling are not simply about seeing the world as it is, but having ideas about it, and interpreting experience to give it meaning. Different communities live differently according to the ideas they have and the meanings they experience. In a literal sense, we create the worlds we live in. We can also re-create them. The great revolutions in human history have often been brought about by new ideas: by new ways of seeing that have shattered old certainties.

Second, realizing our creative potential is partly a question of finding our medium, of being *in our element*. Education should help us to achieve this, but too often it does not and too many people are instead displaced from their own true talents. They are out of their element and out of their minds in that sense.

Finally, there is a kind of mania driving the present direction of educational policy. In place of a reasoned debate about the strategies that are needed to face these extraordinary changes, there is a tired mantra about raising traditional academic standards. These standards were designed for other times and for other purposes – as I will explain. We will not succeed in navigating the complex environment of the future by peering relentlessly into a rear-view mirror. Today, as when the first edition appeared in 2001, I'm convinced that to stay on this course we would be out of our minds in a more literal sense.

Ken Robinson
Los Angeles, May 2017

OUT OF OUR MINDS

"When people say to me that they are not creative, I assume that they haven't yet learnt what is involved."

CREATING THE FUTURE

HOW CREATIVE ARE YOU? How creative are the people you work with? How about your friends? Next time you are at a social event, ask them. You may be surprised by what they say. I've worked with people and organizations all over the world. Everywhere I go, I find the same paradox. Most children think they're creative; many adults think they are not. This is a bigger issue than it may seem.

We are living in a world that is changing faster than ever and face challenges that are unprecedented. How the complexities of the present will play out in future is all but unknowable. Cultural change is never linear and rarely predictable. If it were, the legions of pundits and forecasters would be out of a job. It was probably with this in mind that the economist J.K. Galbraith said, "The primary purpose of economic forecasting is to make astrology look respectable." As the world spins faster, organizations everywhere need people who can think creatively, communicate and work in teams: people who are flexible and quick to adapt. Too often they can't find them. Why not? My aim in this book is to answer three questions.

> **Why is it essential to promote creativity?** Business leaders, politicians and educators emphasize the vital importance of promoting creativity and innovation. Why does this matter so much?
>
> **What is the problem?** Why do people need help to be creative? Young children are buzzing with ideas. What happens as we grow up to make us think we are not creative?
>
> **What is involved?** What is creativity? Is everyone creative or just a select few? Can creativity be developed and, if so, how?

Everyone occasionally has new ideas, but how can creativity be encouraged as a regular part of everyday life? If you are running a company or an organization or a school, how do you make innovation systematic? How do you lead a culture of innovation?

RETHINKING CREATIVITY

To answer these questions, it's important to be clear about what creativity is and how it works. There are three related ideas, which I'll elaborate as we go on. They are *imagination*, which is the process of bringing to mind things that are not present to our senses; *creativity*, which is the process of developing original ideas that have value; and *innovation*, which is the process of putting new ideas into practice. There are various misconceptions about creativity in particular.

Special people?

One misconception is that only special people are creative. This idea is reinforced by histories of creative icons like

Martha Graham, Pablo Picasso, Albert Einstein, Thomas Edison, Virginia Wolf, Maya Angelou and Steve Jobs. Companies seem to think this too. They often divide the workforce into two groups: the "creatives" and the "suits." You can normally tell who the creatives are because they don't wear suits. They wear jeans and they come in late because they've been struggling with an idea. I don't mean that the creatives are not creative. They can be highly creative, but so can anybody if the conditions are right – including the suits. Everyone has creative capacities. The challenge is to develop them. A culture of innovation has to involve everybody, not just a select few.

"My starting point is that everyone has huge creative capacities as a natural result of being a human being. The challenge is to develop them. A culture of creativity has to involve everybody, not just a select few."

Special activities?

A second misconception is that creativity is about special activities, like the arts, or advertising, design or marketing. All of these can be creative, but so can anything, including science, mathematics, teaching, medicine, running a sports team or a restaurant. Some schools have "creative arts" departments. I am an uncompromising advocate of better provision for the arts in schools but creativity is not confined to the arts. Other disciplines, including science and mathematics, can be just as creative. Creativity is possible in any activity that engages our intelligence.

Companies are creative in different areas. Apple is famously good at creating new products. Wal-Mart's creative strength is in systems, such as supply chain management and pricing. Starbucks did not invent coffee; it created a particular service culture around coffee. Actually, it did invent the $8 cup of coffee, which was a breakthrough, I thought. A culture of innovation should embrace all areas of the organization.

Letting go?

Creativity is sometimes associated with free expression, which is why some people worry about encouraging too much creativity in schools. They think of children running wild and knocking the furniture over rather than getting on with serious work. Being creative often does involve playing with ideas and having fun and enjoyment. It is also about working hard on ideas and projects, crafting them into their best forms and making critical judgments along the way about which ones work best and why. In every discipline, creativity draws on skill, knowledge and control. It's not only about letting go, it's about holding on.

Learning to be creative

It is often thought that people are either born creative or not, just as they may have blue or brown eyes, and there's not much anyone can do about it. The fact is, there is a lot you can do to help yourself, and other people, become more creative. If someone tells you they can't read or write, you don't assume they are not capable of it, just that they haven't learnt how. It is the same with creativity. When people say they are not creative, I just assume they have not learnt how. I also assume that they can. Why are these issues important anyway?

THREE THEMES

There are three core themes in this book.

We are living in times of revolutionary change
No matter where you are or what you do, if you live on earth you are caught up in a global revolution. I mean this literally not metaphorically. There are forces at work now for which there are no precedents. Human affairs have

always been turbulent. What is distinctive now is the rate and scale of change. Two of the driving forces are technological innovation and population growth. Together they're transforming how we live and work, changing the nature of politics and culture and putting perilous strains on the earth's natural resources. The outcomes are unpredictable. What is certain is that we and our children are confronting challenges that are unique in human history.[1]

We have to think differently about our talents and abilities

Given the challenges we face, the most profound shift has to be in how we think about our abilities and those of our children. In my experience, many people have little idea of their real talents. Too many think they have no special talents at all. My premise is that we are all born with immense talents but that too few people discover or develop them. Ironically, one of the reasons is education. The waste of talent is not deliberate. Most educators have a deep commitment to helping students do their best. Politicians make impassioned speeches about making the most of every student's abilities. The waste of talent may not be deliberate but it is systemic. Dominant approaches to education and training are preoccupied with certain types of ability that systematically overlook the talents and stifle the creative confidence of untold numbers of people.

We have to run schools, companies and communities differently

Leading a culture of innovation has radical implications for how institutions are organized, whether they are schools or corporations, and for styles of leadership. Business and public sector leaders commonly share three perspectives. They know that one of the biggest challenges they face is the increasing complexity of the global environment, which they expect to accelerate in the coming years. They are concerned that their organizations are not equipped to cope with this complexity. They agree that the most important leadership skill for dealing with this growing complexity is creativity. Many organizations put on occasional training days to encourage their staff to think creatively; but, like the rituals of rain dancing, I believe they may misunderstand the problems they're trying to solve. The problems they face are immediate and there are some immediate things they can do to tackle them, but the long-term solutions lie upstream in the education system.

I've worked with national education systems, with school districts, principals, teachers and students from kindergarten to university and beyond, including community colleges and adult education associations. I've directed national research projects, taught in universities and trained teachers. I also work now with every type of business, including Fortune 500 companies, major banks and insurance houses, design companies, media corporations, information technology organizations, and with retail, manufacturing, engineering and service companies. I've worked with cultural centers in the arts and the sciences; with museums, orchestras, and with dance and theater companies and community arts organizations. My work has taken me to Europe, North America, South America, the Middle East and Asia. I know first hand that the education, business and the cultural sectors face many common challenges. Some are compounded by the fact that they have so little contact with each other.

When I talk with business leaders, they complain that education isn't producing the people they urgently need: people who are literate, numerate, who can analyze information and ideas; who can generate new ideas and implement them; who can communicate clearly and work well with other people. They want education to provide such people and complain that it does not. When I work with educators they complain that the culture of standardization and testing, which politicians usually impose in the interests of the economy, is stifling the creativity of teachers and students alike. They want to provide a more balanced and dynamic form of education that makes proper use of their own creative energies. Too often they feel they can't do any of this because of political pressures of conformity and the disaffection of students who suffer under the same malaise. Meanwhile, parents lie awake at night worrying about the quality of their children's education. They assume that education will help their children to find work and become economically independent. They also want education to help young people to identify their unique talents and to lead a life that has meaning and purpose. This is what young people want for themselves. The best future for all of us lies in deeper forms of understanding and collaboration between all of these groups.

ONLY CONNECT: EDUCATION, BUSINESS AND CULTURE

Education is not always a good word to use socially. If I'm at a party and tell someone I work in education, I can see the blood drain from their face. "Why me?" they're thinking, "Trapped with an educator on my one night out all week." If I ask them about their education, or about their children's schooling, they pin me to the wall. Education is one of those topics that run deep with people, like religion, politics and money. It should. The quality of education affects all of us: it is vital to our own fulfillment, to our children's futures and to long-term global development. It stamps us with an impression of ourselves that is hard to remove.

Some of the most eminent people did not do well at school. No matter how successful they've become, they often worry that they are not as clever as they seem. They include teachers, university professors, vice-chancellors, business people, musicians, writers, artists, architects and many others. Many succeeded despite their education not because of it.

Of course, many people loved their time in education and have done well by it. What of all those who did not? Given the changes that are now engulfing us, governments everywhere are pouring vast resources into education reform. This is good, but it is not good enough. The challenge is not to reform education but transform it.

As the technological and economic revolution gathers pace, education systems throughout the world are being reformed. Most countries have a dual strategy. The first is to increase access to education, and especially higher education. The demand for educational qualifications grows annually; education and training are now among the world's largest businesses. The second strategy is to raise standards. Educational standards should be high and it is obviously a good idea to raise them. There is not much point in lowering them. But standards of what? Educating more people and to a much higher standard is vital, but they have to be educated differently.

Education is not an impartial process of developing people's natural abilities and it never was. Systems of mass education are built on two pillars. The first is economic: they have been shaped by specific assumptions about labor markets, some of which are now out of date. The second is intellectual: they have been shaped by particular ideas about academic intelligence, which often disregard other abilities that are just as important, especially for creativity and innovation.

Before the middle of the nineteenth century, relatively few people had a formal education. Being educated was mainly for the privileged few who could afford it. Mass systems of education were developed primarily to meet the needs of the Industrial Revolution and they mirror the principles of industrial production: linearity, conformity and standardization.

In almost all of them there is the same hierarchy of disciplines, which shows itself in the time given to them; whether they are compulsory or optional; whether they are in the mainstream curriculum or after school; whether they are included in standardized tests and how much they feature in political polemics about raising standards. At the top of the hierarchy are mathematics, languages and sciences; next come the humanities – history, geography and social studies – and physical education; at the bottom are the arts. There is another hierarchy within the arts: art and music usually have higher status than theater and dance. There is hardly a school system in the world that teaches dance every day as a compulsory discipline in the way that mathematics is taught. This hierarchy is not accidental: it is based on assumptions about supply and demand in the marketplace and about intelligence and academic ability in particular.

Many government reforms in education have been doubling down on this model. They have reinforced the hierarchy, imposed a culture of standardized testing and limited the discretion of educators in deciding what and how to teach. This is not a party political strategy. Politicians are curiously united in this respect. They argue over the funding and organization of education, over access and selection and about the best ways to improve standards. It is rare to hear politicians of any party raise questions about the absolute importance of academic standards or the need for standardized tests to secure them. Ironically, they promote these policies in the interests of the economy.[2] I say ironically because these reforms are stifling the very skills and qualities that are essential to meet the challenges we face: creativity, cultural understanding, communication, collaboration and problem solving.

All organizations are competing in a world in which the ability to innovate and adapt to change is not a luxury: it is a necessity.[3] The consequences of being inflexible to change can be severe. Organizations that stand still may be swept aside: corporate history is littered with the wreckage of companies, and whole industries, that were resistant to change. They became stuck in old habits and missed the wave of change that carried more innovative companies forward. It's not only companies that risk decline.

Few would dispute that in the eighteenth and nineteenth centuries, Europe, and especially Great Britain, dominated the world culturally, politically and economically. Britain was the crucible of the Industrial Revolution and its military forces secured the colonies as surely as the English language invaded their cultures. When Queen Victoria ascended to the throne in 1837, she presided over the largest empire in history: the empire on which the sun never set. If you had gone to her court in 1870 and suggested that this empire would be over within a generation, you would have been laughed out of the building. But it was true. By the end of World War I in 1918, the empire was fatally wounded and, by the time I was born in 1950, it was a memory. Culturally, politically and economically, the twentieth century was dominated by the United States, as surely as Europe had dominated the nineteenth. Whether it will dominate the twenty-first century remains to be seen. As award-winning US scientist Jared Diamond has shown, empires tend to collapse rather than fade away.[4] Think of the Soviet Union and its rapid dissolution in the 1980s and 1990s.

All organizations are perishable. They are created by people and they need to be constantly revitalized if they are to survive. When organizations fail, the jobs and communities that depend on them falter too. Among the worst affected these days are young people. Youth unemployment rates are more sensitive than adult rates to economic turbulence, and the recovery of the job market for young men and women tends to lag behind that of adults. For millions of young people, the future seems bleak and despairing. They have no work and see no prospect of it. The International Labor Organization consistently argues that creating jobs for the millions of young women and men entering the labor market every year is a critical component in the path towards wealthier economies. It is not only the quantity but also the quality of jobs that matters. In a world of headlong change, where lifelong employment in the same job is a thing of the past, creativity and innovation are not luxuries, they are essential for personal security and the health of communities.

Thomas Friedman, author of the *World is Flat*, argues that, "Those who have the ability to imagine new services and new opportunities and new ways to recruit work ... are the new Untouchables. Those with the imagination to invent smarter ways to do old jobs, energy-saving ways to provide new services, new ways to attract old customers or new ways to combine existing technologies will thrive." The solution is better education and training. Here, too, the future cannot be business as usual. "We not only need a higher percentage of our kids graduating from high school and college – more education – but we need more of them with the right education. Our schools have a doubly hard task, not just improving reading, writing and arithmetic but entrepreneurship, innovation and creativity. We're not going back to the good old days without fixing our schools as well as our banks."[5]

"The challenge now is to transform education systems into something better suited to the real needs of the twenty-first century. At the heart of this transformation there has to be a radically different view of human intelligence and of creativity."

One of the reasons the old systems of education are not working now is that real life is not linear or standardized: it is organic, creative and diverse and always has been.

Some weeks before our son started at university in Los Angeles, we went along for an orientation day. At one point, the students were taken away for a separate briefing on program options and the parents were taken to the finance department for a form of grief counseling. We then had a presentation from one of the professors about our roles as parents during our children's student days. He advised us to step out of their way and spare them too much of our career advice. His own son had been a student at the university some years before and had originally wanted to study the classics. The professor and his wife were not optimistic about his job prospects. They were relieved when, at the end of the freshman year, he said he'd decided to major in something "more useful." They asked what he had in mind, and he said philosophy. His father pointed out that none of the big philosophy firms were hiring at the time. His son took some philosophy courses anyway and eventually majored in art history. After college he found a job in an international auction house. He traveled, made a good living, loved the work and the life. He got the job because of his knowledge of ancient cultures, his intellectual training in philosophy and his love of art history. Neither he nor his parents could have predicted that path when he started his college studies.

The principle is the same for everyone. Life is not linear. As you live your life you take or avoid opportunities, meet different people, have unexpected experiences and create a unique biography along the way. What we become in the future is deeply influenced by our experiences here and now. Education is not a straight line to the future: it is also about cultivating the talents and sensibilities through which we can live our best lives in the present.

BEYOND IMAGINING

In December 1862, Abraham Lincoln gave his second annual address to Congress. He was writing one month before he signed the Emancipation Proclamation, and in his message he urged Congress to see the situation they faced with fresh eyes. He said this: "The dogmas of the quiet past are inadequate to the stormy present. The occasion is piled high with difficulty. As our case is new, so we must think anew and act anew. We must disenthrall ourselves and then we shall save our country."[6]

I love the word "disenthrall." We all live our lives guided by ideas to which we are devoted but which may no longer

be true or relevant. We are hypnotized or enthralled by
them. To move forward we have to shake free of them. Over
the past few centuries of industrialism, more and more people have moved off the land into cities and seem to believe
that they can live apart from the rest of nature. The climate
crisis reminds us that we cannot. In most respects, we are
like most other organisms on earth. Our lives
are brief; we pass through the same cycle of   *"We may not be able*
mortality from conception to birth to death;   *to predict the future*
we have the same physical needs as other   *but we can help to*
species and we depend on nutrients that the   *shape it."*
earth supplies.

Biologically, we are probably evolving at the same rate as
other species, culturally, we are evolving at a uniquely furi-
ous rate. The cultural lives of dogs and cats are not changing
that much. They seem to do pretty much what they've always
done. There's no need to keep checking in with them to see
what's new. In human life, there is always something new and
the pace of change is quickening every day. The reason is that,
in one respect at least, we human beings are different from
the rest of life on earth. We have powerful imaginations and
unlimited powers of creativity. In imagination we can visit the
past, and not just a single view of the past. We can review and
reinterpret the past. We can enhance our sense of the present
by seeing with other people's eyes. We can anticipate possible futures and we can act creatively to bring them about.
We may not be able to predict the future, but we can help to
shape it.

It may be that some of the challenges we are creating, in
the natural environment, in politics and in our conflicting
beliefs, will overcome us, and maybe sooner rather than later.
If so, it will not be because we have made too much use of
our imaginations but too little. Now, more than ever, we need
to exercise these unique creative powers that make us human
in the first place. The challenges we face are global and personal. As this is my book, let's start with me.

FACING THE REVOLUTION

"*By about 2040, there will be a backup of our brains in a computer somewhere, so that when you die it won't be a major career problem.*"

Ian Pearson[1]

OUT AND ABOUT

MY FATHER WAS BORN IN 1914 in Liverpool, England. He lived his whole life in Liverpool and rarely traveled more than 30 miles from the city. My mother was born in 1919, also in Liverpool. It was only later in her life that she traveled out of the country for holidays. I was born in Liverpool in 1950. Even then, people didn't really go anywhere. A visit to the nearest town was a day's outing. In some regions, dialects were so distinct that it was possible to tell which village or part of town someone came from. I have five brothers and a sister, all born in Liverpool. My brother John has been piecing together our family tree. He found out that in the mid-to-late nineteenth century, seven of our eight great grandparents grew up in Liverpool too, all within a couple of miles of each other, in some cases in adjacent streets. That is how they met. For most of human history, people lived, worked and married locally and expected to live the sorts of lives their parents had led. They were not besieged with media images of celebrities and reality stars that made them hesitate about settling for the person they'd just met at the pub.

I now travel so much for my work that I sometimes cannot remember where I have been or when. A few years ago I went to Oslo in Norway to speak at a conference. I flew overnight from Los Angeles via New York. The plane was delayed and I arrived in Oslo five hours late and tired but looking forward to the event. As I was getting ready to go on stage, one of the organizers asked me whether I had been in Oslo before. I told her that I had not but that the city seemed fascinating. A few hours later, I remembered that I *had* been in Oslo before. For a week! Admittedly it was about 15 years earlier, but even so. You don't usually wander into Norway without noticing. In a week, you do all kinds of things: eat, shower, meet people and talk and think about Norwegian things. I had been to the National Art Gallery and spent time looking at paintings by Edvard Munch, including *The Scream*, which is what I felt like doing when I realized I had forgotten the entire trip. It may be a sign that I am on the move too much. I think it's also a sign of the times.

I used to live in England in a village called Snitterfield (really), which is three miles from Stratford-upon-Avon, the birthplace of William Shakespeare. Snitterfield is where William Shakespeare's father, John, was born in 1531. When he was 20 years old, John left Snitterfield to seek his fortune in Stratford. It is almost impossible to grasp the differences between his view of the world and ours almost 500 years later, when business travelers fly across continents to attend meetings for the weekend and then forget where they've been. For most of human history, social change was snail-like in comparison with now. As we'll see later, there were revolutionary discoveries, expeditions and technological inventions during his lifetime. Even so, John Shakespeare's daily life probably differed very little from that of his parents, grandparents or great grandparents.

My father never left England. For work or pleasure, I've now been to most countries in Europe, to the Far East and to many parts of the United States and Australia. By their early teens, my children had visited more countries than I had by the age of 40. When I was growing up in the 1950s and 60s, I thought of my parents' childhood in the 1920s as the Middle Ages: horses in the street, few cars, steam trains, grand ocean liners, no air travel to speak of, no television and few telephones. When we got our first black and white television in 1959, we felt we'd reached the last stage of human evolution. My own children have a similarly quaint view of my childhood: only two television channels, no color or surround sound, no video games, smartphones, tablets or social media. Their world is inconceivably different from those of my grandparents and great grandparents.

"To understand how hard it is to anticipate the future now, we need only think of how difficult it proved to predict the future in the past."

The differences are not only in the nature of change but also in the pace of it. The most profound changes haven't happened in 500 years, most of them have happened in the past 200 years and especially in the last 50, and they are getting faster. According to one estimate:

- in 1950 the average person traveled about 5 miles per day

- in 2000 the average person traveled about 30 miles per day

- in 2020 the average person will travel about 60 miles per day.

Imagine the past 3000 years as the face of a clock with each of the 60 minutes representing a period of 50 years. Until three minutes ago, the history of transport was dominated by the horse, the wheel and the sail. In the late eighteenth century, James Watt refined the steam engine. This changed everything. It was a major tremor in the social earthquake of the Industrial

Revolution. The improved steam engine vastly increased the power available for industrial production. It paved the way for faster methods of transport by road and sea and made possible the development of railways, the arterial system of the early industrial world. The steam engine impelled vast movements of humanity at speeds that were never thought possible. Since then, the curve of change has climbed almost vertically:

4 minutes ago	Internal combustion engine (François Isaac de Rivaz, 1807)
2.6 minutes	Motor car (Karl Benz, 1885)
2.3 minutes	First powered airplane flight (Wright brothers, 1903)
2 minutes	Rocket propulsion (Robert Goddard, 1915)
1.8 minutes	Jet engine (Hans von Ohain and Frank Whittle, 1930)
1.2 minutes	First man-made object orbits the earth (Sputnik 1, 1957)
58 seconds	First manned moon landing and moon walk (Apollo 11, 1969)
43 seconds	Reusable space shuttle (Discovery, 1981)
10 seconds	Tesla Model S (2009)
8 seconds	Unmanned spaceplane (X-37B, 2010)

The revolution in transport is one index of the pace of change, but it's not the fastest one.

GETTING THE MESSAGE

Human beings have had access to writing systems for at least 3000 years. For most of that time these systems hardly changed. People communicated by making marks on surfaces, using pens on paper, chisels on stone or pigment on boards. Written documents existed in single copies and had to be copied by hand. Only a privileged few had access to them and only those few needed to be able to read. Between 1440 and 1450, about 11 minutes ago on our clock, Johannes Gutenberg invented the printing press. Since then the rate of change has gone into overdrive. Think of the major innovations in communication in the past 200 years, and how the gaps on the clock have shortened:

11.5 minutes ago	Printing press (1440–50) X
3.5 minutes	Morse Code (1838–44)
2.8 minutes	Telephone (1875)
2.6 minutes	Radio (1885)
1.8 minutes	Black and white television (1929)
1 minute	Fax (1966)
48 seconds	Personal computer (1977)
46 seconds	Analog cell phone (1979)
32 seconds	World Wide Web (1990)
28 seconds	SMS messaging (1993)
20 seconds	Broadband (2000)
12 seconds	iPhone/smartphones (2007)
8 seconds	iPad/tablets (2010)

When I was born in 1950, no one had a home computer. The average computer then was about the size of your living room. This was one reason people didn't buy them: they weren't inclined to live outdoors to accommodate a largely useless device. A second reason was the cost. Computers cost hundreds of thousands of dollars. Only government departments and some companies had computers.

In 1950 the transistor was invented. In 1970, the silicon chip was developed. These innovations not only reduced the size of computers, they vastly increased their speed and power. The standard memory capacity has increased exponentially since then, from a few hundred kilobytes to several gigabytes.

The smartphones in your pocket has more computing power than was available on earth in 1940. In 1960, Jerome Bruner and George Miller founded the Harvard Center for Cognitive Studies: the first institute dedicated to cognitive science. The Institute was well funded and purchased the first computer used in America for psychological experimentation: a PDP4 minicomputer. It cost $65,000 in 1962 and came with 2K of memory, upgradable to 64K.[2] Nowadays many children's toys have more computing power than that. The average digital wristwatch has appreciably more power than the 1969 Apollo Moonlander: the space vehicle from which Neil Armstrong took his small step for man and his giant leap for mankind.

It is estimated that something in the order of 10^{17} microchips are being manufactured every year; a number, I'm told, that's roughly equivalent to the world population of ants. I repeat it here in the confident knowledge that it can't be checked. This prodigious rate of production indicates the vast range of applications for which computers are now used. The pace of expansion in computer technology over the past 70 years has been breathtaking. Here's a rough chronology:

1937–42	First electronic digital computer, created at Iowa State University.
1951	First commercially produced computer, The Ferranti Mark 1 sells nine between 1951 and 1957.
1965	First phone link set up between two computers.

1972	First email program created.
1974	The term 'Internet' first used.
1975	The Altair personal computer spawns home-computing culture.
1976	Steve Wozniak builds the Apple I with Steve Jobs.
1981	IBM enters the home-computing market and sells 136,000 in the first 18 months.
1983	Microsoft Word launched.
1984	1,000 Internet hosts.
1989	100,000 Internet hosts.
1990	Microchips are invented in Japan that can store 520,000 characters on a sliver of silicon 15 mm by 5 mm.
1992	Internet hosts exceed 1 million.
1997	Internet hosts rise from 16 million to 20 million by July. www.google.com registered as a domain name.
2002	The first social networking site Friendster launches in USA.
2003	Skype VOIP telephony is launched in Sweden based on software designed by Estonian developers.
2004	The term Web 2.0 is devised to describe an increase in user-generated web content.
2004	Facebook launched.
2005	YouTube launched
2006	Twitter launched.

2007	Google surpasses Microsoft as the most valuable brand.
2010	Global number of Internet users nearly 2 billion.
2017	Facebook has 1.8 billion users.
2017	Global number of Internet users nearly 4 billion.

The Internet is the most powerful and pervasive communication system ever devised. It grows daily, like a vast, multiplying organism; millions of connections are added at an ever-faster rate in patterns that resemble ganglia in the brain. Just like the brain, the most robust synapses are the ones that fire most often. Inventor and futurist Ray Kurzweil points out that the evolution of biological life and of technology have followed the same pattern. They both take a long time to get going but advances build on one another and progress erupts at an increasingly ferocious pace: "During the 19th century, the pace of technological progress was equal to that of the ten centuries that came before it. Advancement in the first two decades of the 20th century matched that of the entire 19th century. Today significant technological transformations take just a few years ... Computing technology is experiencing the same exponential growth." [3]

In the mid-1960s, Gordon Moore co-founded Intel. He estimated that the density of transistors on integrated circuit boards was doubling every 12 months and that computers were periodically doubling both in capacity and in speed per unit cost. In the mid-1970s, Moore revised his estimate to about 24 months. Moore's Law may have run its course around 2020. By then transistors may be a few atoms in width. The power of computers will continue to grow, but in different forms. By the way, if the technology of motor cars had developed at the same rate, the average family car could now travel at six times the speed of sound, be capable of about 1,000 miles per gallon and would cost you about one dollar to buy. I imagine you'd get one. You'd just have to be careful with the accelerator.

IT'S ONLY JUST BEGUN

As breathtaking as the rate of technological innovation in the past 50 years has been, the revolution is only just getting underway. In the next 50 years, we may see changes that are as unimaginable to us now as the iPad would have been to John Shakespeare. One of the portals into this radical future is nanotechnology, which is the manipulation of very small things indeed. Nanotechnologists are building machines by assembling individual atoms. To measure the vast distances of space, scientists use the light year – the number of miles that light travels in a year, which is equivalent to just under 10 trillion kilometers, or 6 trillion miles.

I asked a professor of nanotechnology what they use to measure the unthinkably small distances of nanospace. He said it was the nanometer, which is a billionth of a meter. A *billionth* of a meter. It's almost impossible to grasp how small this distance is. Mathematically it is 10^{-9} meter or 0.000000001 meter. Does that help? I understood the idea but couldn't visualize it. I asked, "What is that roughly?" He thought for a moment and said, "A nanometer is roughly the distance that a man's beard grows in one second." I had never thought about what beards do in a second, but they must do something. It takes them all day to grow about a millimeter and they do not do it suddenly. They don't leap out of your face at 8 o'clock in the morning. Beards are languid things and our language reflects this. We do not say "as quick as a beard" or "as fast as a bristle." We now have a way of grasping how slow they are: about a nanometer a second. A nanometer is very small indeed, but it's not the smallest thing around. If you have a nanometer, you can have half of one. There is indeed a picometer, which is a thousandth of a nanometer; an attometer, which is a millionth of a nanometer and a femtometer, which is a billionth of a nanometer. A *billionth* of a *billionth* of a meter. So if your beard had a beard ...

In 1995, Professor Sir Harry Kroto was awarded the Nobel Prize for Chemistry. With others, he discovered the third form of carbon, a nanotube of graphite called the C60 molecule, also known as the Bucky Ball after the American architect Buckminster Fuller. Fuller made extensive use of geodesic shapes that are similar to the structures of the C60 molecule. The C60 has remarkable qualities. It is a hundred times stronger than steel, a tenth of the weight and it conducts electricity like a metal. This discovery triggered a wave of research in engineering, aerospace, medicine and much else. If it could be produced in industrial quantities, the C60 would make possible the construction of airplanes 20 or 50 times their present size but much lighter and more fuel-efficient. Buildings could be erected that went through the atmosphere; bridges could span the Grand Canyon. Motor cars and trains could be a fraction of their current weight with greater fuel economies through the use of solar power.

Nanotechnology makes it feasible to create any substance or object from the atomic level upwards. While scientists speculate about the practical possibilities, others wonder about the political and economic consequences. Charles Ostman, Senior Fellow at the Institute for Global Futures, notes, "Right now power and influence in the world is based on the control of natural and industrial resources. Once nanotechnology makes it possible to synthesize any physical object cheaply and easily, our current economic systems will become obsolete. It would be difficult to envision a more encompassing realm of future development than nanotechnology." [4]

Nanotechnology promises radical innovations in fields as disparate as engineering and medicine. Its applications range from "molecular computing, to shape-changing alloys, to synthetic organic compounds, to custom gene construction, to ultra-miniaturized machinery." In medicine, nanoma-chines with rotor blades on the scale of human hair are being proposed as scrubbers to swim through veins and arteries cleaning out cholesterol and plaque deposits. In other medi-cal applications, "the implications for modifying the cellular chemistry of almost any organ of the human body to cure disease, prolong life, or to provide enhanced sensory and mental abilities, are almost beyond comprehension." Artifi-cially grown skin cultures are already being produced, and research into the development of an organic artificial heart is taking place in several different locations.

Nanotechnology makes possible the extreme miniaturiza-tion of computer systems and will revolutionize how we use them. In future, computers will be small enough to be worn on the body and be powered by the surface electricity of your skin. The problem will be what to do with the monitor: you won't want a thin film of microprocessors clinging to your wrist and a monitor strapped on your chest. One solution is retinal projectors that use low-level lasers mounted on spec-tacle frames and project the display into your eyes. A version of this technology is already used in advanced aircraft sys-tems. Pilots see the navigation displays on the inside of their visors and can change the direction of the aircraft by moving their eyes. You hope they don't sneeze in hostile airspace.

For more everyday use, computers could be woven into clothing. Shirts could have sensors that monitor heartbeat and other vital signs. Hints of serious ill health could be relayed directly to a doctor. Smart shoes will turn the action of walking into enough energy to power wearable computers. Other innovations will replace the conventional keyboard. Already, interfaces are available that are controlled by the power of thought. Headsets can monitor brainwaves and convert them into instructions. All these devices work out-side their users' bodies. Soon, information technologies may move inside our bodies and even into our brains. Computers may be about to merge with our own consciousness.

USING YOUR BRAIN

The most revolutionary implications of research in information systems, material sciences and in neuroscience lie in the crossovers between them. It is possible to conceive of information technologies modeled on the neural processes of the brain. Future generations of computers may be based not on digital codes and silicon but on organic processes and DNA: computers that mimic human thought.

I was talking recently with a senior technologist at one of the world's leading computer companies. At the moment, he said, the most powerful computers on earth have the processing power of the brain of a cricket. I don't know if this is true and nor does he. I don't know any crickets and if I did I'd have no way of telling what, if anything, is going on in their brains. His point is that even the most powerful supercomputers are still just mindless calculators. They perform tasks that humans can't but they don't have any opinions about what they do. They don't think, in any proper sense of the term. Similarly, airplanes are much better than we are at flying at 35,000 feet but there's no point asking them how they feel about it. They don't. This is all changing.

In the foreseeable future, the most powerful computers may have the processing power of the brain of a six-month-old human baby. In some senses, computers may soon become conscious. It will soon be possible to buy a cheap personal computer with the same processing power as an adult human brain.[5] How's that going to feel when you're working with a computer that's as smart as you are; maybe not as attractive as you are, or as much in demand socially, but as smart as you? You give this machine an instruction and it hesitates, and says, "Have you thought this through? I'm not sure that you have." By 2030, personal computers, whatever form they take by then, could have the processing power of not one but of a thousand human brains.

Neural implants that provide deep brain stimulation (DBS) are now used to counteract tremors from Parkinson's disease and multiple sclerosis. Cochlear implants can replace the functions of a damaged inner ear. Retinal implants can restore some visual perception supplementing damaged photoreceptor cells in the eye. Neural implants and "smart drugs" could improve our general sensory experiences and our powers of memory and reasoning. In future, if you have an important examination coming up, you might be able to buy another 80 megabytes of RAM and have it implanted in your brain. It may be possible to have language implants. Instead of spending five years learning French, you can have it implanted in time for your summer holidays. You would probably have to pay a few dollars more for the style implant.

Ray Kurzweil believes that by "the third decade of the 21st century, we will be in a position to create complete, detailed maps of the 'computationally relevant features of the human brain,' and to recreate these designs in advanced neural computers." There will be a variety of bodies for our machines too, "from virtual bodies in virtual reality to bodies comprising swarms of nanobots ..." Humanoid robots that walk and have lifelike facial expressions have been developed in several laboratories. Before the end of this century, "... the law of accelerating returns tells us, earth's technology-creating species – us – will merge with our own technology. When that happens we might ask: what is the difference between a human brain enhanced a million-fold by neural implants and a non-biological intelligence based on the reverse engineering of the human brain that is subsequently enhanced and expanded?"

As Kurzweil notes, "an evolutionary process accelerates because it builds on its own means for further evolution ... The intelligence that we are now creating in computers will soon exceed the intelligence of its creators." There may come a time, Ostman says, "when machines exhibit the full range

"An evolutionary process accelerates because it builds on its own means for further evolution." of human intellect, emotions and skills, ranging from musical and other creative attitudes to physical movement." In that case, "the very boundaries of philosophical questions concerning where life ends and something else, yet to be defined, begins are at best soon to become a very fuzzy grey zone of definitions, as will the essence of intelligence as it is currently defined."

Some of this may sound far-fetched, but if someone had told you 20 years ago that you could sit on the beach with a small wireless device and search the Library of Congress, send instant mail, download music and videos, book your holidays, arrange a mortgage and check your cholesterol, you might have thought they were taking something. Now we take it for granted. If you could go back in time and hand your iPhone to your great grandparents, they'd think you were Captain Kirk. The impossible yesterday is routine today. Wait until tomorrow.

IT'S GETTING CROWDED

Technological development is one driver of change. There is another: the sheer numbers of people who are now on the planet. We are by far the largest population of people that has ever lived on the planet at the same time.

In the middle of the eighteenth century, at the beginning of the Industrial Revolution, there were just 1 billion people on earth. In 1930, there were 2 billion. It took all of human history until about 1800 for the population to reach the first billion and 130 years to reach the second billion. It took only 30 years to add the third in 1960, 14 years to add the fourth in 1974 and 13 years to add the fifth in 1987. By the night of the millennium celebrations in December 1999, the world's population had reached 6 billion, and continued to climb rapidly. In 2017 it reached 7.5 billion and the

United Nations estimates that in 2050 the world population will be close to 10 billion.

The issue is not only how the human population is growing, but how it is shifting. In 1800, the vast majority of people lived in the countryside; only 5% lived in cities. By 1900, that number had risen to 12%. By 2000, almost 50% of the 6 billion people on earth lived in cities. It is estimated that in 2050, over 60% of the population – about 6 billion people – will be living in cities. These will not be manicured cities of the American Dream. Many will be vast, sprawling mega-cities with populations of over 20 million. The numbers are daunting. It's estimated that by 2050 there will be over 500 cities with more than a million people and over 50 mega-cities with populations of more than 10 million. Already, Greater Tokyo has a population of 38 million, which is more than the entire population of Canada, gathered in one sprawling urban metropolis.

At the same time, the human world is shifting on its axis. The big growth in population is not in the old industrial economies of Western Europe and North America; it is in the emerging economies of South America, the Middle East and Asia. Currently, 84 million people are being added every year to the populations of the less developed countries, compared with about 1.5 million in more developed countries, where populations are projected to remain relatively constant throughout this century.[6] China is the world's most populous nation with a population of 1.4 billion. Its population is increasing by 1% each year, assuming minimal migration, though that rate is bound to accelerate with the phasing out of the one-child policy from 2015.

India's population is more than 1.3 billion and, with a growth rate of about 2%, it may overtake China in population by the middle of the century. In some of the emerging economies, almost half the population is under 25. In the older industrialized countries, the population is aging. Many have extremely slow rates of population growth and even what's known as "natural decrease," where death rates exceed birth rates. Currently, that's the case in 20 countries including Russia, Japan, Germany, Latvia, Austria and Italy. In some countries, immigration is the only source of population growth. The United States is the third most populous country in the world, with a current population of 324 million, which may reach 422 million by 2050. An estimated 4 million babies were born in the USA during 2015, the lowest fertility rate there since records began in 1909. (The general fertility rate is the number of births per 1,000 women between the ages of 15 and 49.) The main growth in the US population is through patterns of migration from Central and South America.[7]

As this century progresses, these massive shifts in populations will put intense pressure on our use of natural resources, on water supplies, food production, energy and the quality of the air we breathe. We will face bigger risks than ever from potential epidemics and new diseases. There will be profound effects on economic activity and trade. If the past is any guide, we will be at risk too from the persistent perils of cultural conflict. Responding to these challenges will demand radically new ways of caring for natural resources, new technologies for generating energy, sustainable methods of food production and new approaches to the prevention and treatment of diseases – and politics. Here, as everywhere, innovation is the key.

THE PERILS OF PREDICTION

On Sunday April 30, 1939, the President of the United States, Franklin D. Roosevelt, stood before an audience of over 200,000 people in Flushing Meadows, Queens, just east of New York City, and steadied himself at the podium. As he did so, an unusual camera was trained on him. His role that day was to open the 1939 New York World's Fair. The theme of the Fair was "Building the World of Tomorrow" and during its two seasons of activity in 1939 and 1940 it attracted 45 million visitors. Among the hundreds of exhibits was the pavilion of the Radio Corporation of America (RCA). The pavilion featured demonstrations of the world's first commercial system of television. Roosevelt's speech that day was the first presidential speech to be televised. In addition to the audience at the Fair he was watched by about a thousand people gathered around a few hundred TV sets in various buildings in New York City. Ten days before the official opening of the Fair, David Sarnoff, the President of RCA, gave a dedication speech for the RCA pavilion in which he heralded the system of television as the dawn of a new age of broadcasting. The pavilion attracted huge interest but not everyone was convinced that the new medium would catch on.

A newspaper article covering the event concluded that television would never be a serious competitor for radio. When you're listening to the radio, it argued, you can get on and do other things. To experience television, people would have to sit and keep their eyes glued on a screen – which was, of course, to become the very attraction of the whole system. Nonetheless, it seemed clear to the writer that the average American family simply wouldn't have time for it. Well, they found time. On average, the average American family went on to squeeze about 25 hours a week from their busy schedules to sit with their eyes glued on the television. The fault line in the paper's assessment of television was to judge it in terms of contemporary cultural values where there seemed to be no place for it. Television was not squeezed into existing American culture: it changed the culture altogether. After the arrival of television, the world was never the same again. Television was a transformative technology, just as print, the steam engine, electricity, the motor car and others before it had been.

It is all but impossible to predict the future of human affairs with any certainty. The forces of change create too many crosscurrents to chart them more than a little way ahead. The effects of transformative technologies are hard to predict for the very reason that they are transformative. To understand how hard it is to anticipate the future now, we need only think of how difficult it proved in the past.

Turning the page

As Gutenberg ironed out the technical wrinkles in his printing press in 1450 in Mainz, Germany, I doubt that he anticipated the full consequences of the invention he was about to unleash on the world. A goldsmith by training, Gutenberg, blended existing technologies with some refinements of his own to develop a system of printing that was quick, adaptable and efficient. His system made it possible for the first time to reproduce documents in volume and for them to be distributed across the continent and then the world. His printing press changed everything. It opened the floodgates of knowledge and ideas and generated a rapacious appetite for literacy. By1500, printing presses across Europe were pumping countless documents on every subject and from every point of view, with seismic implications for politics, religion and culture. In the sixteenth century, the English philosopher and politician Sir Francis Bacon developed the principles of the scientific method. He did so in a world that had been transformed by the proliferation of ideas and intellectual energy that had flowed from the printing presses of Europe. Towards the end of his life, Bacon commented that the advances in printing that Gutenberg had made had "changed the whole face and state of things throughout the world."

Getting around

The internal combustion engine was created 400 years after Gutenberg's first printing press. The impact of that invention was also unforeseen. It struck many people as an interesting innovation, but they struggled to see why it would replace horses and carriages, which seemed to do a perfectly good job of getting people around. One person whose curiosity was piqued by the new horseless carriages occupies an unfortunate place in the history of transportation. Her name was Bridget Driscoll. She was one of the first to be killed in an auto accident.

On August 17, 1896, Bridget, then aged 44, was visiting an exhibition at the Crystal Palace in London with her teenaged daughter, May. The exhibition included demonstration rides by the Anglo-French Motor Carriage Company. As she was walking through the grounds, Mrs Driscoll was struck by one of the vehicles and died of her injuries. The case was highly unusual and was referred to the Coroner's Court for proper consideration. The jury was faced with conflicting accounts of the accident, including the speed of the vehicle. One witness said that the vehicle had been moving at "a reckless pace, in fact like a fire engine." The driver, Arthur James Edsall, denied this and said that he had been traveling at only 4 miles per hour. His passenger, Alice Standing, said that the engine had been modified to make the car move faster than 4 miles an hour, though an expert witness who examined the vehicle contradicted this allegation.

After deliberating for six hours, the jury returned a verdict of accidental death. Summarizing the case, the coroner, Mr Percy Morrison, reflected on the bizarre nature of this tragic episode and said he hoped "such a thing would never happen again." Well, it happened again. In the twentieth century over 60 million people died in auto accidents and millions more were traumatically injured. Like the printing press, the motor car changed the world in ways that its inventors could hardly have imagined.

Digital culture is changing the world just as profoundly as these earlier technologies did. The effects are cumulative. Radical innovations often interact and generate new patterns of behavior in the people who use them. When Tim Berners-Lee laid the foundations of the World Wide Web in 1990, his aim was to help academics collaborate by accessing each other's work. He could not have foreseen the metastasizing expansion of the Internet and the viral spread of social media, and their transmogrifying effects on culture and commerce. The evolution of the Internet has been fueled not only by innovations in technology but also by the imaginations and appetites of billions of users, which in turn are driving further innovations in technology.

New work for old

We cannot always predict the future but some things we do know. One is that the nature of work will continue to change for very many people. Our children will not only change jobs several times in their lives but will probably change careers. In less than a single generation, the nature of work for millions of people has changed fundamentally, and with it the structure of the world economies. When I was growing up in the 1950s and 60s, the majority of people did manual work and wore overalls; relatively few worked in offices and wore suits. In the last 30 years especially, the balance has been shifting from traditional forms of industrial and manual work to jobs that are based on information technology and providing services. The dominant global corporations used to be in manufacturing and oil; many of the key companies today are in communications, information, entertainment, science and technology.

Cisco Systems supplies networking equipment for the Internet. In November 2000 its stock market value was $400 billion, making Cisco worth more than the combined value of all of the world's car companies, steel makers, aluminum companies and aircraft manufacturers at that time. That was just the start. In 2017, five of the top ten companies in the Fortune 500, including the top three, are technology companies. The most valuable is Apple, with a market value of $725 billion, followed by Alphabet (Google), valued at $507 billion and Microsoft at $326 billion. Number five on the list is Facebook, with a market value of $321 billion and Amazon is number seven at $250 billion. What will the Fortune 500 listing look like in 2027, assuming there is one? It's impossible to say.

The emergence of e-commerce and Internet trading in the 1980s swept away long-established ways of doing business. The computerization of the financial markets and the synchronization of the global economies revolutionized financial services, including banks, insurance companies, stockbrokers and dealers. Since the so-called Big Bang in London in 1988, international corporations have swallowed up smaller traditional banks, retail stores have offered financial services of their own, and banks have become insurance and mortgage brokers. The heady expansion of the financial services sector in the five years from 2000 and its precipitous collapse in 2008 was a further illustration, if we needed one, that the course of human affairs, in business as elsewhere, usually defies prediction and often beggars belief.

Getting the idea

Over the last 30 years there has emerged a powerful new force in the world economies. Often described as the intellectual property sector, or sometimes as the creative industries, they include advertising, architecture, arts and antiques, crafts, design, fashion, film, computer games, music, performing arts, publishing, software and computer services, television and radio. This sector is more significant when patents from science and technology are included: in pharmaceuticals, electronics, biotechnology and information systems, among others.[8] The creative industries are labor-intensive and depend on many types of specialist skill. Television and film production, for example, employs specialists in performance, script writing, camera and sound operation, lighting, make-up, design, editing and post-production. The communications revolution, and the new global markets it has created, has multiplied outlets for creative content and increased consumer demand. As the financial significance of this sector grows, so does its employment base, not only in Europe and the United States but in Asia too.

Old workers for new

Throughout the world, business and education are faced with a new generation gap. While the number of people on earth is increasing, there are profound differences between generations. As healthcare improves and life expectancy increases, the boomers are continuing to boom in size and energy. In the UK, for example, by 2020 the number of people over 50 will have increased by 2 million, while the number of those under 50 will have dropped by 2 million. Those now passing 50 are not like their predecessors from generations past. They account for 80% of the nation's wealth, enjoy better health and are more inclined than the heavily mortgaged parents of young children to take on new challenges and adapt to new ways of working. This makes them highly effective new-economy workers. As one study puts it: "Declining birth rates mean that employers are going to have to become more creative if they want to access the knowledge workers they need. And that means abandoning the lazy prejudice of age discrimination."[9]

THE LEISURED SOCIETY?

The promise of a leisured society brought on by labor-saving digital technologies has so far proved elusive. Most people I know are working harder, longer and to shorter deadlines than they were ten years ago. The ability to communicate across time zones means that as you are going to bed someone has started their day and wants to be in touch. Apart from the daily trove of emails, there are the insistent pings and trills of texts, phone calls and notifications on your smartphone or tablet. A senior executive in a major oil company told me that the wind-down to Christmas used to begin in mid-December and the recovery might run on to the middle of January. Now people are fixing meetings in Christmas week and the whole operation speeds back in to action in the first week of the New Year. As he put it, "Standards of living are much higher than when I started out, but the quality of life is lower." Meanwhile, many other people have no work at all. This is a different proposition, which we will come back to in Chapter 3.

There is also the constant deluge of news and information and a nagging pressure to keep abreast of it all. A well-known British journalist was reminiscing about his early days in radio news. He joined the BBC in the 1930s at a time when there was no regular news bulletin. In his first week, a bulletin was scheduled and he arrived at the studio to watch the broadcast. The presenter sat at the microphone and waited until the time signal had finished. He then announced somberly: "This is the BBC Home Service from London. It is one o'clock. There is no news." The news would be broadcast if anything happened to warrant it.[10] Compare this with the fevered news cycle now, reporting 24 hours a day on a multitude of channels and media. The reason is not that there is more happening in the world now than there was in the 1930s. We now have a ferociously competitive news industry, which generates news and opinion around the clock to nourish its own bottom line. All of this adds to the general sense of crisis that permeates twenty-first-century culture.

ANTICIPATING THE FUTURE

In 1970, Alvin Toffler published his groundbreaking book *Future Shock*. The idea of culture shock is well known to psychologists. Political refugees and economic migrants can experience culture shock when they move to a new country and find themselves in an environment where all their normal reference points – language, values, food, clothes, social rituals – are gone. It can be profoundly disorienting and can lead, in extreme cases, to psychosis. Toffler saw a similar global phenomenon in the effects of rapid social change promoted by technology. He argued that being propelled too quickly into an unfamiliar future could have the same traumatic effect on people. The issue is not the fact of change: it was the rate, nature and scale of it.

Our times have released "a stream of change so accelerated that it influences our sense of time, revolutionizes the tempo of daily life, and affects the very way we feel the world around us. We no longer feel life as people did in the past. And this is the ultimate difference, the distinction that separates the truly contemporary person from all others." This acceleration, he believed, lies behind "the impermanence, the transience, that penetrates and tinctures our consciousness, radically affecting the way we relate to other people, to things, to the entire universe of ideas, art and values." Interestingly, in the 1970s, when Alvin Toffler was developing his apocalyptic views on the rate of social change, the personal computer wasn't available, let alone the Internet. He wrote *Future Shock* on a manual typewriter.

LOOKING FORWARD

In the twenty-first century, humanity faces some of its most daunting challenges. Our best resource is to cultivate our singular abilities of imagination, creativity and innovation. Doing so has to become one of the principal priorities of education and training everywhere. Education is the key to the future, and the stakes could hardly be higher. In 1934, the great Swiss psychologist Jean Piaget said, "only education is capable of saving our societies from possible collapse, whether violent or gradual." History provides many examples. Over the course of humanity's relatively brief occupancy of the earth, many great societies and whole civilizations have come and gone. We build our own cultures not only on the achievements of those that have come before but also on their ruins. The visionary novelist, H.G. Wells, put Piaget's point even more sharply: "Civilization," he said, "is a race between education and catastrophe." The evidence suggests that he and Piaget were right.

THE TROUBLE WITH EDUCATION

"Current systems of education were not designed to meet the challenges we now face. They were developed to meet the needs of a former age. Reform is not enough: they need to be transformed."

ACADEMIC INFLATION

I WENT TO COLLEGE IN 1968. I did not look then as I look now. I was not the suave sophisticate that you will find on my website. I was deep into Led Zeppelin and, visually at least, I was channeling the lead singer, Robert Plant. I had shoulder-length hair, wore jeans and a torn combat jacket, and was almost dangerously attractive to women. That was certainly my impression. I was 22 and considering my options. Should I get a job? Not yet, I thought. There was no rush. At that time, college graduates were virtually guaranteed a decent job and it did not matter much what their degree was in. It could have been in Old Norse and it often was. Employers would still snap them up. "You can speak Viking," they'd say, "come and run our factory: your mind is honed to a fine edge."

When I graduated, if you had a degree and didn't get a job, it was probably because you didn't want a job. I did not want a job. I wanted to "find myself." You could do this in the 1970s. I decided to go to India, where I thought I might be. As it happens I didn't get to India, I got to London (where, to be fair, there are a lot of Indian restaurants). I knew that when I wanted a job I could get one, and soon enough I did. A college degree was a passport to a good professional position. Nowadays, college graduates have no guarantee of a job and those who do find work do not expect to be with the same company for long, or even that the company will be around for that long either.

There are many good reasons for gaining academic qualifications. Studying for them should be inherently worthwhile and the best programs are. Academic qualifications are also a form of currency: they have an exchange rate in the marketplace for jobs or higher education. Like all currencies, their value can go up or down according to market conditions and how much currency is in circulation. University degrees used to have a high market value in part because relatively few people had them. The growth in population and the expansion of the "knowledge economy" have led to unprecedented numbers of people going to college. In the 1970s, about one in twenty people went to college. The current target is one in three, rising to one in two. As a result, the market value of degrees is tumbling. Something more is needed to edge ahead of the crowd. Jobs that used to require only a first degree are now asking for masters' degrees, or even doctorates.

Several years ago, I was on a university appointments panel. I asked the chairman of the panel what we were looking for in the candidates. He mentioned the various qualities and qualifications that were essential for the job and then he said, "I think we're also looking for someone with a good PhD." I said, "As opposed to what? A dreadful one?" He meant a PhD from a high-ranking university. There was a time when, if you had a PhD, you were in a tiny fraction of the population.

All PhDs were regarded with reverence. Now, we're getting picky. We want "good" PhDs. What's the next twist on this spiral? Nobel Prizes? Will we eventually see Nobel Laureates applying for clerical jobs and being told, "OK, you've got a Nobel Prize, that's lovely. Can you also handle Excel? We need someone to sort out the payroll."

The assumption is that by expanding education and raising standards all will be well. The end game assumes that when everyone has a PhD, there will be a return to full employment. There will not. The markets will reconfigure as the currency rates fall and employers will look for something else. They're doing this already. The issue is not that academic standards are falling. The foundations upon which our current systems of education are built are shifting beneath our feet.

TWIN PILLARS

We now take it for granted that governments should provide mass systems of education; that they should be funded from the public purse; that all young people should go to school until they are at least 16 and that a high proportion of them should go on to college. As obvious as they may seem now, these assumptions are relatively new.[1] It was only from the 1860s onwards that countries throughout Europe, as well as many of the American states, began to establish mass systems of public education. The history of state education everywhere is an intricate tapestry of economic needs, philanthropic passions, competing movements of social reform and wildly divergent philosophical convictions. Even so, there were some common driving forces.

Pre-industrial societies were dominated by the old aristocracies and the churches, which presided over largely illiterate, poor rural populations. Before the 1860s, the vast majority of Europeans were still illiterate. Only Prussia, some of the other northern German states and the Scandinavian kingdoms boasted widespread literacy.[2] The spread of industrialism generated surging streams of new wealth and a new and ambitious social force: the middle classes. Education was the road to social improvement and economic opportunity. Public education evolved around the interests and ambitions of the middle classes; not only for themselves but also for the industrialized societies they were helping to create. Industrial expansion provided the resources to pay for it all.

As millions of workers migrated from the countryside to the cities, to stoke the fires of industrialism in the factories and shipyards, a third social group began to take shape: the urban working classes. For some pioneers of mass education, schools were a way to raise the aspirations of the working classes and to lift them out of poverty and despair. Others saw it as the best way to promote the values and opportunities that are meant to lie at the heart of healthy democracies. In the United States, Horace Mann saw mass education for all as the natural fulfillment of the principles of the Constitution. Others were less idealistic and saw it as the most efficient way of inculcating the working classes with the habits and disciplines of industrial production. Some argued that it was a waste of public resources to attempt to educate the children of the working classes: such children were essentially uneducable and would not benefit from these efforts. They were wrong about that. Others feared that educating the working classes would give them ideas above their station and lead to a social revolution. They were not wrong about that.

State-supported elementary schools sprang up throughout Europe from the mid-1800s: in Hungary from 1868; Austria from 1869; England from 1870; Switzerland from 1874; the Netherlands from 1876; Italy from 1877; and Belgium from 1879. They grew too in the United States. According to Gerald Gutek, by the time of the Civil War, "the common school movement had accomplished its aim of achieving popular systems of elementary schools in most of the states.

After 1865, schools were established in the southern states. As various new states entered the Union, they too established common elementary school systems."³

From the outset, mass systems of education in Europe and North America were designed to meet the labor needs of an industrial economy based on manufacturing, engineering and related trades, including construction, mining and steel production. Industrialism needed a workforce that was roughly 80% manual and 20% administrative and professional. This requirement influenced the structure of public education. Typically, it was shaped like a pyramid, with a broad base of elementary education tapering to a narrow peak of higher education. The majority of children went to elementary school and a smaller number went on to high school. The majority of those left full-time education at 14 to find work. A few went on to higher education. Those with strong academic qualifications went to universities, others to trade colleges or polytechnics.

In Europe, there were usually two types of high school: academic schools for a minority of pupils who showed an aptitude for such work; and more practical or technically oriented schools for the majority who did not. The academic schools fed the universities, which had higher status, and so too did the students who went to them. It was not that only a minority was capable of going to university: the supply of places was limited by the needs of the labor markets. As these needs have changed, so the number of places in higher education has increased. In the United States and Europe, the expansion began in the 1960s, partly to accommodate the bulging population of baby boomers after the end of World War II. This trend has continued with the burgeoning demands of the "knowledge economy." From the beginnings of state education in the United Kingdom, the expansion of academic "grammar" schools went hand in hand with the founding of new universities in the major industrial centers.⁴ There was a similar pattern of expansion in the United States. Some

American universities, such as Indiana, Madison Wisconsin and Ohio State, are now the size of small towns and are turning out graduates in their tens of thousands every year.

Over the last 40 years, the number of young people capable of achieving university-level education has increased from one in five to one in two. What happened to account for this remarkable flowering in intellectual capacity? Was it fluoride in the water or the rise of organic farming? The fact is that most young people have always been capable of higher academic study, but, until recently, the economy did not need them in such large numbers.

THE CULTURE OF EDUCATION

The rise of industrialism influenced not only the structure of mass education but also its organizational culture. Like factories, schools were planned with special facilities, with boundaries that separated them from the outside world, set hours of operation and prescribed rules of conduct. They were designed on the principles of standardization and conformity. Students were taught broadly the same material and they were assessed against common scales of achievement, with relatively few opportunities for choice or deviation. They moved through the system in age groups: all the 5-year-olds together, all the 6-year-olds together and so on, as if the most important thing that children have in common is their date of manufacture. In high schools, the day was organized into standard units of time, with the transitions marked by bells or buzzers. The curriculum was based on division of labor with specialist teachers of separate disciplines. The systems operated on the manufacturing principles of linearity and conformity. Each stage was designed to build on the one before. If students progressed in the prescribed way through the system, and especially if they completed college, they emerged at the far end educated and ready for work.

The original architecture of these systems is still visible in the way that many school systems work today. When I first moved to Los Angeles, I saw an egregious example of the linear principle in the form of a discussion paper for education entitled, "College Begins in Kindergarten." There is more to say on this issue of linearity, but let me simply say here that college does not begin in kindergarten. Kindergarten begins in kindergarten. The director of The Ark Children's Theatre in Dublin once made a wonderful comment on this theme. "A three-year-old," he said, "is not half a six-year-old. A six-year-old is not half a twelve-year-old." Three-year-olds are three. In some urban centers the competition is so intense for places in the "right" kindergartens that children are being interviewed – for kindergarten. What are the interviewers looking for, evidence of infancy?

The principle of linearity sees education as preparation for something that happens later on. This approach is sometimes called the front-loading model of education: you accumulate educational resources at the beginning of your life and eke them out gradually as you get older. I have also heard it called the gas tank model: you are filled up in your youth with an initial supply of education, which is meant to see you through the rest of life's journey. Sadly, some young people leave school with half a tank; it is basic grade and there are too few gas stations if they run out en route.

It is worth pausing on the analogy with motor cars. Some policy makers talk about reforming education as if they were sorting out the auto industry. They emphasize the need to get back to basics and focus on the core business, to face up to overseas competition and to raise standards and improve efficiency, return on investment and cost-effectiveness. The difference is that motor cars and other lifeless products have no interest in how they are produced. People, on the other hand, are keenly interested in their own lives and education. They have feelings and opinions, hopes and aspirations. Ignoring the human factor is at the root of many of the problems that industrial systems of education have created.

Education is not only a preparation for what may come later; it is also about helping people engage with the present. What we become in our lives depends on the quality of our experiences here and now. For many people there never has been a simple, linear progression from education to a neatly planned career. Our lives are too buffeted by the currents and crosscurrents of social forces and personal impulse and the unpredictable confluences of events and opportunities.

The assumption of a direct line between what is taught in school and the work that young people do afterwards puts a priority on subjects that seem most relevant to the economy. If the economy needs more scientists and technologists, science and technology are given higher priority and other programs, in the arts and humanities, for example, are cut to make way for them. This policy is not in the better interests of young people or of society in general and it is not even the best way to produce good scientists and technologists. It is a mistake to think of the relationship between education and the economy as a straightforward process of supply and demand. While industrial systems may be standardized and linear, human life is not. It runs on different principles.

What's the use?

The Council of Europe is an intergovernmental organization based in Strasbourg. It works with member states across Europe including many of the former Soviet Bloc countries. Some years ago, I directed a research project for the Council of Europe, looking at provision for the arts in the education systems of 22 countries.[5] Someone has to do this sort of thing. There were many differences and some similarities. In all of them, the arts were on the edges of the school curriculum. Most systems included some art and music, very few taught drama and hardly any provided dance lessons. The pattern is the same in the United States, Canada, Mexico, Central and South America and in many parts of Asia: in fact, almost everywhere. Whatever the standards are that most countries want to raise, they don't seem to have much to do with what the arts teach. I know this from my own school experience.

When I was 14, my class teacher told me that I had a problem and sent me to see the head teacher. The issue was my choice of options for the next two years of school. I loved art and was very keen to carry on with it. I also wanted to take German. "Well, you do have a problem, Robinson," the head teacher said. "I'm afraid you can't do art and German." I was baffled. I'd seen films about Germany and there seemed to be pictures everywhere. "No," he said, "you can't do art and German here in this school. They clash on the timetable." I asked him what I should do. "If I were you," he said, "I should do German." I asked him why, and he said, "It will be more useful." I found this exasperating and still do.

I would have understood if he had said German would be more interesting, or that I had an obvious feel for languages, or that it would suit me better. But is German more useful than art? I know it is useful, especially in Germany. Languages are useful, but is art not? Is it useless? The curricula of most school systems seem to divide into two broad groups: the useful disciplines and the useless ones. Languages, mathematics, science and technology are useful; history, geography, art, music and drama are not. When funding is tight or reform movements focus on raising standards, arts programs are usually cut.

In 2001, the Federal Government of the United States passed into law the Elementary and Secondary Education Act (ESEA), generally known as "The No Child Left Behind Act, 2001" (NCLB). Its aims were to raise academic standards in all schools, to make teachers accountable for student achievement, to raise levels of college preparedness and in these ways to reinvigorate the economic competitiveness of the USA. The principal methods were to intensify programs of standardized testing for languages and mathematics and to link funding for schools to students' performance on the tests. NCLB was the result of a cross-party coalition; it was composed by serious people with the best interests of the country in mind and its intentions were admirable. In practice, it failed to meet its own objectives and has been widely condemned for demoralizing teachers and students, and for inculcating a numbing culture of standardized testing, buttressed by financial penalties for underperformance. Overall achievement in literacy and mathematics scarcely budged. Meanwhile, provision for the arts and for the humanities in many American schools was devastated.[6]

Policy makers emphasized that devastating arts education was not the intention of the legislation. I'm sure it was not. I doubt that serious politicians huddled in the committee rooms of Congress planning the downfall of the nation's piano teachers or deciding that dance educators were getting out of hand and had to be curbed. The arts suffered from collateral damage. The minds of the policy makers were focused on the disciplines at the top of the hierarchy. NCLB is a prime example of what some holistic doctors call the septic focus: the tendency to look at a problem in isolation from its context.

The septic focus

I had a friend, Dave, who was an actor. He was a large actor, weighing about 280 pounds. He liked to drink beer and had a particular taste for a powerful brew called Abbot Ale. You could run a small car on Abbot Ale, or a large actor. Dave regularly drank 12 pints of it a day. Some years ago, he developed back pain and went to his doctor, who referred him to a kidney specialist. The specialist examined him and said that he had potentially serious kidney problems. Dave asked what could be causing it. "It could be a number of things," said the consultant. "Do you drink?" Dave said that he did, socially, and mentioned the Abbot Ale. He admitted that he "socialized" quite a lot. The specialist told him he would have to stop drinking or face the prospect of renal failure. Dave said he couldn't stop drinking: he was an actor. "In that case," said the specialist, "why don't you change to spirits?" Dave said he thought that spirits could cause cirrhosis of the liver. "But you haven't come to see me about your liver," said the specialist, "I am concerned about your kidneys." A holistic doctor would have recognized that the problem in Dave's kidneys was a result of his overall lifestyle. Solving one problem by causing another is no solution. The septic focus is evident in the education reform movements that focus on certain parts of the system while neglecting the system as a whole.

Why do the disciplines at the top of the hierarchy get all the attention? Why does this hierarchy exist in the first place? The first answer is economic: some disciplines are assumed to be more relevant to the world of work. Generations of young people have been steered away from the arts with benign advice about poor job prospects: "Don't do art, you won't make it professionally as an artist." "Don't take music, you won't make a living as a musician." Benign advice maybe, but now profoundly wrong, as we will see. The arts are often thought to be important in schools for other reasons: as opportunities for creativity and self-expression or as leisure or "cultural" activities. When times are hard, many people take it for granted that the arts are not relevant to the hard-headed business of making a living. They may be interesting and enriching in themselves but when push comes to shove, they are disposable luxuries – optional at best.

I once had an argument on British television about this with a prominent member of the government. He said that the arts are important because they help to educate people for leisure. One of the many problems with this argument is that leisure is relative to work. If you have less work, you may have more leisure, if you have no work, you are unemployed. At the time, there were something like 2 million people in the UK who were unemployed. They were not organizing themselves as the new leisured classes.

There is another reason for the hierarchy, which is cultural. After all, children are not usually told, "Don't do math, you're not going to be a mathematician," or "Don't take science, you won't make it as a scientist." The disciplines at the top of the hierarchy are assumed to be inherently more important. This assumption is not to do with economics: it has to do with ideas about knowledge and intelligence. These ideas have dominated our ways of thinking for the past 300 years. If one pillar of mass education is industrialism, the second is academicism.

The ivory tower

In everyday language "academic" is often used as a synonym for "education." Politicians talk routinely about raising "academic standards" as if this means "educational standards" in general. The term "academic ability" is often used to mean "intelligence" in general. It is not the same thing at all. Academic work typically focuses on certain sorts of verbal and mathematical reasoning: on writing factual and critical essays, verbal discussions and mathematical analyses. These are important abilities, which education should promote, but if human intelligence were limited to them most of human culture would never have happened. There would be a lot of analysis but not much action. There would be no practical science, no technology, no functioning businesses, no art, no music or dance, no theater, poetry, love, feelings or intuition. These are large factors to leave out of an account of human intelligence. If all you had was academic ability, you couldn't have got out of bed this morning. In fact, there wouldn't have been a bed for you to get out of. Nobody could have made one. They could have written about the theoretical possibility of a bed, but not constructed the thing.

There is an interesting ambiguity in cultural attitudes to academic achievement. On the one hand, it is thought to be vital to personal success and to national prosperity. If academic standards are thought to be falling, media pundits beat their chests and politicians become resolute. On the other hand, "academic" is used as a polite form of abuse. Professional academics are thought to live in ivory towers with no practical understanding of the real world at all. An easy way to dismiss any argument is to say that it is "merely" academic.

How have we become so enthralled by academic ability and so skeptical of it at the same time? As we shall see in the next chapter, the cultural answers lie deep in the Enlightenment: the tumultuous movements in European philosophy and science in the seventeenth and eighteenth centuries. One reason why academic work continues to dominate general education is the tight grip of the universities on the school curricula and assessment. In many ways, the whole of elementary and high school education is a protracted system of university entrance. Those who go to university rather than straight into work or vocational training programs are still seen as the real successes of the system.

If you were to stand back from education and ask, "What is it all for?" you might conclude that the primary purpose of compulsory education is to produce university professors. They are the apotheosis of academic culture. I used to be a university professor and I have huge respect for academics and for academic life, but it is just another form of life. It should not be held up as the standard for other forms of human achievement. I know artists, business leaders, dancers, sportspeople and many others whose accomplishments, intelligence and humanity are as substantial as those of anyone I have met with a post-doctoral degree.

"Thinking of education as a preparation for something that happens later can overlook the fact that the first 16 or 18 years of a person's life are not a rehearsal. Young people are living their lives now."

Many highly intelligent people have passed through the whole of their education feeling that they are not, and many academically able people who've been fêted by the system have never discovered their other abilities.

The roles of education

Education has three main roles: personal, cultural and economic. A great deal could be said about each of these, but let me boil them down here into three basic statements of purpose:

> **Economic:** to provide the skills required to earn a living and be economically productive.
> **Cultural:** to deepen understanding of the world around us.
> **Personal:** to develop individual talents and sensibilities.

Understanding how these roles relate to each other is the key to bringing about systems of education for the twenty-first-century which have creativity and innovation at their center.

ECONOMIC CHALLENGES

Education has critical roles in developing the knowledge, skills and attitudes that are needed for economic vitality and growth. Current systems of education are causing problems that affect people from the top of the labor market to the bottom of it: from those who are highly qualified to those with no qualifications at all.

The over-qualified

Most national policies for education are committed to increasing the numbers of college graduates. The policies may be working, but too often the graduates are not. The sheer volume of graduates has generated an unexpected crisis in graduate recruitment. It is not that there are not enough graduates to go around: on the contrary, there are too many for the available numbers of graduate jobs.

For China, graduate unemployment is a sensitive issue. As part of its economic strategy, the government has encouraged millions of students to go to university to stimulate skills and consumer spending. Their families have invested heavily in their education. Many of these graduates have not found work for which they are qualified and are desperately applying for routine jobs in rural areas, or looking for posts as nannies and domestic helpers in more affluent regions such as Guangzhou. Quoting a housekeeping recruitment agency, the provincial government's newspaper, *Guangzhou Daily*, reported in January 2009 that 500 or 600 people were applying for domestic jobs every month, more than 90% of whom were university students – including 28 masters students.[7]

Graduate vacancies began to increase as the decade ended, especially in large companies, but there is still a considerable gap. In the United Kingdom, in the same period, there were about 20,000 graduate opportunities per annum and about 200,000 graduates a year competing for them. Many ended up applying for jobs for which they were over-qualified. During the recession of the early 1980s, around 30% of all graduates were in non-graduate jobs early on in their careers. Levels of over-qualification are even higher now.

There is a further issue. Too few graduates have what business needs. Complex economies need sophisticated talent "with global acumen, knowledge of different cultures, technological literacy, entrepreneurial skills, and the ability to manage increasingly complex organizations."[8] Employers say they want people who can think creatively, who can innovate, who can communicate well, work in teams and are adaptable and self-confident. They complain that many graduates have few of these qualities. It is hardly surprising. Conventional academic programs are not designed to develop them. Ironically, the demand for new skills is coming at a time when colleges are least able to adapt and provide them because growing student numbers restrict the time available for staff to offer personalized teaching. Nowadays, in most large universities, there are few opportunities for individual teaching. Students attend mass lectures by remote professors and large seminar groups run by poorly paid graduate assistants. Assignments are often graded with little feedback to inform the student. The pervasive culture of multiple-choice assessment makes the process even more impersonal and risk averse.

The war for talent

Many organizations are finding it difficult to find the people they need. When they do find them, they often have trouble keeping them. Executives say there is an increasing shortage of the people needed to run divisions and manage critical functions, let alone lead companies. This problem has been building for some time. One of the consequences is that organizations are fighting a war for talent.[9]

The corporate consultancy company, McKinsey, worked with the human resources departments of 77 large US companies in a variety of industries to understand their talent-building philosophies, practices and challenges. Their original study included nearly 400 corporate offices and 6,000 executives in the "top 200" ranks in these companies. It also drew on case studies of 20 companies widely regarded as being rich in talent.[10] Three-quarters of companies had said they had insufficient talent sometimes, and all were chronically short of talent across the board.[11] The study concluded that executive talent has long been an under-managed corporate asset. Companies that manage their physical and financial assets with rigor and sophistication have not made their people a priority in the same way. Few employees trust employers to provide useful opportunities for professional development. Most take a short-term view of training needs. Only a third of employers provide training beyond the job. In a rapidly changing environment, they worry that their best talent will be poached by other companies. They are wary of investing in developing their own talent since they fear it will primarily benefit their competitors. Staff turnover is often high and vacant posts are

filled with outside talent. According to search professionals, the average executive will work in five companies; in
another ten years it may be seven.

Most companies choose to develop powerful recruitment
and retention processes to get the "right people" on board.
The problem with the short-term model is that "it does nothing to prevent the exodus of the rest – those whose talents are
undeveloped. It assumes a world with an unlimited supply
of talent ... that does not mind working in businesses where
development is not deemed a priority."[12] Even so, according to McKinsey, companies are engaged in a war for senior
executive talent that will remain a defining characteristic of
the competitive landscape for decades to come. Yet most are
ill prepared, and even the best are vulnerable.[13]

The under-qualified

The problems are serious enough for the highly qualified. They
are worse for the unqualified. In the United States an average
of 30% of students who enter the 9th grade in school will not
graduate from high school. In some areas the proportion is
as high as 50%. In some Native American communities it is
higher still. Among those who stay the course, rates of under-
achievement and disaffection are often desperately high.[14]

It is wrong to blame the students for these numbers: they
reflect a problem within the system. Any other standardized process with a 30% wastage rate, let alone 50% or higher, would be
condemned as a failure. In the case of education, it is not a waste
of inert commodities; it is a waste of living, breathing people. As
matters stand, those who don't graduate from high school are
offered few alternatives apart from low-income work if they can
find it, or long-term unemployment if they cannot. The costs of
unemployment create immense burdens for the economy, while
very many productive jobs that could be filled are not.

In 2016, 21 million people in the European Union were
unemployed, nearly a third of them under the age of 25.

According to one study, "One in three Europeans of working age has few or no formal qualifications, making them 40 percent less likely to be employed than those with medium-level qualifications. In the United Kingdom alone, 5.7 million adults of working age have no qualifications at all and 20 percent of all adults in England, around 7 million people, have serious problems with basic literacy and numeracy."[15] Most experts agree that the roots of Europe's jobs dilemma lie in an inflexible education system, high labor taxes and barriers to mobility.

Among the worst affected are young people. Worldwide there are approximately 600 million young people between the ages of 15 and 24. Around 75 million of them (12%) are unemployed, about twice the rate of adult unemployment. According to the International Labor Organization, youth unemployment is a deepening problem everywhere. Unemployment creates its own social hazards from the sense of alienation and prolonged inactivity. Ninety percent of young people live in developing economies, where they are especially vulnerable to underemployment and poverty. "In developing countries," says the ILO, "crisis pervades the daily life of the poor. The number of young people stuck in working poverty grows and the cycle of working poverty persists through at least another generation."[16] The ILO argues that these trends will have "significant consequences for young people as upcoming cohorts of new entrants join the ranks of the already unemployed" and warns of the "risk of a crisis legacy of a 'lost generation' comprised of young people who have dropped out of the labor market, having lost all hope of being able to work for a decent living."

The ILO studies highlight the cost of unemployment among young people: "Societies lose their investment in education. Governments fail to receive contributions to social security systems and are forced to increase spending on remedial services."Young people are the drivers of economic development: "Foregoing this potential is an economic waste and can undermine social stability." The chronically high number of jobless, roughly half of whom have been out of work for more than a year, is more than an economic challenge.

The long-term unemployed are part of a broad group who feel marginalized by the driving forces of change but powerless to do anything about them. These groups tend to be concentrated in particular areas, lessening their shared chances of recovery. (In the UK, the vast majority of unemployed people live on 2,000 housing estates.) In a work-driven society, being without work or the prospect of it can produce an aggressive counter-attack. In many countries, there is a worrying trend in disaffection and aggression among young people in schools.[17] Many teachers feel frustrated and demoralized. In a survey of teachers in the UK, two-thirds wanted to leave the school they worked in and half wanted to leave the profession altogether because of poor discipline in schools.[18]

In the United States, too, there is a smoldering problem of social exclusion. In a number of urban centers the problems of gang violence are growing. In major European cities, gang warfare has become an endemic feature of teenage life. One of the most troubling prospects is the emergence of a permanent underclass, which can become caught in an irrevocable cycle of crime, poverty and despair. There can be a high price to pay in containing the anger and frustrations of those who feel marginalized and hopeless.

The United States has the highest incarceration rate of any country in the world. A startling 1 in every 35 American adults is in the correctional system – which includes jail, prison, probation and supervision – more than double the rate 30 years ago. Prison and jail populations grew 274%, to 2.3 million in 2008, while those under supervision grew 226%, to 5.1 million. The numbers are concentrated among particular groups. Just over 10% of black adults in the US are in the correctional system, about 4% of the Hispanic population and 2% of whites. Large numbers of people in the mushrooming prisoner populations did not complete

high school, or struggled with literacy or numeracy or under-
performed in education because of undiagnosed learning
difficulties.

Over the past 30 years, state spending on penitentiary
systems has been the fastest-growing part of their budgets
after Medicaid, the healthcare program for those with low
income. In California in 2010, spending on the state correctional system overtook spending on the whole of public higher education. The costs of incarceration are vastly
higher than education. On average, keeping an inmate in
prison costs $29,000 a year, compared with an estimated
$9,000 a year for high school education.[19] Some policy mak-
ers clearly prefer to meet the costs of containment rather
than invest in the talents of marginalized communities. Yet,
developing the talents and aspirations of those who are in
trouble is by far the best way to re-engage them in society
and avoid the spiraling costs of recidivism. From every point
of view, social, ethical and economic, it would make vastly
more sense to invest in improving education in the first place
and to give all young people a proper start in life rather than
underfund education and spend incomparably more on the
consequences.[20]

CULTURAL CHALLENGES

I sometimes ask people at conferences to put their hands up
if they are over the age of 30 and to keep them up if they are
wearing a wristwatch. Usually it is the majority. When I ask
teenagers the same question, very few keep their hands up.
As a rule, the current generation of teenagers do not wear
wristwatches. For them, the time is everywhere, on their
smartphones, tablets and games units. They see no need to
wear a separate gadget just to tell the time. "Why would you?"
they say. "It's a single function device. How lame is that?" I
say, "No, it's not, it tells the date as well."

Technology, as was once said, is not technology if it happened before you were born. Digital technologies have created what has been called the biggest generation gap since rock and roll. Mark Prensky and others make a distinction between digital natives and digital immigrants.[21] This is not a hard distinction but it does point to a generational shift. In immigrant communities, the adults often recreate the culture of the old country in the new one, for the sake of nostalgia and security. The children are thrust into the new culture, embrace it more vigorously and teach it to the adults. It is often this way with digital culture. Our children have a lot to teach us about the possibilities of the new tools and ways of thinking. They speak digital as their native tongue, many adults speak it as a second language. Our children do not even consider these devices as technology. They are as natural to them as the air they breathe.

As technologies race forward, economies oscillate and populations shift, so do values and behavior. Education systems everywhere now have to contend with massive waves of cultural change on every front. Some of these are the direct features of digital culture, some are not. In the last 50 years many of the old certainties have also broken down: the nuclear family, patterns of religious involvement, gender roles and the rest. The cavernous inequalities of wealth and opportunity are opening deeper divisions between cultural communities. Everywhere, and for every reason, cultural identities are now complex, interwoven and contested.

PERSONAL CHALLENGES

Young people in school are under much more pressure from testing than my generation was. They work harder to get into college than we did, they work harder when they are there if they want a good result and, when they leave, their qualifications are worth less. This pressure begins when they are 5, if not 3, and continues throughout school. For students in higher education, the pressure can be more intense. As academic inflation continues to rise, students put themselves under immense pressure to succeed. Many take performance-enhancing drugs to stay focused.

There is another pressure. In a study of suicidal behavior among students, Rory O'Connor and Noel Sheehy argue that students "are under pressure to be rounded, happy, successful, talented, bright young things and they want to fit in ... They are under pressure not to appear under pressure." More and more of them are finding all of these pressures too difficult to bear and are suffering from the consequences. The numbers of suicides at universities highlight the toxic pressures to succeed. Some student counselors are joining the call for schools to spend more time helping young people to develop the personal, social and coping skills they need to deal with contemporary life: "Only by getting young people to talk can we tackle the stigma associated with being unable to deal with stress and the reluctance to go to see anyone about it ... By assuming that academic success is the be-all and end-all of life, we are not teaching people how to deal with failure and this is a fundamental oversight."[22]

TAKING STOCK

The current systems of mass education were conceived and built in other times to meet other challenges. They have to be reconceived to meet the challenges we face now. Despite the growing skills gap, the war for talent and the pace of change on every front, many policy makers and others continue to chant the mantra about the need to raise traditional academic standards and scores on standardized tests. The reason, I believe, is that the assumptions underpinning these approaches to education have become so deeply embedded that many people are not even aware of them. They have blended into the everyday ideologies of common sense, as the way things have to be. Like a lot of common sense, what may seem obvious can also be wrong. Raising academic standards alone will not solve the problems we face; it may compound them. To move forward we need to rethink some of our basic ideas about education, intelligence and ourselves. Above all, we need to awaken ourselves from what James Hemming[23] vividly called the "academic illusion." It enthralls us more completely than you might think.

· 4 ·

THE ACADEMIC ILLUSION

"All truth passes through three stages:
First, it is ridiculed. Second, it is violently opposed.
Third, it is accepted as being self-evident."
Arthur Schopenhauer (1788–1860)

HOW INTELLIGENT ARE YOU? This is not an easy question to answer. Intelligence is one of those qualities that we think we can recognize in people, but when we try to define it, it can slip from our grasp. If it's any consolation, there's no agreed definition of intelligence among the many specialists in psychology, neurology, education or other professional fields who devote a good deal of their own intelligence to thinking about it. There may be no agreed definition, but there are two ideas that dominate popular conceptions of intelligence. The first is IQ (Intelligence Quotient); the second is a memory for factual information.

JOIN THE CLUB

Mensa is an international association that promotes itself as one of the most exclusive clubs in the world. Membership is on the basis of "high intelligence" and Mensa claims to admit only 2% of the population to its ranks. The decision is based on applicants' performance in various "intelligence tests" that ask questions like these:

1) What letter should come next?

   M Y V S E H M S J R S N U S N E P?

2) Details of items bought at a stationer are shown below.

   78 – Pencils

   152 – Paint Brushes

   51 – Files

   142 – Felt Tip Pens

   ? – Writing Pads

   How many writing pads should there be?

3) In which direction should the missing arrow point?

   v   >   ∧   v   <

   v   <   >   v   >

   ∧   >   ?   >   v

   >   <   v   ∧   >

   v   >   <   v   ∧

These sorts of question test the ability to analyze logically the principles that govern a sequence of ideas.[1] Philosophers call this logico-deductive reasoning. Thinking "logically" is an important part of the popular view of intelligence. The second is having a good memory for facts.

AS A MATTER OF FACT

Mastermind is one of the best-known quiz shows on British television. Four contestants take it in turn to sit under a spotlight in a darkened studio and face the quizmaster. There are two 2-minute rounds of questions: the first is on a specialist topic chosen by the contestant; the second on "general knowledge." The Mastermind of the Year emerges at the end of each series from an all-winners final and is fêted as one of the cleverest people in Britain. A long-running radio program called *Brain of Britain* has a similar format. Contestants in the phenomenally successful *Who Wants to be a Millionaire?* can win a fortune by giving correct answers to just 12 factual questions. Quiz programs like these draw on the ability to memorize factual information, including names, dates, events and statistics. Philosophers call this propositional knowledge: knowledge *that* something is the case. Academic ability draws on these two capacities for logico-deductive reason and for propositional knowledge.

The term "academic" derives from the name of a grove near ancient Athens called *Academeia*. It was there, 400 years before the birth of Christ, that the Greek philosopher Plato established a community of scholars. Plato's teachings drew on the philosophical methods that had been developed by his teacher, Socrates. Plato's most famous student was Aristotle (who, in turn, was tutor to Alexander the Great). Aristotle further developed these ideas in his own work and teachings, from which there have evolved systems of thought, of mathematics and of science that have shaped the intellectual character of the Western world. But apart from presumably having high ones themselves, Plato, Socrates and Aristotle had never heard of IQ or Mensa. So what is the link between IQ tests, quiz shows, mass education and the groves of *Academeia*?

MEASURING YOUR MIND

Like the motor car, television, the micro-processor and the Coca-Cola bottle, IQ is one of the most compelling inventions of the modern world. It is an idea in four parts.

Each of us is born with a *fixed* intellectual capacity or quotient: just as we may have brown eyes or red hair, we have a set amount of intelligence.

How much intelligence we have can be calculated by a series of "pencil-and-paper" tests of the sort illustrated above. The results can be compared against a general scale and given as a number from 0 to 200. That number is your IQ. On this scale, average performance is between 80 and 100; above average is between 100 and 120 and anything above 130 gets you into Mensa's Christmas party.

IQ tests can be used to predict children's performance at school and in later life. For this reason, various versions of IQ tests are widely used for school selection and for educational planning.

IQ is an index of general intelligence: that is, the scores on these tests point to a person's overall intellectual capacities. For this reason, some people think that it is enough to announce their IQ score for everyone to grasp how bright they are, or not.

Since the idea of IQ emerged about 100 years ago, it has had explosive consequences for social policy and especially for education. Where did the idea come from in the first place; how did it come to dominate the popular conception of intelligence; and is it a fair and accurate measure across all cultures?

Brave old world

The foundations of the modern intelligence test were laid in the mid-nineteenth century by Sir Francis Galton, a cousin of Charles Darwin. After reading *The Origin of Species* in 1859, he wondered if human life followed the principles of natural selection that Darwin had described in the rest of nature. Galton concluded that if heredity played a decisive role in human development, it should be possible to improve the human race through selective breeding procedures. (He first used the word *eugenics*, with the meaning "good" or "well" born, in 1883.[2]) With that end in mind, he turned to developing scientific ways of isolating and measuring "general intelligence" and of comparing it between individuals. The modern intelligence test builds on Galton's work and more especially on that of Alfred Binet.

At the beginning of the twentieth century, Binet was working with children in elementary schools in Paris and wanted to identify those who might need special educational support. He began to develop short tests for children of different ages that could be easily administered. His aim was practical and his method "was pragmatic rather than scientific."[3] By 1905, he had produced his first scale of intelligence based on a test of 30 items designed for children aged from 3 to 12 years. The tester worked through the items with each child until the child could do no more. Performance was compared with the average for the age group to which the child belonged. If a child could pass the test expected of a 6-year-old, say, the child was said to have a mental age of 6. Binet used the difference between the mental age and the chronological age as an index of "retardation."

In 1912, German psychologist William Stern proposed using the ratio of mental age to chronological age to yield the now familiar intelligence quotient:

$$IQ = \frac{\text{mental age}}{\text{chronological age}} \times 100$$

Within a few years, translations of Binet's work were starting to appear in other parts of the world. The restricted uses for which it was originally designed were soon forgotten and it was applied in every sort of setting, especially in the United States. One hundred years later, IQ remains the principal basis of selection for different forms of education, for many different types of employment and for roles in the military.

IQ has been used to support and to attack theories of racial, ethnic and social difference. Early IQ tests in the UK and the USA suggested that poor people and their children have low IQs and that the rich and their offspring have high IQs. Researchers wondered if IQ somehow determined levels of affluence and of material success. An important variable, of course, is that poor people could not afford to educate themselves and rich people could, which is something of an oversight from a methodological point of view.

For a time, these findings provided a powerful rationale for political initiatives based on eugenics to "improve" the human stock by selective breeding and population control. In the early twentieth century, leading intellectuals including Winston Churchill and George Bernard Shaw supported the eugenics movement, arguing that the breeding of the poor should be carefully controlled. Some states in the USA legislated to sterilize people classified as "idiots" or of low intelligence. With different motives, the Third Reich embraced eugenics as a key element in the Final Solution.

A major controversy about IQ tests flared up in 1992 with the publication in America of *The Bell Curve* by Charles Murray and Richard Hernstein.[4] *The Bell Curve* argued that IQ tests point to significant racial differences in human intelligence. It argued that IQ is linked to low moral behavior and that there is a connection with the cultures of some ethnic groups, especially Black and Hispanic communities. *The Bell Curve* was widely condemned as a racist tract and generated an inferno of debate, which is still smoldering.

From the outset, IQ has been a powerful and provocative idea, and it remains so, even though there is no general agreement on exactly what IQ tests measure, or on how, whatever it is they do measure, this relates to general intelligence. Nonetheless these ideas of academic ability and of IQ have come to be taken for granted as the natural order of things, rather than as the product of particular scientific enquiries and cultural perspectives. How has this happened? The answer lies in the triumph of science in the last 400 years and in its roots in the groves of *Academeia*.

THE TRIUMPH OF SCIENCE

Historians conventionally think of Western history in three main periods: ancient, medieval and modern. These periods are not separated by sharp boundaries or exact dates, but they are recognizable phases in the cultural evolution of humanity. They are marked by different ways of seeing the world and by the different worlds that were created as a result.

The philosopher Susanne Langer[5] argues that intellectual horizons of a society, or of an historical period, are not set simply by events or human desires. They are set by the basic ideas that people use to analyze and describe their lives. Theories develop in response to questions and a question, as Langer notes, can only be answered in a certain number of ways. For this reason the most important characteristic of an intellectual age is the questions it asks – the problems it identifies. It is this, rather than the answers it provides, that reveals its underlying view of the world. In any intellectual age there will be some fundamental assumptions that advocates of all the different ways of thinking unconsciously take for granted. These deep-seated attitudes constitute our ideology, and they set the boundaries of theory by inclining us to this or that set of issues and explanations. If our explanations are theoretical, our questions are ideological.

"Copernicus, Galileo and Kepler did not solve an old problem: they asked a new question."

The term "paradigm" was popularized in the 1970s by the American philosopher of science, Thomas Kuhn (1922–1996).[6] A paradigm is an accepted framework of rules and assumptions that define established ways of doing things. In the history of science, a paradigm is not a single theory or scientific discovery, but the underlying approach to science itself, within which theories are framed and discoveries are verified.

Kuhn describes science as a puzzle-solving activity in which problems are tackled using procedures and rules that are agreed within the community of scientists. He was interested in periods in history when there was a shift either in the problems or in the rules of science or both. He saw a difference between periods of "normal science," when there is general agreement among scientists about problems and rules, and periods of "extraordinary science," when normal science begins to generate results that the accepted rules and assumptions cannot explain. If these anomalies accumulate, there can be a loss of confidence in the accepted methods and a professional crisis in science, which can unleash periods of enormous creativity and invention. Periods of "extraordinary science" create opportunities for new questions and theories about the nature and limits of science itself. These are times of scientific revolution.

A new paradigm may emerge when new ideas or methods – what Susanne Langer calls *generative ideas* – runs with tumultuous force through existing ways of thinking and transforms them. Truly generative ideas excite intellectual passions in many different fields because they open up whole new ways of seeing and thinking. As Susanne Langer said, "a new idea is a light that illuminates things that simply had no form for us before the light fell on them and gave them meaning. We turn the light here, there and everywhere and the limits of thought recede before it."[7]

Paradigm shifts tend to run a characteristic course. They are triggered by new ideas that reconfigure basic ways of thinking. Initially, there is a period of intellectual uncertainty and excitement as the new ideas are applied, stretched and tested in different areas of inquiry. Eventually, the revolutionary ways of thinking begin to settle down and their potential becomes clearer and more established. They become part of the new way of thinking: the new paradigm. Eventually, the ideas become drained of their excitement, leaving a residue of established ideas and new certainties. They enter the culture as taken-for-granted ideas about the way things are and provide the framework for a new period of normal science.

The transition from one intellectual age to another can be traumatic and protracted. Some people never make the transition and remain resident in the old worldview: their ideological comfort zone. New ways of thinking do not simply replace the old at clear points in history. They may coexist with old ways of thinking for a long time, creating many tensions and unresolved problems along the way. Each major period of intellectual growth has been characterized by revolutionary ideas that have driven forward the sensibilities of the times.

In the ancient and medieval periods it was taken for granted that Ptolemy (c. AD 90–c. AD 168) was right: the sun orbited round the earth. There were two reasons for this belief. To begin with, that is exactly what it seemed to do: the sun came up in the morning, passed through the sky and went down again at night. It was obvious to everyone that the sun was moving, not the earth. People were not being flung off the planet on the way to work; there was not a network of ropes to cling to on the way to the shops. It was plain common sense that the earth was motionless. There were religious reasons too for this assumption.

In the medieval worldview, the earth was the center of creation and human beings were God's last word: the jewel in the cosmic crown. Theologians assumed a perfect symmetry in the universe. The planets, it was thought, revolved around the earth in perfect circular orbits. Poets expressed this harmony in the rhythms of verse; mathematicians from the early Greeks developed elegant formulae to describe these motions; and astronomers based elaborate theories upon them. The problem was that there were worrying variations in these movements. The planets would not behave.

Astronomers made increasingly intricate calculations to account for these variations. As perplexed as everyone else, Nicolaus Copernicus (1473–1543) made a radical proposal. What if the sun was not going round the earth, he asked? What if the earth was going round the sun? This startling idea solved, at a stroke, many of the old problems that had plagued astronomers. Heliocentrism had arrived. Later, Johannes Kepler (1571–1630) showed that the planets did not move in circles but in elliptical orbits, a phenomenon that Isaac Newton (1643–1727) was eventually explain by the effects of gravitational attraction.

The Copernican theory caused few ripples until Galileo Galilei (1564–1642) took an interest in Heliocentrism. His telescope enabled scientists to see the truth of Copernican theories and the ideas began to take hold. Unfortunately, they were heretical: an affront to God's design and to humanity's view of itself. Galileo was persecuted and put on trial twice for his views. Nonetheless, over time more people came to accept that these theories were correct. Copernicus, Galileo and Kepler did not solve an old problem: they asked new questions and in doing so they changed the paradigm within which the old questions had been framed. The old theories were shown to be wrong because the assumptions on which they had been based were mistaken. They were built on a false ideology. As this realization spread, it ushered in a new intellectual age: a new paradigm.

The Renaissance of the fourteenth and fifteenth centuries marked a shift away from the medieval worldview and from the ideologies in which they had been conceived. The insights of Copernicus and Galileo proved to be the dawn of a new age. The transition from Ptolemy's first-century view of the universe with the earth at its center, to the universe of Copernicus, repositioned not only the earth in space but also humanity's place in history.

The shock waves did not stop with astronomy: they rolled through all areas of cultural life including philosophy, politics and religion. Though they both denied being atheists, the arguments of Copernicus and Galileo raised serious doubts about many aspects of religious teaching. Five hundred years later, Darwin's theory of evolution was to issue a more profound challenge to religious belief: a theory that was framed in the paradigm of objective science that had been heralded by the Copernican revolution. The medieval world-view that had been held together by dogma and faith was eventually shaken apart by a new one, based on logic, reason and evidence.

BORN AGAIN

The period which we now think of as the Renaissance was so called because it marked a rebirth of interest in the methods and achievements of the ancient world in philosophy, literature and mathematics. In little more than 150 years, the Renaissance gave rise to some of humanity's most luminous figures and most enduring works: lives and achievements that have shaped the world that we now live in. Between 1450 and 1600 Europe saw the birth of Leonardo da Vinci, Michelangelo, Raphael, Galileo, Copernicus, Shakespeare and Isaac Newton. They produced works in art and literature of unsurpassed beauty and depth, and created the foundations of modern science, technology and philosophy.

The modern idea of a Renaissance person is someone who is learned in a range of disciplines including the arts and sciences. The quintessential Renaissance figure is Leonardo da Vinci, who was gifted in painting, sculpture, mathematics and science. When Michelangelo was painting the Sistine Chapel, he was also working on scientific theorems and on designs for new technological devices. The Renaissance and the cultural movements that flowed from it were impelled not only by surpassing accomplishments in the arts and letters, but by a succession of startling innovations in technology. Four in particular were to prove decisive: the printing press, the magnetic compass, the telescope and the mechanical clock.

Spreading the word

Before the printing press, only a small, literate elite, largely confined to the Church, had access to books, ideas and learning. The power of the Church was rooted in its exclusive access to scriptures and through them to the word of God. This gave the clergy unrivalled control over the people's minds. The printing and distribution of books unleashed a voracious appetite for literacy and disseminated ideas across national and cultural boundaries on a scale that was previously unimaginable. As the flow of ideas increased, the iron grip of the Church began to loosen.

The invention of the portable book by Aldus Manutius (1450–1515) of Venice facilitated the personal library and revolutionized the control of knowledge. The venerable institution of the medieval library began to be replaced by an independently published and commercial product. As Juan F. Rada puts it: "A new technological and intellectual transition started, which reinforced the conditions of the scientific revolution and accompanied the great period of the discoveries. The portable book had a subversive impact, created the conditions for the Reformation, for the use of vernacular language, for the diversification of publishing and allowed for a great individual expression of authors and readers." The portable library created the instruments that were necessary for the development of complex bureaucracies and large organized states: "Publishing became the vehicle for the transmission of ideas and debate, for proselytism and for scholarly recognition. The seeds for the Enlightenment were sown and with them the belief in education and, in this century, the belief in universal education and literacy."[8]

Getting our bearings

The Renaissance was an era of eye-opening discoveries. The fleets of the European powers journeyed across the oceans on speculative expeditions of exploration and colonization.

These forays into the unknown were made possible by new navigational tools, including the magnetic compass (developed originally by the Chinese some 200 years earlier and only recently surpassed by GPS), which revolutionized orientation, especially at sea, by measuring points of direction with great precision.

As some explorers were mapping the earth, others took their lead from Galileo and were surveying the heavens with a new sense of scientific precision. The telescope made possible more accurate observations of the movements of the planets and of the place of the earth in the heavens. These innovations interacted with the evolution of new theories in science and mathematics. So too did a more complex invention, which may also have its roots in Chinese technology.

During the sixteenth and seventeenth centuries, people started to think differently about time. Until then the most reliable ways of keeping track of time were sundials and water clocks. Versions of these devices had been in use around the world since ancient times and they varied both in sophistication and in how they framed the passing of time. In 1656, Christiaan Huygens, a Dutch philosopher, mathematician and scientist, perfected his design for a mechanical clock, regulated by a pendulum. Huygens' clock was complex, precise and reliable, and it helped to revolutionize humanity's sense of time. The idea that the day is divided into 24 equal segments of 60 minutes is an indissoluble part of how we see the world. Mechanical clocks released people from organizing their time by the natural rhythms of day and night: a change that had profound significance for patterns of work and industry. The clock also suggested new ways of thinking about the universe.

In 1687, Isaac Newton published his *Principia* in which he set out his monumental theories about the workings of nature and of our place in the cosmos. In doing so, he conceived of the universe as a great clock-like mechanism, an idea that had a deep impact on subsequent developments in science and philosophy. Implied in this image were ideas about cause and effect and about the importance of external as against internal stimuli: ideas that now shape everyday thinking and behavior. As Alvin Toffler notes, the invention of the clock came before Newton published his theories and had a profound effect on how he framed them, though Newton himself warned against using his theories to view the universe as akin to a great clock. He said, "Gravity explains the motions of the planets, but it cannot explain who set the planets in motion. God governs all things and knows all that is or can be done."

The rise of the individual

In the medieval period, Church and State were locked in a close embrace. One force that began to erode the power of the Church was the spread of literacy. Another, which literacy fomented, was a growing unrest with the spiritual and political corruption of the Church. In the early fifteenth century, the German cleric Martin Luther sparked a revolt against Rome that spread rapidly throughout Europe and split Christianity in two. Luther argued that no third party, and least of all a corrupt and self-serving Church, should stand between individuals and their relationship with their creator. The Reformation emphasized the need for individuals to reach their own understanding of the scriptures and to deal directly with God. The emphasis on empowering the critical judgment and knowledge of the individual underpinned the growth of scientific method in the seventeenth and eighteenth centuries in Europe; the period now known as the Enlightenment.

Being reasonable

As the old certainties of the Church were shaken, the intellectuals of the Enlightenment began to ask fundamental questions about the nature of things. Specifically, what is knowledge and how do we know? They tried to take nothing for granted. The aim was to see the world as it is; stripped of superstition, myth and fantasy. Knowledge had to conform to the strict dictates of deductive logic or be supported by the evidence of observation. The French philosopher René Descartes (1596–1650) argued that nothing should be taken on trust. If a new edifice of knowledge was to be constructed, it must be built brick by brick with each element fully tested. He set out a logical program of analysis where nothing would be taken for granted, not even his own existence. His starting point was that the only thing he could know for certain was that he was actually thinking about the problems: *cogito ergo sum.* "I think, therefore I am." I must be alive because I am thinking.

The rationalist moves through logical sequences, building one idea on another in a mutually dependent framework. The empirical method similarly looks for patterns in events, suggesting movements from known causes to known effects. *Rationalism* and *empiricism* were the driving forces of the Enlightenment and they ran with irresistible force through science, philosophy and politics, bowling over traditional methods of thought and opening up vast new fields of adventure in science, technology and philosophy. They led, in due course, to the Industrial Revolution of the eighteenth and nineteenth centuries and to the dominance of science in our own times. Along the way a fissure opened up between two modes of understanding that had previously been almost indistinguishable: the arts and the sciences.

The shaping of the modern world

The achievements of the rationalist scientific worldview have been incalculable. They include unparalleled leaps in medicine and pharmaceuticals and in the length and quality of human life; the explosive growth in industrial technologies; sophisticated systems of communication and travel; and an unprecedented understanding of the physical universe. There is clearly much more to come as the catalogue of achievements in science and technology continues to accumulate. There has been a heavy price too, not least in the schism of the arts and sciences and the domination of the rationalist attitude, especially in the forms of education to which it has given rise.

The union of the arts and sciences, which seemed so natural in the Renaissance, gradually dissolved during the Enlightenment. In the late eighteenth and early nineteenth century, there was a powerful cultural reaction to cold logic and its mission to demystify the world. In music, art, dance, drama, poetry and prose, the disparate band of the Romantics reasserted the power and validity of human experience, of feelings, emotions and transcendence. Whereas the Enlightenment was represented by the great rationalist philosophers and scientists, including Hume, Locke and Descartes, Romanticism was carried forward in the powerful works of Beethoven, Schiller, Wordsworth, Coleridge, Byron, Goethe and many more.

In contrast to the rationalists, the Romantics celebrated the nature of human experience and existence. The divisions are alive and well in contemporary attitudes to the arts and sciences. Typically, the sciences are associated with fact and truth. The image of the scientist is a white-coated clinician moving through impersonal calculations to an objective understanding of the way the world works. In contrast, the arts are associated with feelings, imagination and self-expression. The artist is pictured as a free spirit giving vent to a turmoil of creative ideas. In education, the impact of these assumptions has been far reaching.

THE RISE OF EDUCATION

Before the Industrial Revolution, relatively few people had any formal education. In the Middle Ages in Europe, education was provided largely by the Church in what were known as grammar schools. Originally, a grammar school was literally one that taught grammar and especially Latin grammar.[9] The Kings School, Canterbury, claims to be the oldest grammar school in England. It traces its origins to the coming of St Augustine in AD 597, though such institutions may have originated more than 1,000 years earlier. Grammar schools of various sorts can be traced back to the ancient Greeks.

Many of the grammar schools in Europe were founded by religious bodies. Some were attached to the larger or collegiate parish churches, others were maintained by monasteries. The primary purpose of these grammar schools was to educate boys for the Church, but medieval clerics followed careers in many fields. The Church was the gateway to all professions including law, the civil service, diplomacy, politics and medicine. In the ancient and medieval schools, the principal focus was on learning Greek and Latin literature and the aim was to be fluent enough in these to gain a foothold in professional life. Latin was the international language of the Church and fluency was a requirement. Given their specialist functions, grammar schools have always been selective through some form of entrance test.

By the close of the fifteenth century, there were 300 or more grammar schools in England: the Church was involved in most of them. As the fifteenth and sixteenth centuries unfolded, and skepticism of religious doctrine deepened, nonreligious organizations began to establish their own schools for their own purposes. Many of these were related to trade.[10] The growing influence of grammar schools was accompanied by gradual changes in what they actually taught.

The curriculum of the medieval grammar schools was specifically classical. Classical education was based on the seven liberal arts or sciences: grammar, the formal structures of language; rhetoric, composition and presentation of argument; dialectic, formal logic; arithmetic; geometry; music; astronomy.[11] For centuries, the classics dominated the very idea of being educated and attempts at reform were resisted. As James Hemming notes, schools were in thrall to the "classical illusion," the idea that "only those are educated who can read Homer in the original."

During the Renaissance some pioneering head teachers tried to loosen the grip of the classics on the grammar school curriculum by introducing other subjects and more practical approaches to teaching them. Richard Mulcaster was the first headmaster of the Merchant Tailors' School from 1561 to 1586. He made valiant efforts to have English taught at grammar schools, arguing that it was essential to regulate its grammar and spelling. He pressed the case for drama in schools and his boys performed before Elizabeth I on a number of occasions. The curriculum of the Merchant Tailors' School came to include music and drama, dancing, drawing and sport of all sorts – wrestling, fencing, shooting, handball and football.

Francis Bacon (1561–1626) argued for the inclusion of other subjects in the school curriculum, including history and modern languages and especially science. The headmaster of Tonbridge School published a book in 1787 arguing for the curriculum to include history, geography, mathematics, French, artistic training and physical training. In Britain, attempts to broaden the curriculum beyond the classics made little progress until the mid-nineteenth century. Charles Darwin (1809–82) went to school at Shrewsbury. Reflecting on the experience, he said: "Nothing could have been worse for my mind than this school, as it was strictly classical; nothing else being taught except a little ancient geography and history. The school as a means of education was to me a complete blank. During my whole life I have been singularly incapable of mastering any language ... The sole pleasure I ever received from such [classical] studies was from some of the odes from Horace which I admired greatly."[12]

The pressure for change came from elsewhere. Three developments in particular were to reshape public opinion about schooling and to reform the grammar school curriculum. The first was the growing impact of science and technology, and the changing intellectual climate of which they were part. Second, the rampant growth of industrialism was changing the international economic landscape. The Exhibitions of 1851 and 1862 illustrated the rapid industrial progress of other European countries, a movement that had begun in Britain but was now threatening to outrun it. Third, new theories were developing about the nature of intelligence and learning. The new science of psychology was proposing new explanations about the nature of intelligence and how it should be cultivated. These theories challenged the benefits of a strictly classical education rooted in learning grammar and formal logic.

During the nineteenth and twentieth centuries the classics became almost extinct in secondary education. In their place, the school curriculum settled into the now-familiar hierarchy: languages, mathematics, science and technology at the top, the humanities and the arts at the bottom. As James Hemming put it, it was then that the classical illusion was replaced by the academic illusion.

THE IRRESISTIBLE RISE OF IQ

In 1870, the British Government passed an Act of Parliament to develop provision for primary schools. In 1902, it turned its attention to secondary education and began to establish county grammar schools. Forty-two years later, at the height of World War II, the government passed the 1944 Education Act, which provided free secondary education for all. The Act was designed to produce a workforce that met the needs of the post-war industrial economy.[13] It established three types of school: grammar, secondary modern and technical. The grammar schools were to educate the "top 20%": the prospective doctors, teachers, lawyers, accountants, civil servants and managers of post-war Britain. It was assumed that they would need a rigorous academic education and that is what the grammar schools were intended to give them. Those who went to the secondary modern schools were destined for blue collar and manual work. They were given a more basic education that was effectively a watered-down version of the grammar school curriculum. Many European countries made similar sorts of provision.[14]

It was during the massive expansion of education in the postwar years in the United Kingdom that IQ took such a firm hold on the whole system. The large numbers of young people who were streaming into compulsory education had to be channeled into the various types of schools that were available. IQ testing was a quick and convenient method of decision-making. Like the SATs (Scholastic Assessment Tests) in the United States these tests took no account of social background or previous educational opportunity.[15] They were also very limited. High scores relied on standard verbal and logical operations. Success relied as much on knowing the techniques involved as on natural aptitude. Despite their obvious shortcomings, challenging the authority of these tests was never an easy matter. Then, as now, they had the backing of government and of the scientific establishment. They were assumed to be "above reproach or beyond social influence, conceived in the rarefied atmosphere of purely scientific inquiry by some process of immaculate conception."[16]

"Success relied as much on knowing the techniques involved as on natural aptitude."

For all their sway over education, IQ tests and SATs do not assess the whole range of a student's intellectual abilities. They look for particular sorts of ability. The same is true of the forms of education that they support. For generations, students have spent most of their time writing essays, doing comprehension exercises, taking tests of factual information and learning mathematics: activities that involve propositional knowledge and forms of logico-deductive reasoning. The most common form of assessment is still the timed written examination, in which success mainly depends on a good short-term memory. Some students labor for months to pass these tests – others glide through them with relatively little effort. This pattern continues into higher education, and especially in universities. Some disciplines promote other sorts of ability, especially those with a practical element. Most schools have art lessons and some music – perhaps playing an instrument or being in a choir – and sport. They are at the margins of formal education, and seen as dispensable when the academic chips are down. The arts are an important test case.

THE NARROWING OF INTELLIGENCE

Some years ago, I was a member of a university promotions committee, a group of 20 professors from the arts, sciences and social studies. A university lecturer is expected to do teaching, administration and research. A case for promotion has to include evidence of achievement in all three. One of my roles as head of department was to make recommendations about members of my own faculty. I had recommended an English lecturer, who I thought was a sure case. Committee members had to leave the room when their own recommendations were being discussed. I thought this was a routine matter so I slipped out of the room and was back within a few minutes ready to rejoin the meeting. I was kept waiting outside for nearly half an hour: clearly there was an issue.

Eventually I was called back into the room and sat down expectantly. The vice-chancellor said, "We've had a few problems with this one. We're going to hold him back for a year." Members of the committee are not meant to question decisions that concern their own recommendations, but I was taken aback. I asked why, and was told there was a problem with his research. I wasn't prepared for this, and asked what was wrong with it. I was told there was so little of it.

They were talking about an English lecturer who, in the period under review, had published three novels, two of which had won national literary awards; who had written two television series, both of which had been broadcast nationally and one of which had won a national award. He had published two papers in conventional research journals on nineteenth-century popular fiction. "But there is all of this," I said, pointing to the novels and the plays. "We're sure it's very interesting," said one of the committee, "but it's his research we're worried about," pointing to the journal papers. "But this is his research too," I said, pointing to the novels and plays. This led to a good bit of shuffling of papers.

By research output, most universities mean papers in academic journals or scholarly books. Apparently, the idea that novels and plays could count as research had not occurred to them. A good deal hangs on this. The issue was not whether these novels or these plays were any good, but whether novels and plays as such could count as research in the first place. The common-sense reaction was that they could not. But what is research? In universities, research is defined as a systematic enquiry for new knowledge. I asked the committee whether they thought that novels and plays, as original works of art, could be a source of new knowledge. If so, does the same apply to music, to art and to poetry? Were they saying that knowledge is only to be found in research journals and in academic papers? This question is important, for a number of reasons. It relates particularly to the status of the arts and sciences in universities and in education more generally.

There is an intriguing difference in research in arts and science departments in universities. If you work in a physics or chemistry department, you work in a laboratory and you "do" science. You do not spend your professional life analyzing the lives and times of physicists. If you are a mathematician, you don't scrutinize the mood swings of Euclid or his relationships with his in-laws when he developed his theories. You do mathematics. This is not what goes on in many arts departments. Professors of English are not employed to produce literature: they are employed to write about it. They spend much of their time analyzing the lives and drives of writers and the work they produce. They may write poetry in their own time, but they are not normally thanked for doing it in university time even though it may raise the profile of the university. They are expected to produce analytical papers about poetry. Producing works of art doesn't often count as appropriate intellectual work in an arts department, yet the equivalent in a science department, doing physics or chemistry, does. So why is it that in universities writing about novels is thought to be a higher intellectual calling than writing novels; or, rather, if writing novels is not thought to be intellectually valid, why is writing about them?

I mentioned earlier that a distinction is commonly made between academic and non-academic subjects. Science, mathematics and the social sciences are seen as academic subjects; and art, music and drama as non-academic. There are several problems in this approach. The first is the idea of subjects, which suggests that different areas of the curriculum are defined by their subject matter: that science is different from art because it deals with different content. Mathematics is not defined only by propositional knowledge. It is a combination of concepts, methods and processes *and* of propositional knowledge. The student is not only learning about mathematics but also how to do mathematics. The same is true of music, art, geography, physics, theater, dance and the rest. For these reasons alone, I much prefer the idea of disciplines to subjects.

The idea of disciplines also opens up the dynamics of interdisciplinary work. It is because of these dynamics that disciplines keep shifting and evolving. This is what the linguist James Britton[17] had in mind when he said, "we classify at our peril. Experiments have shown that even the lightest touch of the classifier's hand is likely to induce us to see members of a class as more alike than they actually are and items from different classes as less alike than they actually are. And when our business is to do more than merely look, these errors may develop during the course of our dealings into something quite substantial."

Disciplines are constantly merging, reforming, cross-fertilizing each other and producing new offspring. When I first arrived at my last university, I went to a meeting of the professorial board, a committee of all professors in the university across all disciplines. There was a proposal from the professor of chemistry that the university should establish a new professorship in chemical biology. The board nodded sagely and was about to move on, when the professor of biological sciences argued that what the university really needed was a chair in biological chemistry. As Britton implies, our categories of knowledge should be provisional at best.

The second assumption is that some subjects are academic and some are not. This is not true. All issues and questions can be considered from an academic point of view and from other viewpoints too. Universities are devoted to propositional knowledge and to logico-deductive reasoning. Academics can look at anything through the frame of academic enquiry: plants, books, weather systems, particles, chemical reactions or poems. It is the *mode of work* that distinguishes academic work, not the topic. The assumed superiority of academic intelligence is obvious in the structure of qualifications. Traditionally, universities have rewarded academic achievement with degrees. Other institutions give diplomas or other sub-degree qualifications. If you wanted to do art, to paint, draw or make sculptures, you went to an art college and received a diploma for your efforts. If you wanted a degree in art, you had to go to university and study the history of art. You didn't create art at university; you wrote about it. Similarly, if you wanted to play music and be a musician you went to a conservatoire and took a diploma; if you wanted a music degree you went to a university and wrote about music. These distinctions are beginning to break down. Arts colleges do now offer degrees and some university arts departments do offer practical courses. Even so, in some cultures and institutions there is still resistance to giving degrees for practical work in the arts.

CHANGING OUR MINDS

The modern worldview is still dominated by the ideology that came to replace medievalism: the ideology of rationalism, objectivity and propositional knowledge. These ideas frame our theories just as much as myth and superstition underpinned the painstaking calculations of the medieval astronomers. Just as their ideology created the framework for their questions, so does ours. We ask how we can measure intelligence. The assumption is that intelligence is quantifiable. We ask how we can raise academic standards but not whether they will provide what we need to survive in the future. We ask where we can find talented people but ignore the talents of people that surround us. We look but we do not see, because our traditional common-sense assessment of abilities distracts us from what is actually there. We ask how to promote creativity and innovation but stifle the processes and conditions that are most likely to bring them about. Caught in an old worldview, we continue to lean on the twin pillars of mass education, despite the evidence that the system is faltering for so many people within it.

The popular idea of intelligence has become dangerously narrow and other intellectual abilities are either ignored or underestimated. Despite all the attempts to promote parity between academic and vocational courses, the attitude persists that academic programs are much higher status.[18] Yet, intelligence is much richer than we have been led to believe by industrial/academic education. Appreciating the full range and potential of human intelligence is vital for understanding the real nature of creativity. To educate people for the future, we must see through the academic illusion to their real abilities, and to how these different elements of human capacity enhance rather than detract from each other. What are these capacities and what should be done to release them?

KNOWING YOUR MIND

"Now, more than ever, human communities depend on a diversity of talents; not on a singular conception of ability."

LIZ VARLOW IS A VIOLA PLAYER with the London Symphony Orchestra and winner of the prestigious Frink Award. She was born in Birmingham, England, and started playing the violin at the age of 8. She won two scholarships to the Royal College of Music, and went on to win numerous prizes. Fellow musicians describe her as a very fine musician who has developed her musical sensitivity to the highest levels. What sets her apart even further is that she is profoundly deaf. Her hearing began to deteriorate at the age of 16. By the time she was 19, she had become deaf for reasons that have never been established. Nonetheless she has maintained her capabilities as an outstanding professional musician. How does she perform without hearing?

"How does anyone play?" she says. "I know how to make sounds and also know how what I'm doing sounds. A 'normal' hearing player does this too. They make sounds and use hearing to check it. It's too late afterwards if the note is out of tune. With the benefit of a fine aural memory, a solid technique and a good sense of humor I have been able to deal with all professional situations and found deafness to be little handicap."

Dame Evelyn Glennie is one of the world's most accomplished percussionists. She travels the world giving virtuoso concerts to huge acclaim. Her recordings have sold millions of copies and she has won a variety of awards from professional music organizations including Musician of the Year. She is in demand worldwide to lead master classes on musicianship. She too is deaf. She became profoundly deaf at the age of 12 just as she was beginning to develop her musical abilities. She persisted in developing these abilities despite the lack of the one sense that most people would consider critical to their fulfillment.

Such examples defy logic. How can someone who is deaf become an outstanding musician? The achievements of Liz Varlow and of Evelyn Glennie demonstrate the extraordinary flexibility and virtuosity of the human mind. It is these qualities that underpin the uniquely human capacities for creativity and innovation.

LIVING IN TWO WORLDS

One of the founding perceptions of modern philosophy is that we live in two distinct worlds. There is a world that exists whether or not you exist: the world of material objects, events and of other people. This world existed before you were born and it will continue to exist after you have gone. There is another world that exists only because you exist: the world of your own private consciousness, feelings and sensations. Your world is one in which, as the psychologist R.D. Laing put it, there is only one set of footprints.[1] Your world came into being when you were born and it will end when you do. We share the first world with other people; we share the second with no one. Recognizing the difference between *your* world and *the* world marks an important stage in the development of personal identity. How do we come to see the external world as we do? How do we know it is there and not just in our minds?

Some philosophers of the Enlightenment worried whether the outer world was there at all. One of the most celebrated was Bishop Berkeley (1685–1753). His theory of idealism proposed that the whole world might be no more than an elaborate idea in the mind of God. His theory was greeted with amusement by the celebrated wit, Dr Johnson (1709–84). One of the Bishop's supporters attacked Dr Johnson's flat rejection of idealism saying that Berkeley's theory "could not be refuted." Dr Johnson turned to a nearby boulder, kicked it with his foot and said, "I refute it thus." To Dr Johnson and everyone else, even idealist philosophers seem to carry on living in the world and doing their shopping despite their uncertainty about its existence.

The outer world may be an illusion but for everyday purposes we assume it is not: we accept that the people and things we see about us are real and appear to us all in the same way. However tantalizing these problems may be for philosophers, they are only problems if we think about them as such. For most of the time, we live our lives in what has been called the *natural attitude*.[2] While some seventeenth- and eighteenth-century philosophers were questioning the existence of the material world, a new breed of scientists set about bringing it under our control. As Bertrand Russell (1872–1970) commented, the scientific outlook is not so much a rejection of philosophical doubts: it is more an illustration that, in daily life, we assume as certain many things that, on closer scrutiny, we find to be full of apparent contradictions. How do we bridge these two worlds?[3]

Consciousness and the brain

These days it is taken for granted that consciousness and the brain are intimately related. This is a relatively recent idea. The ancient world saw only a tenuous link. The brain is an unpromising sight. It is a crinkled ball of flesh with no moving parts, which lives remotely from the rest of the body in a cage of bone. Normal human brains are about the size of a melon and look like a large walnut. The upper side is in two halves, or hemispheres, and has a surface of convoluted folds. This is the cerebral cortex or new brain. It is thought of as being in four regions or lobes: *parietal, frontal, posterior* and *anterior.* A shaft of nerve fibers known as the corpus callosum connects the two hemispheres. Underneath the brain and to the back is a smaller, cauliflower-shaped area called the cerebellum in an area known as the old brain. Coming out of that and connecting it to the spinal cord is the brain stem.

The functions of the mind that we now associate with the brain were assumed by ancient anatomists to be located in the heart and the lungs. The brain was thought to be the home of the soul that endured physical death and passed into the afterlife. The brain had no obvious functions otherwise. By the Middle Ages, anatomists had concluded that the brain played a more practical role in this life too. As anatomical studies advanced, they gradually revealed the physical connections through the spinal cord between the brain, the central nervous system and the rest of the body. The debate still goes on about the relationship between the motionless gray substance of the material brain, and the vibrant thoughts, feelings and desires that constitute human consciousness. The fact that there is a relationship is easy enough to establish. Removing the brain does bring consciousness to an abrupt end. How the conscious mind arises from the physical matter of the brain is not yet known. How is it that a ball of flesh the size of a melon can generate the insights of Isaac Newton, the music of Mozart, the dance of Martha Graham, the poetry of Shakespeare and the spiritual longings of Gandhi? How do we account for what has been called the ghost in the machine?

There is a common-sense distinction between mind and consciousness. In one sense, consciousness is what you lose when you go to sleep and regain when you wake up. Consciousness has a second meaning, that of understanding. It is in this sense that we talk of raising consciousness of an issue. The brain has more on its mind than conscious thought. A good deal of the brain's activities are not apparent to the conscious mind. Conscious thought accounts for only a proportion of what the brain is doing at any given moment. Much of its work is silent traffic within the rest of the body's automatic functioning: with the involuntary processes of metabolism, glandular functions and the complex perceptions of taste, smell, touch, vision, hearing and so on. Although the relationships between consciousness and the brain are still a mystery, more is known than ever before about what the various parts of the brain do and how they relate to each other as they are doing it.

MAPPING THE MIND

In the Middle Ages it was believed that the mind consisted of different faculties, and that each of them was located in a different part of the brain. These faculties included memory, imagination and logical reasoning. This theory was used as a justification for the classical curriculum of the grammar schools. Memory, it was thought, was trained by learning Latin vocabulary; logical reasoning by geometry; and imagination by poetry and music.[4]

Just as most human brains are similar in appearance, most skulls are the same general shape. On closer inspection they vary in size and have distinctive bumps and hollows across the surface. In the eighteenth century, the Austrian scientist Franz Gall studied the brains of hundreds of dead people and tried to match their shapes with the personalities of their former owners. From these he developed a detailed theory of personality, brain shape and the patterns of bumps on the skull, a theory known as *phrenology*; literally the "study of the mind."

Gall identified 32 personality traits associated with different patterns of bumps on the skull. Phrenologists believed there was a direct link between specific functions, such as speech, and different regions of the brain. Gall's phrenological speculations were later discounted by more considered studies of the brain. Studies of people with brain damage in the nineteenth century showed that the idea of exclusive locations for particular brain functions was misleading.

The capacities of the brain are more complex and dynamic than initial theories suggested. For generations, scientists developed their understanding of the brain by dissecting dead brains on laboratory tables, a method with some obvious limitations. Over the last 30 years the technologies of brain scanning have made it possible to study living brains by tracking patterns of electrical activity and blood flow during different activities. Scientists now understand much more about the gross functions of the brain: which parts are used in different activities and in which combinations; in speech, for example, in recognizing faces, listening to music or doing mathematics. Neuroscience is using nanotechnology to explore brain activity at the molecular level including the transfer of electrical charges at the neural synapses. These studies are generating new approaches in psychology, in the design of drugs and in the treatment of pain. They also suggest three crucial themes for understanding creativity. Intelligence is highly *diverse, dynamic* and *distinct*.

DIVERSITY

The view of the Enlightenment philosophers was that knowledge of the world could only be derived from systematic logic and the empirical evidence of the senses. This approach has a powerful appeal to common sense. In practice, there are other factors to take into account.

There is more to the world than meets the eye, or any of our senses. We do not see the world as it is but as our particular senses present it to us. The nature of our senses determines our *field of perception*: what we are able to perceive and how. We live in a rich sensory environment but can perceive only some of it because our senses are limited. We experience the world as we do partly because of the way we are built. As human beings we are typically between five and six feet tall, we stand upright and our bodies are broadly symmetrical. Unprotected, our bodies can endure only small variations in heat. Although it is commonly taken for granted that we have five senses – sight, taste, touch, hearing, smell – we have at least four more: balance, orientation, pain and temperature. Our eyes are at the front of our heads and we have binocular vision. We can see light that has a wavelength from about 400 nanometers (extreme violet) to about 770 nanometers (extreme red). Our ears can normally hear sounds in the range 20–15,000 Hz. Our senses are the channels through which information flows between the outside world and our own consciousness. If those channels were different, other sorts of information would flow through them and our view of the outside world could well be transformed.

Other animals have different and often more specialized senses and inhabit different sensory worlds. Some mammals, such as bats, can detect ultrasonic frequencies well above 15,000 Hz. Some animals and birds can detect infrasound or low-frequency sound. Pigeons can detect sounds as low as 0.1 Hz. Elephants communicate using sounds as low as 1 Hz. Two animals living in exactly the same physical environment may have entirely different views of what's going on. A seahorse and a killer whale, living in the same stretch of ocean, inhabit the same environment but live in different worlds. One factor is their relative size and strength. They are also equipped with entirely different sensory capacities. Your view of the world would be different too if you could hear the sounds that bats hear, or see the world as cats do, or had the smell receptors of a dog; if you could see sounds, or breathe underwater or fly.

Our physical configuration determines what we *can* perceive of the world; there are other factors that affect what we *do* perceive. Human intelligence is not just a process of perception but of selection. Otherwise there would be too much information coming in, like a radio tuned to an open frequency. When you look at a room, a landscape, the street, you don't pay equal attention to everything in your field of perception. You notice some things, not others. Two people standing in the same street may perceive it in completely different ways. A traffic warden may see a landscape of offenders; a window cleaner a land of opportunity. A bird fancier wandering through a wood will see it differently from a botanist interested in rare plants. If you drive a yellow car, you are likely to see yellow cars everywhere. What we do perceive is affected by a range of factors, many of which are cultural. We'll come back to them in Chapter 8.

The constitution of our senses, our bodies and of our brains deeply affects what we think about. It also affects *how* we think. The rationalist view of knowledge is focused on the logico-deductive powers of mind. While this may seem reasonable in itself, there is more to consciousness than these particular powers. The brain is an organic entity that interacts with all the physical states and processes of our bodies. Our health, physical condition and appetites can deeply affect our states of mind.

The academic life tends to deny the rest of the body. In many schools, students are educated from the waist up and attention eventually comes to focus on their heads, and particularly the left side. Many academics live in their heads, and slightly to one side. They are disembodied in a certain way. They tend to look upon their bodies as a form of transport for their heads: it's a way of getting their heads to meetings. If you want real evidence of out-of-body experiences, sign up for a residential conference for senior academics and go along to the dance on the final night. There you will see it. Grown men and women, writhing uncontrollably, off the beat, waiting for it to end so that they can go home and write a paper about it.

In contrast, dancers exult in their bodies and in the forms of understanding that can only be manifested through movement. I used to be on the board of the Birmingham Royal Ballet in England and had the privilege of watching professional dancers at work. The rigor, precision and sensibility of their work are breathtaking. I mentioned earlier that dance does not have the same status in schools as "academic" subjects, but dance gives form to ideas and feelings that cannot be expressed in any other way. As Martha Graham once said, dance is the hidden language of the soul.

There may be no agreed definition of intelligence, but we might agree here that intelligence includes the ability to formulate and express our thoughts in coherent ways. We can do this using words and numbers. We can also think visually, in sound, in movement and in all the many ways in which these different modes interact. Musicians are not trying to express in sound ideas that would be better put into words. They are having musical ideas: ideas for which there may be no words. Visual artists think visually and have visual ideas.

Intelligence includes the ability to engage effectively with the practical challenges of living in the world. Developmental psychologist Howard Gardner, best known for his theory of multiple intelligences, defines intelligence as the ability to solve problems in a given context. Consider a 12-year-old Puluwat in the Caroline Islands, he says, who has been selected by his elders to learn how to become a master sailor: "under the tutelage of master navigators he will learn to combine knowledge of sailing stars and geography so as to find his way around hundreds of islands. Or consider the 14-year-old adolescent in Paris who has learnt how to program a computer and is beginning to compose works of music with the aid of a synthesizer." A moment's reflection, says Gardner, reveals that each of these individuals "is demonstrating a high level of competence in a challenging field and should by any reasonable definition of the term be viewed as exhibiting intelligent behaviour."[5] Gardner argues that there are least seven different types of intelligence. In later work he accepts that there are others too.

I mentioned my reservations about Mensa, the organization for people with high IQs. I am not against an organization for people who enjoy IQ tests. I am all for clubs and societies. It is good that people with common interests should get together and benefit from each other's passions. There are clubs for everything: cooking, chess, athletics, politics, philately, dog breeding, astronomy, you name it. Certainly there should be an IQ club. My problem is with the branding of Mensa. It is promoted as the club for the most intelligent people on earth. Really? If there were such a club, no doubt we would all like to be considered for membership. But shouldn't there be some other questions on the application forms? For example, can you compose a symphony? Could you play in an orchestra? Could you start and run a successful business? Could you write poetry that will move people to tears? Could you choreograph or perform in a dance that speaks to our inner humanity? All of these are examples of the manifest diversity of human intelligence and of the many ways in which we engage with each other and with the world around us. Shouldn't they count too in any comprehensive conception of intelligence? And shouldn't people who are exceptionally good at any of these things be welcomed in the club that aims to celebrate the highest levels of intelligence?

The point is that intelligence is multifaceted, rich, complex and highly diverse. It includes and goes well beyond conventional conceptions of academic ability and IQ, which is why the world is full of music, technology, art, dance, architecture, business, practical science, feelings, relationships and inventions that actually work.

DYNAMISM

Roger Sperry (1913–94) was awarded the Nobel Prize for his groundbreaking research into the structure and functions of the brain. In the 1950s, he conducted a series of experiments that involved people whose brain hemispheres had been separated by cutting the corpus callosum. I assume they had had their hemispheres separated before they agreed to help Sperry and not as a result. If not they were far more committed to these issues than I am. Sperry found that the "split-brain" subjects could perform two unrelated tasks simultaneously; for example, drawing a picture with one hand while writing with another. He concluded that the two hemispheres of the brain fulfilled different but complementary functions. The left side of the brain was largely involved in logical procedures including language and mathematics; the right-hand side of the brain was more concerned with holistic operations such as the recognition of faces and orientation in physical space.

This research provoked massive interest, not least in education. It suggested a physical correspondence in the brain to the two great traditions in Western European culture. The left hemisphere seemed to relate to the logico-deductive analysis of the Enlightenment and the scientific method; the right hemisphere to the Romantic impulses of beauty, intuition and spirituality. Educational reformers were quick to argue that the academic education system was almost wholly left-brained. James Hemming drew a striking conclusion. Educating people entirely through the left-brain activities of the academic curriculum was, he said, like training somebody for a race by exercising only one leg while leaving the muscles of the other leg to atrophy. Others went too far. I remember reading an article by someone who had half-digested the implications of this research. She said she had written the piece in blank verse because she had only used the right-hand side of her brain; a remark that suggested she hadn't used.

either side. The point is not that the two halves should work separately but together.

Carl Sagan captured this exactly. There is no way to tell, he said, "whether the patterns extracted by the right hemisphere are real or imagined without subjecting them to left hemisphere scrutiny." On the other hand, "mere critical thinking without creative and intuitive insights, without the search for new patterns is sterile and doomed. To solve complex problems in changing circumstances requires the activity of both cerebral hemispheres. The pattern to the future lies through the corpus callosum."[6]

Brain-scanning techniques show that the brain lights up in different configurations according to the activity in hand and that even simple actions draw simultaneously on different regions of the brain. Different areas of the brain are associated with particular mental functions but they participate in other processes too. The interdependence of functions is obvious in the effects of damage to the brain. The right frontal lobe is focally responsible for music; if it is damaged, musical abilities are impaired. If you were to remove this section of the brain and hold it in your hand it would not hum a tune. It relies on its connections with the rest of the brain and body to function at all. Speech is an example of how patterns of brain activity vary. When someone is speaking in their native tongue, their brain configures in one way; it configures differently when they speak a second language learned after infancy.

We experience these dynamics of intelligence constantly. Speech is usually accompanied by a symphony of physical movements, facial expressions and gestures. Dance seems to be quintessentially kinesthetic but choreographers design dances with a passionate attention to visual design and to the qualities of the music, often with mathematical precision. For the audience, dance is also a visual art. Mathematics may seem to be quintessentially abstract, but many mathematicians depend on keen visual imaginations.

I remember watching a teacher in Hong Kong taking a Saturday morning class in mathematics. The children, aged between 8 and 12, each sat with an abacus on their desks. The teacher called out calculations for them to do: 1,289 multiplied by 15,822; 22,348 divided by 4,019. As soon as he finished calling the numbers, a forest of arms shot into the air. Every child had the correct answer. The children used only the abacus for their calculations, flicking the beads across the bars at lightning speed. Another boy was asked to use an electronic calculator for comparison. He was slower every time. The teacher asked the children to put the abacus away. The answers came just as quickly and always faster than the boy with the calculator. The children had internalized the operation, visualizing the abacus in their minds' eyes and "seeing" the answers.

In learning to speak, the relationships between speech, song and music are very strong. Brain imaging shows that the areas of the brain that are primarily concerned with music and language overlap considerably. Diana Deutsch is Professor of Psychology at the University of California. She says, "A person's native tongue influences the way he or she perceives music. The same succession of notes may sound different depending on the language the listener learned growing up."[7] Speakers of tonal languages including Mandarin are more likely than Westerners to have perfect pitch. In one study, 92% of Mandarin speakers who began music lessons at or before the age of 5 had perfect pitch, compared to 8% of English speakers with comparable music training.

When they are born, babies are already familiar with the melody of the mother's speech. Audio recordings from inside the womb at the beginning of labor reveal that the sounds produced by the mother can be heard loudly: "The phrases reaching the baby have been filtered through the mother's tissues, so that the crisp, high frequencies which carry much of the information important for identifying the meanings of words, are muted, whereas the musical characteristics of speech – its pitch contours, loudness variations, tempo and rhythmic patterning – are well preserved." In addition to forging a nascent connection between mother and child, early exposure to musical speech sounds may begin the process of learning to speak. According to Deutsch, after birth the melodies of speech are vital to communication between mother and child. When parents speak to their babies, they use exaggerated speech patterns known as "motherese," and these differ considerably between languages.

Perhaps the most compelling evidence of the holistic functioning of the brain comes from those with sensory impairments. Evelyn Glennie experiences the music with her whole being. Playing in bare feet she absorbs the musical vibrations and rhythms through her body in ways that transcend ordinary concepts of sensory perception. In a way, intelligence itself is like an orchestra. The whole is more than the sum of the parts. It is composed of many specialized elements but only functions as it should when they work together in concert.

The brain is not a mechanical object: it is an organic entity. The mind is not a calculator: it is a dynamic process of consciousness. Creativity is not a single ability that lives in one or other region of the body. It thrives on the dynamism between different ways of thinking and being. Intelligence is not only diverse and dynamic, it is unique and distinct in each of us as individuals.

DISTINCTIVENESS

Martha Graham said, "There is a vitality, a life-force, an energy, a quickening that is translated through you into action and because there is only one of you in all of time, this expression is unique. And if you block it, it will never exist through any other medium and be lost."

I have had the honor and pleasure of working at times with Robert Cohan, the gifted partner of Martha Graham and

founding principal of the London School of
Contemporary Dance. I asked him how he
came to be involved in contemporary dance.
In the early 1950s, he left the US army and
was living in New York. He had always enjoyed
dancing and had a conventional training. A
friend told him of a woman who was running
dance classes downtown and suggested he
might enjoy them. He went, and his life was
changed. After the first three-hour session in
Martha Graham's studio, his body was shak-
ing almost uncontrollably with excitement.
He discovered in her methods and forms of
dance a capacity in himself that he had never
suspected. Through meeting Martha Graham he found himself and spent his artistic life in the world he helped her to
create. He went on to become her principal partner in dance
and to promote her methods in Europe in the 1970s and
1980s as principal of the London School of Contemporary
Dance.

"There is a vitality, a life-force, an energy, a quickening that is translated through you into action and because there is only one of you in all of time, this expression is unique. And if you block it, it will never exist through any other medium and be lost."
– Martha Graham

Cohan's exhilaration in dance illustrates a more general
point. Each of us is a unique moment in history: a distinctive blend of our genetic inheritance, of our experiences and
of the thoughts and feelings that have woven through them
and constitute our unique consciousness. We each have great
natural capacities, but we all have them in different forms.
Does this mean that no one can be thought of as more intelligent than anyone else? Of course not. Some people have
strong abilities in many areas, music, mathematics, verbal
reasoning, visual thinking and so on. High ability in one area
does not entail it in others nor does it exclude it. A good
mathematician may or may not be a good painter or poet;
a gifted poet may have no feel for dance or be a virtuoso in
salsa. We should not stereotype people for having or lacking
academic ability, or label someone with high academic abilities as more intelligent than someone with high abilities in

music or dance. People are so much more than either academic or non-academic. I am not arguing against developing
academic abilities; I am arguing for an expanded conception
of intelligence that includes but goes beyond them.

Children with strong academic abilities may fail to discover
their other abilities; those with less academic ability may have
equally powerful capacities that lie dormant. They can all pass
through the whole of their education never knowing what these
are. They can become disaffected, resentful of their "failure"
and conclude that they are simply not very bright. Some of
these educational failures go on to have great success in adult
life. How many do not? They may never know what they are
capable of and who or what they might become.

Many people are diverted from their natural paths in life by
the preoccupation in education with academic intelligence
and the hierarchy of disciplines. It shows itself especially in
the distinction between academic and vocational programs
and the idea that doing practical work or studying for a trade
is lower grade than taking an academic degree. And yet,
the ability to construct buildings, to wire a house, to install
plumbing systems, to make things grow, to make things that
work, to provide practical services, is exactly what resonates
with very many people and all these skills are fundamental to
the vitality and sustainability of human life. Sometimes this
is literally true.

A couple of years ago, I was in San Francisco for a book
signing. One of the people in line was a man in his mid-30s
and I asked him what he did for a living. He said he was a
fireman. I asked him when he had decided to be a fireman
and he said he had always wanted to be a fireman. "Actually,"
he said, "in elementary school it was a problem because at
that age everyone wanted to be a fireman. But I really did
want to be a fireman and as I grew up I couldn't wait to leave
school to join the fire service." He said that when he was
in his senior year of high school, one of the teachers asked
his class what they were all planning to do when they left.

Almost everyone talked about going to college; he said he was applying to join the fire service. The teacher said that he was making a big mistake; that he was academically smart, had a bright future and would be wasting it if he joined the fire service. The fireman said it was an embarrassing moment and he felt humiliated in front of his friends, but he went ahead with his plans and has been in the fire service and loving it ever since. "But I was thinking about that teacher when you were talking just now," he said. "Because six months ago, I saved his life. He was in a car wreck and my unit was called out. I pulled him from the car, gave him CPR and saved him. I saved his wife's life too." He said, "I think he thinks better of me now."

Rethinking disability

One of the consequences of a narrow view of ability is a correspondingly wide view of disability. Identifying latent abilities is all the more important when conventional forms of communication are restricted. Some years ago, I was involved in a study of art and disability that was chaired by the film director, Sir Richard Attenborough, and funded by the Carnegie Foundation. The study celebrated the artistic capabilities of people with disabilities and argued for greatly improved provision. Some people with disabilities have difficulties with conventional forms of expression: in writing, for example, or in speech, hearing or vision. Often they are branded by their disability: they are not seen as people with a disability but as disabled people.

Dr Phil Ellis conceived and directed a unique music education research initiative at the University of Sunderland. Touching Sound explored new approaches to sound therapy for children who have severe learning difficulties (SLD) and profound and multiple learning difficulties (PMLD).[8] It used low-level laser beams linked to sound synthesizers. When the beams were touched, sounds were generated automatically.

The sensors could be triggered by movements as small as the blink of an eye, so that even people with profound and complex needs could experience being in control of the music and visuals.

The project worked with children whose movements are limited to only a few muscles or even an eyelid. People with a normal range of movement take for granted the ability to affect their environment and to externalize their thoughts and feelings. Those with limited muscular control spend their lives having other people do things to or for them, and have profound difficulties in expressing themselves. Touching Sound enabled them to affect their environment and to be expressive. The feelings of liberation could be overwhelming and the developmental effects could be dramatic. As Marie Watts, one member of the team, put it: "It allows the individual to take control of the environment. It's all about control and empowerment. The technology was also motivating for staff, as it enabled them to get instant feedback from the people they assist."[9]

More than we know

Derek Paravicini was born in England in 1979, prematurely, at 25 weeks, weighing just a pound and a half. He is blind, autistic and an astounding musical prodigy. His blindness is thought to have been caused by oxygen therapy given in the neonatal intensive care unit. The therapy also caused severe learning disabilities. He has absolute pitch, can recognize up to 20 notes played at once and can play any piece of music after hearing it only once. He can also transform them seamlessly into the styles of different musicians. Asked to change into the style of another player, like Oscar Peterson, he will change style mid-song, playing "My Favorite Things" in Peterson's distinctive style. "It's like he's got libraries of pieces and styles in his head," says Adam Ockelford, Derek's teacher. "He can just whip out a piece book and a

style book and bring them together. It just kind of explodes."
How Derek's fingers can do this but can't button a button or
zip a zipper is not known. If he is asked how old he is now, he
does not know.

Derek began playing the piano as a toddler, when his nanny
gave him an old keyboard. His father says, "My daughter
suddenly said one day, 'He's just played one of the hymns
we heard in church this morning.'" Derek was 3 years old
at the time. "And he didn't know, because he couldn't see,
and no one had told him, that you're meant to use your fingers to play the piano. So he used karate chops and elbows,
and even his nose, I seem to remember." At first he resisted
any of Ockelford's attempts to teach him but before long, he
says, "Derek seemed to get it; this was not someone trying
to take away his precious piano. This was someone trying to
reach him. I think suddenly it clicked that he could have a
conversation in sound and he just blossomed ... From all
this confusion that he must have experienced as a child, not
understanding much language, suddenly here was a language
that he could control, he could play with, he could dialogue.
All the things that we normally do with words, Derek did
with notes."

His progress was astounding. After three years of daily lessons, Derek was invited to play at a charity fundraiser. It was
there that Ockelford first saw the thrill Derek got from performing and from feeling the love of the crowd. Derek was
trembling with excitement and elation and he has been performing ever since – in jazz halls, at benefits, in churches –
connecting with audiences and taking requests, with a twist.
He will ask an audience member to select a song, then let a
second audience member choose what key he will play it in
and then let a third select a style. At one event, Derek was
asked to play "Ain't No Sunshine" in B major in ragtime style.
He executed it perfectly. "It's like having three computers all
working at once and you could just put them together straight-
away, without thinking," Ockelford comments. "Sometimes he

does something quite funny musically. You can see a little sparkle. I think he's actually quite pleased with himself what he comes up with."[10]

"Savants" are people with exceptional ability in some areas of intelligence and below-average ability in others. Though autism is thought to be a factor in Derek's prodigious musical ability, his blindness may contribute. The part of his brain that would normally be used for sight and light detection could be used for extra auditory ability. There are other cases of savants with egregious abilities in drawing, memory, and mathematical calculation. Each of them has specific skills that are off the chart, combined with well below average abilities in other areas.[11] These are all examples of the distinctive ways in which intelligence configures in all of us as unique individuals.

PLASTICITY AND POTENTIAL

Jeff Lichtman is Professor of Molecular and Cellular Biology at Harvard University. He directs a wide-ranging program of research to create a detailed map of the circuitry of the human brain. The research is part of a new field called "connectomics." A piece of technology called the Automatic Tape Collecting Lathe Ultra Microtome (ATLUM) cuts samples of brain tissue into very thin slices which are then placed under a scanning electron microscope to create images of individual cells and all their connections to other cells. Professor Lichtman says that this technology "gives us an opportunity to witness this vast complicated universe that has been largely inaccessible until now."

"As children grow, their brains are customized around the uses they make or do not make of them."

One of the aims of the study is to understand the processes of neural growth and pruning. At birth the human brain consists of about 100 billion brain cells. During infancy the child's brain is tremendously plastic. To begin with, each neuron has dozens of connections, but these connections pare down to just a few strong ones as the brain develops and according to how it is used. According to Lichtman, each baby nerve cell connects to 20 times the number of nerve cells that it will have as an adult: "We try to understand what the rules of pruning are. If the nerve cell has a hundred connections and needs to prune that down to five, the question is, which five?" The neurons fight to stay connected and each competition affects the outcome for the rest of the cells. "So to understand the competition's impact on one cell, you have to understand all the competitions." The net effect of all that new neural "hand-to-hand combat" is what we call brain development and it's what transforms a baby who can't walk or talk into a modern adult human being. It's this process that provides us with the flexibility that Lichtman calls "the magic of being human." When a dragonfly is born, he says, it has to know how to catch a mosquito. "But for us, none of this is built-in. Our brains have to go through this profound education that lasts until our second decade. What is changing in our brains?"[12]

The plasticity of the brain is evident in our use of language. If children are born into multilingual households, they learn all the languages they are regularly exposed to. Parents don't teach children to speak in the way they are taught languages in school. Mothers do not teach their babies the principles of grammar and have them practice lists of vocabulary. They prompt and guide and teach particular words. Learning a language is so complex that teaching it formally to an infant would be impossible. Teaching them three or four languages would be unthinkable. Yet infants do learn three or four languages and more if necessary. They don't reach a point of saturation or ask for their grandmothers to be kept out of the room because they can't handle another dialect. They absorb them all. This is because they have a language instinct. It is not that multilingual households produce linguistically gifted children by some random process of good luck. All "normal" children have the capacity to learn not only one but many languages. If a child is born into a home where only one language is spoken, that is the language they learn. Learning a second language in adolescence is much more difficult.[13]

As children grow, their brains are customized around the uses they make or do not make of them. If the language capacity is not used, it may fade as the brain's neural capacities are turned to other uses. The same can be true of music or mathematics or any other capacity. Susan Greenfield gives a startling example of the plasticity of the brain.[14] She tells of a 6-year-old Italian boy who was blind in one eye. The cause of his blindness was that at a crucial period in his infancy his eye was covered with a patch. The neural networks, which facilitate sight from that eye, became redeployed, causing permanent blindness.

In the South Pacific, many young children are accomplished underwater divers. They develop the ability to swim underwater for long periods so that they can gather pearls. In New York, most children do not have this ability. There are very few skilled pearl divers in the Bronx. There is no demand. It's reasonable to assume that the average New Yorker translated at an early enough age to the South Pacific would learn the necessary skills. Living in the Bronx they may have the capacity but not the need and, as a result, not the ability.

"Now, more than ever, human communities depend on a diversity of talents not on a singular conception of ability."

DARRYL'S DANCE

Statistically, there is a higher than normal chance that those who pull out or fall out of education may move in to the criminal justice system. The conventional strategy is to incarcerate offenders, even though it incurs immense social and economic costs and recidivism rates are high. There are more creative approaches to the problem, which are based on an understanding that ability is diverse, dynamic and distinct and that strategies for dealing with disaffection and alienation should be equally sophisticated. One that I admire particularly expresses a special irony. It brings together young offenders – who have often been failed by education – and dance, the discipline that lies at the lowest point in the hierarchy of educational priorities. The results illustrate how often the offenders and the discipline are under-estimated in education.

Dance United is a professional contemporary dance company based in Bradford in the United Kingdom. The company provides a dance-based education program, called The Academy, as an option for young offenders within the local criminal justice system. The Academy was designed for young people who have failed in conventional educational settings and who may be offenders or at serious risk of offending. The participants have included young people convicted of robbery, drug offences, burglary and assault. The Academy team is made up of professional dance artists and teachers working alongside support workers from the Bradford Youth Offending Team (YOT) and other agencies.

The aim of The Academy is not simply to help young people to avoid re-offending, but to help them to discover their innate capacity to succeed. The Academy aims for profound changes in the participants by raising their beliefs in what they are capable of achieving. The young people on the program are treated not as offenders in remediation but as professional dancers in training.[15] The program is based on methods that are used to educate and train professional contemporary dance artists and is highly disciplined and rigorous. For example, the ground rules include the requirement to dance in bare feet. Wearing jewelry, hats or other personal artifacts is not allowed. The physical and creative demands of dance itself are at the core of the program, which aims to promote work of a high artistic standard. The program helps them to learn to trust and support others too.

The Academy works with up to 15 young people at any one time on a program that takes 25 hours each week, for a period of 12 weeks. Each cycle begins with an intensive, three-week performance project, at the end of which the production is presented in professionally staged performances, either in The Academy studio theater, or at a local or regional theater venue. From the fourth week, the program expands into a broader dance and educational curriculum including jazz, African dance, capoeira, circus skills, choreography and more. The program includes input from visiting artists, including photographers, film makers and musicians.

Many people greeted the idea of The Academy program with flat skepticism. How could dance possibly have any effect on people who had shown no regard for other people or property? Wasn't this just groundless romantic nonsense that pandered to the offenders? Surely the obvious answer was prison. For Jim Brady, a professional member of the Bradford Youth Offending Team, who knows something about these issues, the obvious answer was wrong. "If prison worked," he says, "that would be the solution to youth crime. Unfortunately all the evidence suggests that prison doesn't work."[16] To begin with, his colleague, Dave Pope, was also skeptical about the power of dance. He says now that he has seen many other strategies for dealing with young offenders, but none that are as powerful or as effective: "I've seen offenders working on building sites, offenders joining in team sports, offenders doing offender behavior courses and I've seen offenders doing anger management courses. Contemporary dance, much to my surprise, has turned out to be the one thing where I've seen people make the most progress over the shortest period of time."

Why should this program make such a difference where others have not? Tara Jane Herbert, the artistic director of Dance United, is clear about what the program really does. Although the participants are treated as professional dancers and put through a comparable regimen, The Academy is not about turning all of them into performers: "It's about giving those young people the opportunity to do something practical and the skills to be able to choose. Most of the young people that we work with don't make clear choices. They react. Dance training gives them the opportunity to actually think and then make an action. You have to be able to sit still before you make a choice, before you make an action." She says that typically the young people on the program do not know how to focus their physical energy. "They're very fidgety, or very floppy. They're not grounded. There's not a strength and a stillness behind them and that's what focus is about. It's about actually stopping before you begin something. It's like an orchestra. It's the silence before you begin playing and it's exactly the same in dance and in life."

The program helps to build their sense of self-worth by facilitating creative achievement. As one member of the team explains, "They've often been told they're worthless and can't really achieve anything. They learn here that they can. By getting up in the morning they've achieved structure, discipline, being able to take orders, the confidence to go out and approach difficult situations. It's not easy for some of them because they've never danced before."

Dance is highly collaborative. As Helen Linsell, one of the dance artists, explains, "There are different people they have to get on with: people who are older, younger, and different members of staff that they might not connect with." Rhiana Laws, another of the dancers, emphasizes that "There is no room for them to hang out or lean against the wall or sit down because they're tired, or giggle in the middle of an exercise because they did it wrong. We're absolutely rigid and that is what I experienced when I was training professionally."

Tara Jane Herbert says that the public performance at the end of the first three weeks is a massive step. "We invite friends, family; and for most of them it's the first time that they'll be seen in a positive light. It's vital that the quality, the standard of work is excellent, so that they can shine. At the end of the performance their confidence has grown enormously and they suddenly understand why we've pushed for focus, why we've demanded cooperation and all the things that we've been pushing at them suddenly become clear."

One of the participants on the program was a young man named Darryl. When Jim Brady first met Darryl and his mother to consider his options as a young offender, it was hard to know what Darryl might have been thinking. "He didn't engage. He virtually didn't speak," says Brady. "Mom did all the talking. In among the menu of choices I said would be available, was dance." His mother said immediately that Darryl would not dance. Darryl said nothing. In the event, he went to The Academy. And Darryl danced. The results were remarkable, says Brady. "He's physically transformed by it. He's now concerned about nutrition and diet and general health. He's articulate and he's speaking. He carries himself very differently. He's confident and that all happened in the space of three weeks. That's quite a transformation."

Darryl himself is in no doubt. "You do one good session here," he says, "and you ache. But it's a good ache because you know you've done something good. After a few weeks you start to notice your body getting healthier, muscles are coming up and you can feel them growing. It makes you think that there is something you can do and enjoy and it passes time away." The physical and artistic rigors of dance have changed Darryl's view of himself. They've also changed his view of other people; "I've probably learned to consider what other people think," he says, "and look at things from the other person's point of view."

Darryl's father has noticed the difference too. "We really had a lot of friction with Darryl. Now we all have a really good relationship and we're just looking forward to the little spell at college and hoping he motivates himself that little bit more to try just that little bit harder." The parents of one of the other young men on the program saw a change in him too. After the performance, they were a little overwhelmed. "He was just full of life," said his father. "He said it was brilliant and that he'd go back and do it again." His mother agreed.

"He's a changed lad. I can't believe it's my son. I feel like that cloned him and made him good."

For the Chairman of the Youth Justice Board, Professor Robert Morgan, the moral of The Academy is clear: "We need to treat these young offenders as people with potential. Anyone who has observed the sort of work that is being done here realizes the huge untapped resources that we need to develop." After a young lifetime of failure and conflict, Darryl sees the potential in very personal terms. "You can make a difference," he says. "Depending on how you look at it. If you want to keep an open mind and leave everything behind you, it'd be like a new world."

REALIZING WHO WE ARE

We all have profound natural capacities, but we all have them differently. If we fail to promote a full sense of people's abilities through education and training, some, perhaps most, will never discover what their real capacities are. To that extent they do not really know who they are or what they might become. Now, more than ever, human communities depend on a diversity of talents not on a singular conception of ability. When we talk of realizing our potential, we should aim to do so in both senses of the word. We need to understand its range and variety. We also need to turn it into reality. This is why creativity should be center stage in school, work and life.

I said in Chapter 1 that there are many misconceptions about creativity. So what is creativity? How does it relate to intelligence and how does it work in practice? Let's begin with Las Vegas.

BEING CREATIVE

"When people find their medium, they discover their real creative strengths and come into their own. Helping people to connect with their personal creative capacities is the surest way to release the best they have to offer."

M Y WIFE TERRY AND I have lived and worked together for over 40 years. In 2007, it was our 25th wedding anniversary and we decided to renew our vows at the Elvis Chapel in Las Vegas. We went with 30 friends and family, including our two children, James and Kate. It was a great weekend. We had the Blue Hawaii package. There are others, but we liked this one. The package included the Elvis impersonator, four songs and smoke. As we came into the chapel there was a puff of smoke from a pipe near the altar, presumably to add to the air of mystery and sacredness. There was also a hula girl, who was optional. I had opted for her, for reasons I was rather pleased about in the event. For another $100 we could have had a pink Cadillac, but we thought that was a bit tacky. It could have lowered the tone of the whole occasion.

After the ceremony, we had a reception at the Venetian Hotel, which is the size of a small town and includes, on the second floor, an indoor replica of San Marco's Square in Venice, complete with the Grand Canal, gondolas and gondoliers. I have been to Venice, and in some ways the Venetian Hotel is better. It's more authentic and it doesn't smell of sewage.

I mention Las Vegas for a reason. If you think of it, there is no reason for it to be there. Most other cities have a reason to be where they are. Some cities, like New York or Barcelona, are in natural harbors, so they're good for trade. Others are in fertile plains or valleys that are perfect for agriculture; or on major rivers, so they're good for transport and settlement; or on hilltops, so they're good for defense. None of these are true of Las Vegas. As far as I know, nobody is trying to invade Nevada. Las Vegas is in the middle of an arid wilderness. It has no natural water supply, no local sources of agriculture and it suffers from extremely high temperatures. It is the most unlikely place on earth for a major city. Yet for years Las Vegas has been one of the fastest growing cities in America and is known all around the world. In one sense, Las Vegas really does occupy the most fertile place on earth: the human imagination.

"In one respect at least, human beings are radically different from the rest of life on earth. We have the ability to imagine. As a result, we have unlimited powers of creativity."

Las Vegas began life as an idea. It proved to be such a compelling idea that it has generated a maelstrom of imaginative energy. I'm not asking you to approve of the idea of Las Vegas: simply to recognize that it's wholly the product of human imagination. So too is every uniquely human achievement.

THE VEIL OF CONCEPTIONS

We see the world not as it is, but through a veil of conceptions. The nature of our senses determines what we can perceive. Even so, people often see the same events differently, because they have different points of view. They may be in different physical places and literally have a different angle on what is going on. If there was no more to it than that, any dispute could be settled by comparing everyone's point of view and putting together an objective overview. In theory this is what's meant to happen in a court of law. In practice, comparing everyone's points of view often deepens the dispute. Our own view of what is going on is influenced by the ideas, values and beliefs through which we interpret our experience. These affect what we actually do perceive and what we make of it all.

If you take your dog outside and point at the moon, the dog will probably look at your finger and then at you. If you take a young child outside and point a finger at the moon, the child will look at the moon. This is called *joint attention*: the ability to share words and a point of focus. As the brain develops, children learn to understand the idea that one thing can represent another. This ability is the foundation of the most significant achievement of the creative mind: the power of symbolic thought. Language is the most obvious example. When learning to speak, a child learns that the sounds can have meaning and, eventually, that letters represent sounds. Other animals have only a limited capacity for this. If you say, "fetch" to a dog, it will sit up and be ready to move. If you were to talk to it about the importance of fetching or great fetchers you have known, it would sit blankly until you threw the stick. Show it a picture of the stick and it will probably sniff it. The dog's abilities don't go far beyond the association of sounds with actions. They don't extend, as they quickly do for children, to sophisticated powers of thinking and communication.

The power of representation has given rise to intricate forms of thought and communication, which permeate human consciousness and frame our ideas and feelings about the world. We don't just look at the moon, we locate it within complex theories of the universe; we don't just have feelings for each other, we can capture them in music and poetry. We don't just live in communities: we construct elaborate political theories and constitutions.

"Creativity involves putting your imagination to work. In a sense, creativity is applied imagination."

Some theories of intelligence argue that there is a direct line from the senses to the brain to the actions we take. Susanne Langer argues that there is an intermediate process. The brain, she says, is like a great transformer: "The current of experience that passes through it undergoes a change of character not through ... the sense by which the perception entered but by virtue of a primary use, which is made of it immediately. It is sucked into the stream of symbols which constitute a human mind."[1] Take language.

SPEAKING YOUR MIND

There is a common-sense assumption that language is principally a system of communication: first we have our thoughts and then we find the words to convey them. While language is a sophisticated way of communicating, its role in what and how we think is more complex. As a child learns to speak she does more than learn that things have names. She absorbs ways of thinking that the words make possible. For example, the word "camel" in Arabic can be expressed in many different ways. As well as the standard Arabic word *djemal*, the spoken language uses several hundred other nouns, depending on the local dialect. Having the words to describe the nuances makes it easier to see the differences between them.[2] Languages consist of more than the names of things. They are made up of grammatical structure, tenses, moods and syntax, which vary between languages, often profoundly. In some North American Indian languages, for example, the simple idea "I see a man" cannot be expressed without indicating with other parts of speech whether the man is sitting, standing or walking.[3] The Greek language has tenses and moods that are not available in English.

These differences illustrate the different "natural" ways of thinking within different language communities. It is relatively easy for an English speaker to learn French or Italian, in part because many of the words are similar, but also because the conventions of these languages are similar. All three are part of the family of Indo-European languages. It can be harder for a European to learn Chinese, because the conventions are so different. Chinese is a monosyllabic and tonal language. Indeed, Chinese is tonal *because* it is monosyllabic. Each word is limited to one syllable and is represented by a single character in the written language. The number of similar-sounding words would be unmanageable without some means of differentiating for meaning, which is where the voice itself comes in. Words are given a pitch – high, medium, low – and a tone or contour. The voice stays level or rises or falls as the word is pronounced. Almost literally, Chinese is sung. If you sing a wrong note, the person you are speaking to will hear a different meaning altogether. The foreigner first learning to speak Chinese cannot avoid frequent misunderstandings and gaffes; some more serious than others.

Unlike English, French or Italian, Chinese does not use inflections to show agreement, tense or number; these have to be inferred from the context and word order. Written Chinese also differs from European languages in that there is no alphabet. Each word is a distinctive character, which has to be learned *in toto* without the benefit of letters to guide pronunciation. For this reason, a number of different dialects have developed over the centuries in China, all based on a common written language. Chinese people from different parts of the country may have difficulty in understanding each other in conversation yet are still able to communicate in writing. An easy way to grasp this concept is to look at the keypad on a computer: whether English, French or Italian, everyone would understand the letters and numbers even though they would give the letters different names and sounds if they read them out loud.[4]

As they grow into their cultures, children absorb ways of thinking that are embedded in the particular languages they learn. In this way, languages play a central role in the growth of consciousness. Important as they are, words are not the only way in which we think.

WHAT DO YOU MEAN?

Language is a system of symbols. A symbol is something that represents something else. Anything may be a symbol. Symbols may be informal or formal. Informal symbols are not intended to mean anything in particular; we just see them that way. A sunset may symbolize sadness for you and euphoria for someone else, according to personal associations or state of mind. Formal symbols are intended to mean something and there is some level of agreement among those who use them about what they do or can mean. Let me suggest a broad distinction between forms of symbolic representation that are *systematic* and those that are *schematic*.

Systematic symbols

Words and numbers are examples of systematic symbolism. Systems of numbers are built from a small set of basic units that can be combined in an infinite variety of ways to express precise meanings. Just as numbers have accepted values, words too have conventional meanings that are definable in terms of each other, and rules that affect how they can be used and still mean something. In verbal language, one word follows another in sequences that are governed by conventions of grammar and syntax, which divide sense from nonsense. In such systems there are only certain ways in which the various elements can be composed and still have meaning. We may not be able to understand every word in a given sentence, but we can generally recognize that the sentence means something because we understand the rules of the system. If we meet a new word, we can look up the definition, and find its meaning described in other words. Often we don't need to look it up because what it means is clear from its context.

The systematic nature of language is illustrated by the scientist and philosopher, Michael Polanyi, who asked what would happen if we were to replace each different sentence in the English language by a unique word. "We must first envisage," he said, "that from an alphabet of 26 letters we could construct 26^8 eight-letter words: that is about 100 billion." That number is roughly the number of neurons in a human brain, of course. This million-fold enrichment of the English language "would completely destroy it not only because nobody could remember so many words but for the important reason that many would be meaningless. For the meaning of a word is formed and made clear by repeated use and the vast majority of our eight-letter words would be used only once or too rarely to acquire a definite meaning."

Chemistry, for example, says that the millions of different compounds are composed of about 100 chemical elements: "Since each element has a name and characteristic symbol attached to it, we can write down the composition of any compound in terms of the elements it contains. To classify things in terms of features for which we have names, as we do in talking about things, requires the same kind of connoisseurship as the naturalist must have for identifying specimens of plants or animals. Thus, the art of speaking precisely, by applying a rich vocabulary exactly, resembles the delicate discrimination practised by the expert taxonomist."[5]

Schematic symbols

Paintings, poems, music and dance are examples of *schematic* symbols. Words and numbers work well for ideas that can be laid out sequentially. Visual images present the whole pattern of ideas simultaneously. In visual form we can express thoughts that do not fit the structures of words. Their meanings are uniquely expressed in the forms they take. If you want to understand the meaning of a painting, you can't turn to a dictionary of colors to see what blue and green usually mean when they are put together. There is no manual of chords and harmonies that will tell us what a symphony is driving at and no dramatic codebook to tell us what a play means. There are no fixed meanings for the symbolic forms of art, to divide sense from nonsense. The meaning of a work of art is available only in the particular form in which it is expressed. The sound and feel of work in the arts is inseparable not only from *what* it means but from *how* it means. A painting, a play, a symphony, a novel are complex and unique forms created out of a sense of form and cultural knowledge rather than from systematic meanings.

Schematic forms may use systematic symbols. Plays, novels and poems are written in words, after all; and musical notation allows us to see each note in written form. The score is not the music, just as the text is not the play. They are the systematic symbols in which the schematic work is encoded and from which it must be interpreted either in performance or by the reader. Words can be used in a functional way to get the world's business done. Few of us spend much time refining a quick note or email to a friend or someone we work with. Our interest is in what is being said rather than in how it is expressed: in content rather than form. Poetry is a different matter. Consider this by W.B. Yeats:

When You Are Old
When you are old and grey and full of sleep,
And nodding by the fire, take down this book,
And slowly read, and dream of the soft look
Your eyes had once, and of their shadows deep;
How many loved your moments of glad grace,
And loved your beauty with love false or true,

But one man loved the pilgrim soul in you,
And loved the sorrows of your changing face;
And bending down beside the glowing bars,
Murmur, a little sadly, how Love fled
And paced upon the mountains overhead
And hid his face amid a crowd of stars.

W B Yeats (1865–1939)

Poets are concerned not only with literal meanings but also with the layered associations of words and of the rhythms and cadences of the poem as a whole. We do not only respond to a poem, or a play, or to music, line by line or note by note. It is a feature of schematic symbols that we respond to them as a whole. The complete work is more than the sum of its parts.

We use different modes of representation to express different types of ideas. It is said that the composer Gustav Mahler was sitting in his studio completing a new piano piece. As he was playing, one of his students came into the room and listened quietly. At the end of the piece the student said, "Maestro, that was wonderful. What is it about?" Mahler turned to him and said, "It's about this," and he played it again. If the ideas in music could be expressed in words, there'd be no need to write the music in the first place.

Some ideas can only be expressed in mathematics. As the Nobel physicist, Richard Feynman, put it: "If you're interested in the ultimate character of the physical world, at present time our only way to understand it is through a mathematical type of reasoning. I don't think a person can appreciate much of these particular aspects of the world, the great depth and character of the universality of the laws, relationships of things, without an understanding of mathematics. There are many aspects of the world where mathematics is unnecessary, such as love, which are very delightful and wonderful to appreciate and to feel awe about. But if physics is what we are talking about, then not to know mathematics is a severe limitation in understanding the world."[6]

Mathematics is the best medium for some forms of understanding but relatively poor for others. If you want to describe the movement of electrons, you need algebra. If you want to express your love for someone, it would be better to use poetry. If someone asks you, "How much do you love me?" don't give them a calculator and say, "Here, you work it out."

YOUR CREATIVE MIND

Our ideas can liberate or imprison us. As psychologist George A. Kelly put it: "to make sense out of events we thread them through with ideas and to make sense of the ideas we must test them against events."[7] He describes this process as one of successive approximations. In this way we create the worlds in which we live; and there is always the possibility of re-creation. The generative ideas in human history have transformed the worldview of their times and helped to reshape their cultures. This may be what the comedian George Carlin had in mind when he said, "Just when I found out the meaning of life, they changed it."

What is true of the long cycles of creative change in a social culture is also true of the shorter cycles of creative work by individuals and groups. Creativity is a process of successive approximations.

IMAGINATION, CREATIVITY AND INNOVATION

Imagination is the source of our creativity, but imagination and creativity are not the same thing. Imagination is the ability to bring to mind things that are not present to our senses. Creativity is putting your imagination to work.

Imagination includes mental experiences that are *imaginal*, *imaginative* and *imaginary*. We can imagine things that have existed, do exist, might exist or do not exist at all. If I ask you to think of an elephant, your old school, or your best friend you can bring to mind mental images that are drawn from real experience. We would not normally think of mental images of real experiences as *imaginative*. More properly, they are *imaginal*. If I ask you to think of a green polar bear wearing a dress, you can imagine that too. Now you are bringing to mind something you haven't experienced; at least I assume not. These sorts of images are of possibilities composed *in* the mind rather than recalled to mind. They are *imaginative*. Sometimes we mistake imaginative experiences for real ones. These sorts of experience are *imaginary*.

Imagination enables you to step out of the here and now. You can revisit and review the past. You can take a different view of the present by putting yourself in the minds of others and can try to see with their eyes and feel with their hearts. In imagination you can anticipate many possible futures. You may not be able to predict the future, but by acting on the ideas produced in your imagination you can help to create it.

Creativity is a step on from imagination. Imagination can be an entirely private experience of internal consciousness. You might be lying motionless on your bed in a fever of imagination and no one would ever know. Private imaginings may have no outcomes in the world at all. Creativity does. Being creative involves *doing* something. It would be odd to describe as creative someone who never did anything. To call somebody creative suggests they are actively producing something in a deliberate way.[8] People are not creative in the abstract; they are creative *in* something: in mathematics, in engineering, in writing, in music, in business, in whatever. In a sense, creativity is applied imagination. How does creativity work?

THE CREATIVE PROCESS

I define creativity as the process of having original ideas that have value. There are three key terms here: *process*, *original* and *value*. Creativity is a process more often than it is an event. To call something a process indicates a relationship between its various elements, so that each aspect of what happens affects every other. Being creative involves two main processes that interweave with each other. The first is generative, the second is evaluative. In most creative work there are many shifts between these two modes. The quality of creative achievement is related to both. Helping people to understand and manage how they leaven each with the other is a pivotal task of creative development.

"Creativity is the process of having original ideas that have value."

Generating ideas

Professor Sir Harry Kroto won the Nobel Prize for Chemistry. He was also a professional designer. I asked him what differences there are, if any, between creativity in the arts and sciences: in the studio and the laboratory. He said that for him the process is the same, even though the outcomes are different (as we'll see in Chapter 7). In all creative processes we are pushing the boundaries of what we know now, to explore new possibilities; we are drawing on the skills we have now, often stretching and evolving them as the work demands.

In the early stages, being creative may involve playing with an idea, doodling or improvising around the theme. It may begin with a thought that is literally half-formed: with a sketch, a first plan or a design; the first notes of a melody or the intimation of a solution to a problem. There may be several ideas in play and a number of possible starting points. Creativity doesn't always require freedom from constraints or a blank page. A lot of creative work has to conform to a specific brief or set of conventions, and great work often comes from working within formal constraints. When President Kennedy declared in September 1962 that America would land a man on the moon and bring him safely back to earth, he mobilized a ferment of creativity and innovation that involved billions of dollars, millions of individuals and hundreds of institutions embracing scores of disciplines. The challenge was clear and so were the constraints. No one asked if he could adjust the laws of gravity or possibly move the moon a little closer.

The sonnet has a fixed form to which the writer must submit. Japanese haiku makes specific formal demands on the poet, as do many other forms of poetic structure. These do not inhibit the writer's creativity; they set a framework for it. The creative achievement and the aesthetic pleasure lie in using standard forms to achieve unique effects and original insights.

Because being creative involves *doing* something, it will always involve using some form of media. These may be physical media, such as steel, wood, clay, fabric or food; they may be sensory media, like sound, light, the voice or the body; they may be cognitive media, including words, numbers, or notation. Whatever the media, there is an intimate relationship between the ideas and the media through which they take shape. This is true whether the task is designing a building, developing a mathematical theorem, a scientific hypothesis or a musical composition. Creativity is a dialogue between the ideas and the media in which they are being formed. Dancers do not begin from a verbal proposition and try to dance it. Dance evolves in the making. It is a material process of movement and reflection on movement. Often it is only in developing the dance, the image or music that the idea emerges at all.

Making judgments

Creativity is not only about generating ideas; it involves making judgments about them. It involves elaborating on the initial ideas, testing and refining them and even rejecting them in favor of others that emerge along the way. Sometimes creative works arrive in the world more or less fully formed and need no further work. It's said that Mozart made few revisions to many of his compositions. The poet John Milton was blind. Each morning he dictated whole sections of his

"If you're not prepared to be wrong, it's unlikely that you'll ever come up with anything original."

epic work *Paradise Lost* to his daughters and made only minor changes to the text. Good for them. Usually, creative work is more tentative and exploratory.

Evaluating which ideas work and which do not can involve standing back in quiet reflection, it can be individual or collective, involve instant judgments or long-term testing. There are likely to be dead ends: ideas and designs that do not work. There may be failures and changes before the best outcome is produced. You can see examples of the iterative nature of creative work in the successive drafts of poems and novels, of scholarly papers or in designs for inventions and so on. Thomas Edison famously ran through dozens of ideas and designs for the light bulb before settling on the final version.

Terrance Tao may be the greatest living mathematician. In 2002, at the age of 31, he received the Fields Medal for Mathematics, the equivalent of the Nobel Prize. He says that discovery in mathematics is always about trial and error: "You come up with a wrong idea," he says, "work on it for a month and realize it doesn't work and then you come up with the next wrong idea and then finally, by process of elimination, you come up with something that does work." I asked Sir Harry Kroto how many of his experiments failed. He said about 95% of them. Of course failure is not the right word, he said: "You're just finding out what doesn't work." Albert Einstein put the point sharply: "Anyone who has never made a mistake has never tried anything new." I don't mean to say that being wrong is the same thing as being creative, but if you are not prepared to be wrong, it is unlikely that you'll ever come up with anything original.

Michael Polanyi makes a distinction between *focal* and *subsidiary* awareness. If you're knocking a nail into a piece of wood with a hammer, the focus of your attention is on the head of the nail. You also have to be aware, in a subsidiary way, of the weight of the hammer and the arc of your arm.

It is important that this relationship is the right way round. If you start to focus on what your arm is doing, you're likely to miss the nail. Polanyi continues: "Subsidiary awareness and focal awareness are mutually exclusive. If a pianist shifts his attention from the piece he is playing to the observation of what he's doing with his fingers while playing it, he gets confused and may have to stop. This happens generally if we switch our focal attention to particulars on which we had previously been aware only in their subsidiary role."[9]

In any creative work the focus of our attention has to be right. Although there are always points where criticism is necessary, generative thinking has to be given time to flower. At the right time and in the right way, critical appraisal is essential. At the wrong point, it can kill an emerging idea. Similarly, creativity can be inhibited by trying to do too much too soon or at the same time. The final phases are often to do with refining the detail of the expression: with producing the neat copy so to speak. Trying to produce a finished version in one move is usually impossible. Unless you are dealing with John Milton, asking people to write a poem right away in their best handwriting can inhibit the spontaneity they need in the initial phase of generating ideas. They need to understand that creativity moves through different phases, and to have some sense of where they are in the process. Not understanding this can make people think that they are not creative at all.

"At the right time and in the right way, critical appraisal is essential. At the wrong point, it can kill an emerging idea."

Judging value

When I was a teenager, one of my cousins came to the house flushed with excitement. He'd thought of an invention that he was convinced was going to make us all rich. He'd been walking down the road and was watching an elderly woman inching painfully along with a walking stick. In a moment of inspiration, he thought how much easier it would be if the walking stick had a little wheel on the end of it. Instead of lifting it every time she took a step she could just push it along. He couldn't believe that no one had thought of it before. We made him some tea to drink and broke it to him gently. It was a good idea but for the one catastrophic flaw.

Judging the value of new ideas can be difficult. By definition, creative ideas are often ahead of their times. In the mid-1830s, Michael Faraday gave the first demonstration of electromagnetism at the Royal Institution in London. He stood in a gas-lit lecture theater before a distinguished audience of scientists and showed bright blue sparks leaping between two copper spheres. The audience was impressed but many were at a loss to know what to make of it all. "This is all very interesting, Mr Faraday," said one of them. "But what use is it?" "I don't know," Faraday is purported to have said, "What is a newborn baby?" A world without electricity is now unthinkable. Our lives depend on it in almost every way, from food supplies to transport to heating, lighting and telecommunications. The nineteenth century saw few of the uses of electricity that we now take for granted. It was not as if people's homes were cluttered with dormant dishwashers and televisions, waiting for Faraday to complete his experiments so they could be switched on. The applications of electricity followed the harnessing of electricity itself. Faraday's discoveries helped to create circumstances in which these applications were developed. At the time, many people couldn't see the point of it. This is often the way with creative insights. They run ahead of their times and confuse the crowd.

Original thinkers are often appreciated more by subsequent generations because values change. Many scientists, inventors, artists and philosophers were ridiculed in their own times, though their work has been revered by later generations. Think of Galileo, whose work on heliocentrism was denounced as heretical and not considered science at all. Avant-garde artists are constantly asked, "But is it art?"[10] There are many examples of artists who died in penury, whose work now changes hands for fortunes. People who were thought of as visionary in their own times can be discredited by history for exactly the same reason. Think of phrenology. Few scientists now take seriously the idea that personality can be interpreted by bumps on the human skull. But in the mid-nineteenth century it was highly influential in shaping ideas about psychiatry.

Our view of the past is rarely settled. We live in a perpetual present tense. Our knowledge of other periods can never match their vast complexity as they were experienced and understood at the time. Our perception of the past is selective and always open to revision, often because of changes in contemporary values. Individuals long forgotten or overlooked may be reinterpreted as key agents of cultural progress because of a shift in current fashion or political outlook. The strong sentiment and self-assurance of Raphael, for example, endeared him to many Victorians as the central figure in the Renaissance. There are those today who think more of Michelangelo, for his restless self-doubt, and build their image of the period around him. In these ways, our sense of history and of ourselves involves a continual selection and reselection of ancestors. History is not dead because the present is so alive.

Being original

Creativity is about coming up with new ideas. What qualifies them as new? Do you have to come up with something no one has thought of before? Common sense suggests not. A creative outcome can be original on different levels: for the person involved; for a particular community; for humanity as a whole. The towering figures of science, the arts, technology

"Creativity moves through different phases. Trying to produce a finished version in one move is usually impossible. Not understanding this can make people think that they are not creative at all."

and the rest produced works of historic originality. Teachers do not expect that of young children. Some may be capable of historic originality – Shakespeare was in someone's English class. But generally they try to encourage work that is original for the children themselves.

Making connections

Creative insights often occur by making unusual connections between things or ideas that have not previously been related. All of our existing ideas have creative possibilities. Creative insights occur when they are combined in unexpected ways or applied to questions or issues with which they are not normally associated. Arthur Koestler describes this as a process of bi-association.[11] It happens when we think not on one plane, as in routine linear thinking, but on several planes at once. As I noted in Chapter 5, some modes of thinking dominate in different types of activity: the aural in music, the kinesthetic in dance and the mathematical in physics. Often they draw on different areas of intelligence simultaneously. Mathematicians often talk of visualizing problems and solutions. Dance is closely related to musical understanding; visual arts draw deeply on spatial intelligence. The composition of music is often informed by mathematics.

FREEDOM AND CONTROL

Creative achievement is related to control of the medium. Simply asking people to be creative is not enough. Children and adults need the means and the skills to be creative. I can't play the piano. I don't mean I'm incapable of playing; I have never learnt how to do it. To that extent, I cannot be creative on the piano. I can make noises on it and give vent to my immediate feelings but not be musically creative in the same way as those who can play it.

Many people have problems with mathematics. They see it as a sort of puzzle, the point of which is not wholly clear. Trying to appreciate equations if you do not "speak" mathematics is like trying to appreciate a musical score if you do not read music. Non-musicians see a puzzle; musicians hear a symphony. Those who speak mathematics look through equations to the beauty of the ideas they express. They hear the music. For some of us, grasping mathematical beauty is like trying to read Proust with a French phrasebook.

Many adults say they can't draw. They're right, they can't. They are not incapable of it any more than I am of learning the piano. They don't know how. Given adequate hand–eye co-ordination, most people can learn to draw, but most people have not acquired the necessary skills. The problems they face are often of two kinds. The first is *perceptual*. They try to draw in a photographic way rather than seeing the object more schematically. The second problem is *technical*. Like learning to write, learning to draw is a technical and cultural achievement not a biological one. Unless these things are taught and learnt, the creative possibilities of drawing remain limited.

If they don't practice or have guidance, most children's drawings follow a recognizable pattern up to the age of 13 or so. At about the age of 8, for example, they begin to develop a sense of perspective. As they mature, they pay increasing attention to details and attempt more sophisticated pictures. At about the age of 12 or 13, their drawings often reach a plateau. Many people give up drawing altogether at this point, often through frustration. Their creative ambitions outrun their technical abilities. As a result, most adults have the graphic skills of a young adolescent. This is hardly surprising. Children don't develop these abilities just by getting older, any more than they wake up on their 16th birthday to discover they know how to drive a car.

None of this means that people with limited skills can't be creative. There are different levels and phases of creative development. Some people produce highly creative work with relatively undeveloped techniques. In general though, creative development goes hand in hand with increasing technical facility with the instruments or materials that are being used. Here, as everywhere, it is a question of balance. Technical control is necessary for creative work but it is not enough. Being creative is about speculating, exploring new horizons and using imagination. Many highly trained people – musicians, dancers, engineers, scientists – are very skilled but not especially original. They may not be working in their best medium. A musician may be competent in an instrument but not excited by it. There are other possibilities. One of them is bad teaching. I know many would-be musicians who endured the drudgery of practicing scales and harmonies only until they could put the instrument away forever. Facilitating creative development is about finding a balance between exploring new ideas and acquiring the skills to realize them.

THIS TIME IT'S PERSONAL

There is a difference between *general* and *personal* creativity.

General creativity

Original thinking is possible in anything that we do. In the general run of our lives we settle into routines of behavior and habits of thought. When we encounter a new problem or situation, our established habits can make it difficult to see novel solutions. There are various techniques to help unblock conventional ways of thinking and encourage what Edward de Bono has called lateral thinking.[12] In logico-deductive thought, ideas build on each another in consistent steps and lead to a limited number of answers and sometimes to only one. Lateral and divergent thought works by making freer associations: often by thinking in metaphors or analogies, or even reframing the question itself to open up more possibilities. There are some tests for divergent thinking just as there are for IQ. You might be asked how many uses you can think of for a paperclip. An average score might be 10 or 15, all involving paper. People who are good at these tests might come up with over 100 ideas, and be able to see beyond the conventional use of a paperclip. They might consider a use for a paperclip that is 50 feet high and made out of rubber. The question didn't say it couldn't be.

Some of the most interesting breakthroughs in science, technology and the arts come from reframing the question, just as Copernicus and Galileo chose to question whether the earth was at the center of the universe. As Susanne Langer observed, the questions we ask are as important as the answers we search for. Every question leads to particular lines of inquiry. Change the question and whole new horizons may open up to us. The true value of a generative idea is that it leads to new sorts of questions.

These general techniques of creative thinking can be used to generate a flow of ideas and possibilities, especially in groups and committees. They include the repertoire of thinking skills developed by Edward De Bono, and Synectics, developed by William Gordon and George Prince.[13] Used properly they can have genuine benefits in business, in the community and in our personal lives. Often they focus separately on identifying and analyzing problems, generating solutions and evaluating the best options. They also focus on giving positive rather than negative responses to people's ideas and the value of sharing multiple points of view.

Personal creativity

Herb Alpert is one of the great musicians of his generation. When he plays the trumpet, it's as if he's speaking to you. In a sense, he is. His personal creativity as a musician is indivisible from his passion for the expressive qualities of the trumpet itself. He's also a distinguished sculptor and painter. In each medium, his creative achievements have been inspired by his love for the materials he uses and the possibilities he sees in them. For other musicians, their best medium may be the guitar, the piano, or the violin. There are many examples of people whose creativity is fired by particular media: not water colors but pastels, not mathematics in general but algebra in particular. I spoke once with a professor of physics from California. He described himself as a native speaker of algebra. When he came across algebra at school, he had an intuitive feel for it. He said that English has become his second language. He now spends most of his life speaking algebra.

In addition to general capacities for creative thinking, we all have unique talents and passions and our own personal creative potential. It may be for a particular form of music or specific instrument, or music in general; it may be for mathematics or chemistry or contemporary dance; you may have a vocation for becoming a fireman, a homemaker, a physician or a teacher. We each have skills and abilities that can be developed. In *The Element*, I talk about this personal dimension of creative achievement: the point where individual talent meets personal passion. Personal creativity often comes from a love for particular materials. A sculptor will feel inspired by the shape of a piece of wood or the texture of stone; musicians love the sounds they make and the feel of the instruments. Mathematicians love the art of mathematics just as dancers love to move; writers may feel inspired by a love of the expressive power of words; and painters by the potential of a blank canvas and their color palette. Discovering the right medium is often a tidal moment in the creative life of the individual.

The composer and conductor, Leonard Bernstein, once talked about the moment when he fell in love with music. When he was a young child, he came downstairs one morning to find an upright piano in the hallway of his home.

Bernstein's family was not especially musical but his parents had agreed to look after the piano while some friends were out of the country. He had never been close to a piano before. With a child's curiosity he lifted the lid and pressed on the keys and felt the sounds vibrate from the instrument. A wave of excitement rushed through him. He didn't know why this happened but he knew then that he wanted to spend as much time as he could making such sounds. He had found his medium. In doing so he opened the door to his own creative potential.

Porcelain was introduced into Britain in the eighteenth century. Some of the most exquisite pieces of porcelain were made in the Chelsea Porcelain Factory, which was founded by Nicholas Sprimont in 1743. Before Sprimont discovered porcelain, he was a silversmith by trade. He was a competent silversmith and made a good living. He came upon this new material and it fired his imagination like nothing before. He loved the feel of it and the possibilities it held. Over the next 20 years he produced beautiful objects that far surpassed his achievements in silver. His creative accomplishments were driven by his relationship with the material itself.[14]

Equally, creativity can be inhibited by the wrong medium. Some years ago, I worked with an outstanding literary editor on a book I had written. She was an excellent judge of style and added hugely to the quality of the book, as good literary editors do. She had become a literary editor in her 40s. Before that she was a concert pianist. I asked why she had changed professions. She said she had been giving a concert in London with a distinguished conductor. After the concert they had dinner. Over the meal, he mentioned how good her performance had been and she thanked him. "But you didn't enjoy it, did you?" he said. She was taken aback. This hadn't occurred to her. She said she hadn't enjoyed it particularly, but then she never did. He asked why she did it and she said, "Because I'm good at it."

She'd been born into a musical family and taken piano lessons. She showed a talent and went on to take a music degree, then a doctorate of music and, as the night follows the day, went on to a career as a concert pianist. Neither she nor anyone else had stopped to ask whether she wanted to do this or whether she enjoyed it. She did it because she was good at it. The conductor said, "Being good at something isn't a good enough reason to spend your life doing it." In the weeks that followed she wrestled with this idea and decided that he was right. She finished the season, closed the lid of the piano and never opened it again. She turned instead to books, the art form she really loved. When people find their medium, they discover their real creative strengths and come into their own.

"The capacity for creativity is essentially human and it holds the constant promise of alternative ways of seeing, of thinking and of doing."

CONCLUSION

Intelligence is diverse, dynamic and distinct. So too is the creative process. It can operate in all fields of human intelligence, it is about making dynamic connections, and the results are always in some way unique. Creativity is not a single power that people simply have or do not have. It involves many different mental functions, combinations of skills and personal attributes. We all have creative capacities but many people conclude that they're not creative when they haven't learnt and practiced what's involved. The capacity for creativity is essentially human and it holds the constant promise of alternative ways of seeing, of thinking and of doing. It means, as George Kelly put it, that no one needs to be completely hemmed in by circumstances: "No one needs to be the victim of their own biography." As Carl Jung once said, "I am not what has happened to me. I am what I choose to become." That is the power and the promise of being creative.

FEELING BETTER

"Being creative is not only about thinking: it is about feeling."

I USED TO SUPERVISE DOCTORAL PROGRAMS in the humanities. The university had set a maximum length for doctoral dissertations of 80,000 words. This was necessary because candidates had to be stopped. I once interviewed a candidate who had a PhD from another university. I asked if there was a maximum length for the dissertation. He was startled and said of course not. They were as long they needed to be. I asked him how long his dissertation needed to be. He said 370,000 words. That's roughly the length of the Old Testament. I asked him the title. It was called *Further Education in Dombey: Some Issues.* Dombey[1] is a regional city in England with a population at the time of about 220,000 people. That's a little short of 1.5 words each. What he discovered there that took over a third of a million words to explain, I don't know, but according to his subtitle this wasn't even a comprehensive study, merely a promissory note for a fuller work yet to be composed.

I once asked a professor of mathematics how he assessed PhDs in pure mathematics. My first question was, "How long are they?" He said, "They're as long as they need to be." I asked how long they are typically. He'd reviewed one recently which was 26 pages. That's page after page after page of math with an equals sign at the end. I asked him how he assessed these dissertations. I assumed they were "right." You'd be depressed if you'd spent four years completing a PhD in pure math and it was marked "wrong." "No," he said, "They're normally right." *Normally.* "So how do you assess one?" I asked. "Originality is a key factor," he told me. "Like all PhDs, they have to break new ground and tell us something we didn't know before." In other words, one criterion is how creative the work is. Another, he said, is aesthetic. It is the elegance of the proof, the beauty of the argument.

I asked him why that is such an important consideration in math. He said that mathematicians believe that mathematics is one of the purest ways we have of understanding the truths of nature. Since nature is inherently beautiful there's an assumption that the more elegant the proof, the more likely it is to correspond to the beauty of nature and to be true. He could have been discussing a sonata, or a poem or a dance, and in a way he was. Aesthetics is a powerful force in all forms of creative work: for scientists and mathematicians as it is for musicians, poets, dancers and designers. It's one of the ways in which being creative is not only about thinking: it is about feeling.

"Aesthetics is a powerful force in all forms of creative work: for scientists and mathematicians just as for musicians, poets, dancers and designers."

THE EXILE OF FEELING

The leading figures of the Enlightenment and of Romanticism saw clear water between intellect and emotion. The Rationalists distrusted feelings; the Romantics trusted little else. In their different ways, they saw intellect and feelings as separate from each other. The consequences of this division are still felt to this day.[2]

Rationalist philosophers wanted to dispel the illusions of myth and superstition. In the natural sciences, feelings, intuition, values and beliefs were seen as dangerous distractions: the froth of undisciplined minds. David Hume put it bluntly: "If we take in hand any volume; of divinity or school metaphysics, for instance, let us ask, does it contain any abstract reasoning concerning quantity or number? No. Does it contain any experimental reasoning concerning matters of fact and existence? No. Commit it then to the flames, for it can contain nothing but sophistry and illusion."[3] This meant, for example, that the biological sciences should make no metaphysical assumptions about the origins and functions of life, which should be explained in material terms. If there is a force beyond logic and evidence that is responsible for life on earth, science should make no presumptions about it and take no interest in it.

In the human sciences, there was a similar rejection of religious ideas and of all forms of transcendentalism. Pioneering psychologists, including Ivan Pavlov (1849–1936), J.B. Watson (1878–1958) and B.F. Skinner (1904–90), set out to examine human behavior in ways that set aside all ideas about immaterial spirits or souls. They looked at human behavior as learned responses to the practical needs of survival. B.F. Skinner developed his theory of behaviorism in the 1920s. He showed that people could be conditioned into particular forms of behavior. Pavlov's experiment with dogs came to a similar conclusion. When he gave food to the dogs in his laboratory, Pavlov rang a bell. Soon the dogs salivated at the sound of the bell alone. Pavlov argued that human beings have conditioned responses too.

Sigmund Freud (1856–1939) conceived of the mind as a mental apparatus for engaging the individual with the outside world. He distinguished between *the id*: the basic instinctual drives of human behavior, which operate on the pleasure principle; *the ego*: the conscious mind, which operates on the reality principle and manages our executive functions and relationships in the world; and *the super ego*: which is the seat of moral values, spirituality and conscience. According to Freud, the ego is in a constant state of tension as it strives to manage the primitive impulses of the id, the moral tendencies of the super ego and the competing demands of the external world. Being rational depends on controlling these complex psychological drives. Freudian psychology sees emotions as potential sources of disturbance to a balanced personality.

Despite the influence of these ideas in the human sciences and in popular culture, by the mid-twentieth century growing numbers of academics and therapists alike were questioning these mechanistic approaches to human behavior. In 1960, Jerome Bruner and Frank Miller established the Center for Cognitive Studies at Harvard University, to move beyond the behaviorist paradigm and explore the intrinsic nature of mind and consciousness. Jean Piaget had long argued for more qualitative approaches to understanding how children and adults learn and experience the world.

Other psychologists and therapists objected to what they saw as negative conceptions of feelings and emotions that came from the rationalist and behaviorist traditions; what R.D. Laing called "the negative psychology of affect." Some, like Laing, saw rationalist models of psychology as symptoms of a larger problem: "that our civilization represses not only the instincts, not only sexuality, but any form of transcendence." From the beginning of the twentieth century there had been alternative theories of human well-being. William James (1842–1910), Viktor Frankl (1905–97), Carl Jung (1875–1961) Abraham Maslow (1908–70), Carl Rogers (1902–87) and many others had argued in their own ways for more harmonious conceptions of feelings, spirituality, mind and body. Some, like Alan Watts (1915–73) and Aldous Huxley (1894–1963), drew on ancient Eastern teachings where the divisions between mind, body and spirit had not been so sharply drawn in the first place. By the 1960s, a complicated cultural reaction against rationalism was beginning to gather pace, a reaction that manifested in far-reaching changes in what the cultural historian, Raymond Williams, would have called the "structure of feeling" of the time.

THE PERSONAL GROWTH MOVEMENT

The personal growth movement began in the 1940s and mushroomed during the 1960s, first in America and then in Europe. "Personal growth" refers to various sorts of group encounter activities that aim to explore the relationships between people and increase their knowledge of themselves and each other. Encounter or T-groups encouraged members to see the world through the eyes of others and to rethink their own perceptions of themselves. These encounters often made use of role-play techniques, of art and other "creative" activities; they drew on the alternative theories of psychoanalysts such as Jung and Rogers; and often integrated Eastern techniques of meditation and of physical relaxation including yoga. The principles and practices of the personal growth movement are now the basis of coaching, mentoring and publishing programs around the world.

The two touchstones of personal growth are individuality and authenticity. An individual desiring a personal growth experience "may consider himself less emotionally, physically, or sensually spontaneous than he would like. He may be lonely and find it difficult to communicate honestly with another. The values of sensitivity training and group encounter are honesty and the presentation of the authentic self."[4] Group encounters attracted large numbers of paying customers to the search for more authentic relationships. The personal growth movement is also impelled by a hunger that many people feel to connect with their own natural strengths and with their own creativity.[5]

"The two touchstones of personal growth are individuality and authenticity."

According to Carl Rogers, the burgeoning of personal growth was stimulated by the decline of organized religious beliefs and the need to find alternative sources of meaning in existence. Victor Frankl believed that unknown numbers of people were suffering from what he called the "existential vacuum": the loss of an ultimate meaning to existence that would make life worthwhile. As Frankl saw it, "the consequent void, the state of emptiness is at present one of the major challenges to psychiatry."[6] Carl Jung agreed. During his long professional practice as a psychoanalyst, he was consulted by people "from all the civilized countries of the earth." Among all his patients in the second half of life, "that is to say over 35, there has not been one whose problem in the last resort was not one of finding a religious outlook on life. It is safe to say that every one of them fell ill because he had lost that which the living religions of every age have given their followers, and none of them has been really healed who did not regain his religious outlook."[7]

Holistic therapists argued for systems of analysis that addressed a person's total being in the world, including the expression of personal feelings. The implicit ethic is to live in the here and now. Rather than being wholly existentialist, the counter-culture, as it came to be known, was rooted as much in metaphysical interests. Rethinking materialist values and the search for transcendence, especially through alternative religions, were at the heart of these movements. As traditional religious structures have been eroded, esoteric beliefs, fundamentalist religions and cults of all sorts have proliferated. So too has interest in the so-called para-sciences, in extrasensory perception and in alternative states of consciousness.

EMOTIONAL DISTURBANCE

Despite the best efforts of the counter-culture, the mainstream culture of mental health continues to focus on emotional disturbance, to the delight of the pharmaceutical industries. For over a hundred years, the complex edifice of mental healthcare has been built on the concept of emotional illness. Counselors, therapists, psychologists and psychiatrists of every sort are kept afloat on a rising tide of people needing help with problems of purpose, self-image, relationships or trauma across a scale from short-term depression to complete breakdown. These problems are not the confine of the clinically disturbed. Multitudes of people who otherwise seem to be on top of their lives have trouble handling their feelings and relationships.

SOFT SKILLS

There is a growing movement in "positive psychology" – the study of happiness and well-being. Daniel Goleman is one of the leaders of this movement. He argues that the dominant emphasis on IQ should be tempered by an equal emphasis on EQ: emotional intelligence. Emotional intelligence means being able to understand and express personal feelings; being able to get along with other people, to communicate clearly and with empathy for the listener; and responding positively and with sensitivity to new situations. These "soft skills" are now seen as crucial in productive relationships at home, in the workplace and in leadership.

Business leaders often say that people entering the workforce seem weaker in these areas than earlier generations. The "exile of feeling" may be more pronounced than ever. Goleman reports on a survey of pupils and teachers that shows "a worldwide trend for the present generation of children to be more troubled emotionally than the last: more lonely and depressed, more angry and unruly, more nervous and prone to worry, more impulsive and aggressive."[8] People around the world, he says, are facing the same kind of problems.

There are many reasons. In the developed economies especially, the nuclear family is disappearing. Fewer people are getting married and among those that do, divorce rates are at historically high levels. Adults are spending longer hours at work, and have less time with their children. Young people often spend more time bonding with computers than physically playing with other children. Parents' fear of crime means that fewer children are allowed outside to play unless accompanied by an adult. According to Goleman, they miss out on the games that used to be commonplace in residential streets "that furnished children with all sorts of life skills such as an ability to control anger and settle disputes."[9]

The fact that we are embodied beings and not just beings in bodies was made clear to me when our son James was 12 and preparing for end-of-year examinations at school. A few weeks before they were due to take place, he asked whether, if he did well in the examinations, he could have a games computer. We said no. He asked what his incentive would be in that case, and we said that we'd be very pleased with him. He wasn't impressed. As it happens, he did well and a few weeks later he asked about the computer again. This time we relented, mainly because I wanted one too. We bought the computer and a set of games and I spent an hour setting it all up and left him to try it out.

Downstairs, our daughter Kate, who was 8, was standing with a length of old rope she had found in the garden shed. She asked if I would make her a swing. I found some wood for a seat and wrapped the rope around the bough of an apple tree and left her swinging happily backwards and forwards. A couple of hours later, James saw her on the swing and dashed out to join her. They spent the rest of the day, the whole of the next day and virtually the entire summer on the swing. They invented games, new moves, tricks, circus routines and fantasy situations, all of which revolved around that swing. They laughed, argued, made up and carried on, and gouged a trench in the ground beneath it. Playing outdoors opened their imaginations and gave them more pleasure than the hundreds of dollars worth of computer that was left upstairs. Mind you, I doubt that James would have been particularly motivated, if I'd said to him a few weeks earlier, that if he did really well in his examinations he could have the piece of old rope that was in the shed.

Students now spend more hours on desk study than on physical activities and engaging face-to-face with their peers. Many school systems have cut back on practical programs in the arts and the opportunities they offer for engaging with feelings. There have been severe cuts, too, in physical education programs and all that they offer in connecting physical and mental energies.

Not all of this is new. The cultivation of feeling has long been marginalized by academic education. In the 1970s, Dr Anthony Storr, a lecturer in psychotherapy at Oxford University, saw many examples of what he called "the Oxford neurosis," which he described as "intellectual precocity combined with emotional immaturity."[10] While it would be rash to attribute all forms of emotional disturbances to academic education, there is no question that it has played a part. The conventional academic curriculum largely ignores the "soft skills." This is not an oversight. It is a structural feature of academicism.

TWO TRADITIONS

For the past 250 years, there has been a tension between the worldviews of the Enlightenment and of Romanticism. A common theme of both is a commitment to individualism but they offer different views of what a true individual is and what it takes to become one. I distinguish them as the "rational" and the "natural" individual. Both views tend to compound the division of intellect and emotion.

The rational individual

In the rationalist worldview, the individual possesses certain qualities of mind, and these are what education should promote. The rationalist ideology has given rise to many different theories within philosophy and science. For all their differences they have common characteristics: logic and deduction are the hallmarks of independent thought; these powers are the only reliable source of knowledge of oneself and of the material world; true knowledge is objective and independent of cultural values and personal feelings. Approaches to education based on rational individualism make common assumptions:

- Education should focus on the powers of logico-deductive reason.

- A rational mind is developed by exercising these powers and by absorbing the various bodies of knowledge that they have generated.

- The main role of teachers is to transmit these bodies of knowledge. In this sense, education is a form of initiation.

The natural individual

Natural individualism makes completely different assumptions. In this view, every child is, by nature, a unique individual with innate talents and sensibilities. Education should draw out these qualities rather than suppress them with the values and ideas of the adult world. Education should not be knowledge-based but child-centered. Naturalist models of education make the following assumptions:

- Education should develop the whole child and not just their academic abilities. It should engage their feelings, physical development, moral education and creativity.

- Knowledge of the self is as important as knowledge of the external world. Exploring personal feelings and values is essential and so are opportunities to exercise imagination and self-expression.

- One of the main roles of teachers is to draw out the individual in every child. In this sense, education is a process of self-realization.[11]

Like those of rational individualism, the roots of natural individualism run deep. At the center of eighteenth-century Romanticism was the idea of the natural world. In 1780, Jacques Rousseau published *Emile*, in which he argued for a new approach to education that was based on play, games and pleasure. Rousseau wanted forms of education that cherished childhood and did not impose adult values on young minds. Over the next 200 years, many other pioneers of "child-centered" education argued, from different perspectives, for the importance of play and creativity. Some developed their own proprietary systems to promote it. They included: Johann Pestalozzi (1746–1847), Friedrich Froebel (1782–1852), Maria Montessori (1870–1952), Rudolf Steiner (1861–1925), Carl Orff (1895–1982) and John Dewey (1859–1952).

For all of them, the essential role of education is to develop children's natural abilities and personalities. Children should be allowed to follow a natural pattern of development rather than a standard course of instruction. Like a sculptor, the teacher should follow the unique grain of each child's personality, slowly revealing the individual within. Above all, naturalists wanted to address the whole child: mind, body and spirit.

The value of physical and imaginative play has been recognized by philosophers back to Plato and Aristotle. The nineteenth century brought a new perspective. Darwin's theories of evolution made human development a subject of scientific study. All behavior was assumed to relate somehow to the survival of the species. As babies and children spend so much time playing, play was assumed to have some biological function. In the 1920s and 1930s, developments in the psychology of play combined with "progressive" theories of education to influence mainstream education policy. Throughout the last 100 years there has been a continuous line of people pressing for more creative approaches to education.

In the USA, John Dewey developed new methods of teaching at his Laboratory School. At the Dalton School in New York and the Porter School in Missouri, teachers encouraged "learning by doing." These ideas were part of a broader movement in the 1930s to encourage creativity and self-expression in schools. While John Dewey and others were promoting more liberal approaches to education, A.S. Makarenko (1888–1939) was developing his own system in Russia. The revolution had left millions of children orphaned and homeless. Makarenko devised a system of education based on practical work and collective responsibility. Recognizing the appalling emotional suffering of the children, he found tremendous value for them in creative activities, beauty and pleasure and organized an influential program of music groups, and productions of plays and dance.

A report on elementary school education in the UK in 1931 said that education had to look to the whole child. It emphasized the importance of play, self-expression and creative activities, which "if the psychologists are right are so closely associated with the development of perceptions and feelings."[12] The dominant tendency to see the school curriculum as a jigsaw of separate subjects had to be questioned and so too did presenting work to children simply as lessons to be mastered. Education had to start from the experience, curiosity and the awakening powers of children themselves.

Naturalist attitudes gained ground in education during the 1950s and 1960s, partly because they were seen as representing a more egalitarian approach to education. Naturalists argued that academic education marginalized feelings, intuition, aesthetic sensibility and creativity – the very qualities that make human beings human. In the 1960s and 1970s, the argument for self-expression and creativity in education was rooted in a concern to promote the life of feeling. This concern connected with far-reaching cultural developments in the personal growth movement outside formal education.

EDUCATING THE EMOTIONS

The various pioneers of naturalist approaches in education did not share a single philosophy or promote common practices, any more than all proponents of rationalist philosophies had a single point of view. Each had their own conceptions of human development and their own methods of teaching and learning. As their approaches filtered into public education, the general ideals of rational and natural individualism came to represent two distinct options: a choice between a traditional, subject-based, academic education and progressive, child-centered education. In their extremes, they seem to have little in common; but in two respects at least, they do share common ground.

Both promote the idea of the individual breaking free from the constraints of culture. For the rationalists, the individual becomes independent of cultural influences by the power of rational, objective thought. Since objective knowledge is assumed to exist independently of people and culture, the rational individual is free of bias and sees the world just as it is. For the naturalist, the aim is to liberate the individual spirit from the pressures of culture and reveal the authentic self. Since every person is unique, the authentic self will emerge like the butterfly from the chrysalis provided there's enough creative space in which to grow. In this respect, both of these ideals are a-cultural.

Both reinforce the division between intellect and emotion. Personal growth and natural individualism were reactions against *objectivism*: against treating knowledge as impersonal.

I'll come back to this idea later. The danger lies in moving too far the other way, towards *subjectivism*: to thinking of individual consciousness as completely independent from the world of others.

Laing describes as *schizoid* the person who experiences a rent in her relationship with the world and with herself. The schizoid is unable to experience herself together with the world but rather in despairing isolation from it. If this exaggerates the dangers of subjectivism, the underlying principle still applies: that if a person does not exist

"Feelings are a constant dimension of human consciousness. To be is to feel."

objectively as well as subjectively but only as a subjective identity, "he cannot be real." In other words, there has to be a positive relationship between our knowledge of the external world and our knowledge of ourselves.

So what is the relationship between knowing and feeling and what does it mean for being creative?

KNOWING AND FEELING

Descartes said, "I think therefore I am." As Robert Witkin points out, an equally powerful starting point would be, "I feel therefore I am."[13] To be is to feel. Feelings are a constant dimension of human consciousness. From calm intuitions to raging furies, feelings are forms of perception. How we feel about something is an expression of our relationship with it. Feelings are evaluations: for example, grief at a death, elation at a birth, pleasure at success, depression at a failure, disappointment at unfulfillment.[14] Fear differs from anger because seeing something as threatening differs from seeing it as thwarting. These perceptions have different consequences both physiologically and in the behaviors that result.

 Emotions are *intense states of feeling*, which can involve strong physiological responses. Two people falling into a canal may experience very different emotions. A good swimmer may feel

angry or frustrated. Someone who cannot swim may panic.
In both cases, they experience an emotional *arousal*. These
are related to, but different from, emotional *attitudes*.

In fear or anger, the release of adrenaline primes you for
vigorous action. Blood flow is diverted from the digestive system to the muscles, the heartbeat quickens, sugar is released
by the liver, the sweat glands are stimulated, and so on. The
floods of hormonal changes are not conscious decisions but
ancient instincts that are born out of the need for survival.
They prepare us for action, literally without thinking: to
either "fight" or "take flight." If the physical action doesn't
happen, or is suppressed, we're left with a feeling of pent-
up energy. The increased hormonal levels in the body, which
would have been used up by those actions, slowly disperse as
our systems calm down. Emotional arousals subside as the situation changes and our physical condition settles; the pent-up
feeling will persist until this is over. If the incidents that provoked the arousal are repeated often enough – if you are continually bitten by dogs or frequently fall in canals – you may
develop an emotional attitude towards dogs or canals, which
can flare up when they're nearby or brought to mind.

The seat of many of our emotional responses is deep within
the parts of the brain that were among the first to evolve.
This area of the "old" brain includes the amygdalae: almond-
shaped groups of nuclei in the medial temporal lobes of the
brain that are part of what is sometimes called the limbic
system. The older regions of the brain have roles in regulat-
ing the bodily functions that sustain life, including breathing and the metabolism of other organs. Rational, abstract
thought developed much later in the evolution of the brain
and is associated with the neo-cortex, the convoluted folds
lying across the surface of the two cerebral hemispheres, and
the development of the frontal lobes.

The old brain does not think in the usual sense. As Goleman notes, it is more a set of pre-programmed regulators
that keep the body running and reacting to ensure survival.

This does not mean that feeling and reason are insulated from each other. All areas in the brain are connected through intricate neural circuitry. There is a "continual dance between intellect and emotions, feeling and reason, which is essential to the proper functioning and maintenance of both." In a sense, we do have two different ways of knowing the world and interacting with it: the rational and the emotional. This distinction roughly approximates to the folk distinction between heart and head: "knowing something is right in your heart is a different order of conviction, somehow a deeper kind of certainty, than thinking so with your rational mind." The more intense the feeling, the more dominant the emotional mind becomes and the more ineffectual the rational. This arrangement seems to stem from "the eons of evolutionary advantage to having emotions and intuitions guide our instantaneous response in situations where our lives are in peril, and where pausing to think over what to do could cost us our lives."

 As we mature, the balance between reason and emotion changes, or should do. Newborn babies are convulsed by feelings of hunger, distress or contentment. They express them through noises, facial expressions and movement. Toddlerhood and adolescence are famously times of turbulent emotions and mood swings. As the adult emerges from the child, there is normally a growing control of emotions. We're alarmed if adults act like infants, howling in meetings or crying in frustration at not getting their own way; and we are right to be disturbed by adults whose emotions are out of control.

Becoming mature is not about suppressing feelings, or discounting their importance. In the intricate ecology of consciousness, "the emotional faculty guides our moment-to-moment decisions, working hand in hand with the rational mind, enabling or disabling thought itself."[15] Likewise, the thinking brain plays an executive role in our emotions, except in those moments when emotions surge out of control and

the emotional brain runs rampant. The intellect cannot work at its best without emotional
intelligence. Maintaining a balance between
them is essential to a balanced personality.
The relationships of thinking and feeling are
at the heart of the creative process in all fields,
including the arts and the sciences.

"The relationships of thinking and feeling are at the heart of the creative process in all fields, including the arts and the sciences."

ARTISTS AND SCIENTISTS

Among the legacies of the Enlightenment and Romanticism
are many common-sense but mistaken assumptions about
the arts and sciences. The sciences are thought to be about
knowledge, facts and objectivity; the arts about emotions,
self-expression, being and subjectivity. The sciences apparently lead to pure knowledge, the arts to personal introspection: the sciences are useful, the arts dispensable.[16] Scientists
are pictured as methodical, clinical and objective; artists as
expressive, impassioned and creative. In reality, there are
much closer connections between the arts and sciences than
is commonly thought. Both have objective and subjective elements; both draw on knowledge and feelings, intuition and
non-logical elements.

Creativity in any field is not a strictly logical business. It
draws on feelings and intuitions as well as on existing ideas;
playfulness, as well as on knowledge and practical skills.
Our most original ideas sometimes come to mind without
our thinking consciously about them at all. If we can't work
something out, it is often better to sleep on it or put it to the
"back of our minds" where our subconscious mulls it over
and may deliver a solution to us unbidden. Feelings, hunches
and intuitions play a part in all creative work. So too does a
sense of aesthetics, of elegance and of beauty. This is true in
all fields, from dance to calculus.

The sciences and the arts both involve personal passions and both can be highly creative. Science as well as the arts can have considerable influence on how we feel about the world and on the world we have feelings about. These features of arts and sciences have implications for how we should think about creative processes and for how they should be provided for in education and training.

Discussing the arts and sciences opens up complex issues of definition. Science covers an enormous range of disciplines and fields of interest, from the natural sciences to the physical, to the study of human personality and social systems. The arts, too, cover a wide range of practices, styles and traditions both historically and in different cultures: from the fine arts, to craft and design, to traditional folk arts. For the sake of this discussion, let me compare the extremes of each spectrum: the physical sciences, which are concerned with the inanimate world, and the fine arts, which are concerned with human sensibilities.

The work of the sciences

The main process of science is *explanation.* Scientists are concerned with understanding how the world works in terms of itself. Science aims to produce systematic explanations of events, which can be verified by evidence. In the natural sciences, at least, the assumption is that it is possible to develop "a theory of everything" and that individual scientists are contributing to a collaborative mosaic of explanatory ideas. Scientists aim to stand outside the events they are investigating and to produce knowledge that is independent of them and would be validated by whoever repeated their observations. The dominant mode of scientific understanding is logico-deductive reasoning and the production of propositional knowledge.

As I mentioned earlier, about the impact of intelligence tests, it's sometimes assumed that the sciences are "above reproach, beyond social influence, conceived in the rarefied atmosphere of purely scientific inquiry by some process of immaculate conception."[17] The reality is rather different. Science is the work of living, breathing human beings. The apparently impersonal process of scientific inquiry involves a personal commitment by the scientist in four ways: the choice of problems; the methods of scientific inquiry; personal judgment; and standards of objectivity.

Whose problem is this?
One of the scientist's first moves is to identify an area of inquiry, a set of problems which engages his or her interest. This decision may be wrapped in a web of personal interests and motivations. Michael Polanyi talks of the intellectual passions of science. Passions are expressions of value. Positive passions mean that something is important to us. People who have achieved great things in a given field are generally driven by a love for it, a passion for the nature of the processes involved. The term "flow" has been used to describe times when we are immersed in something that completely engages our creative capabilities and draws equally from our knowledge, feelings and intuitive powers. The excitement of the scientist making a discovery "is an intellectual passion telling us that something is precious and more particularly that it is precious to science."[18] This excitement is not a by-product of scientific investigation but part of the personal commitment to the issues being investigated.

The scientific method
Scientists, like everyone else, are rational only to the extent that the conceptions to which they are committed are true. Descartes wanted to see through common-sense assumptions about the world to achieve a more rational sense of reality. His method was to substitute one set of assumptions with another, in this case the principles of deductive reasoning of mathematics and geometry. He wrote in his *Discourse on Method*: "The long chains of simple and easy reasoning by

which geometers are accustomed to reach their conclusions of their most difficult demonstrations lead me to imagine that all things to the knowledge of which man is competent are mutually connected in the same way."[19] Scientists accept the legitimacy of certain methods and modes of procedure. They identify themselves with particular frameworks of interpretation and rely on their reliability. The astronomer "presupposes the validity of mathematics, the mathematician, the validity of logic and so on."[20] The whole framework of scientific inquiry would collapse if these structures were proved faulty. This does happen. The great paradigm shifts in scientific understanding described by Thomas Kuhn (see Chapter 4) have come about precisely when the existing, dominant structures of thought have proved inadequate.

Personal judgment

These frameworks don't determine the course of any particular scientific inquiry. Scientists need to frame hypotheses and design experiments. In doing so, they exercise considerable personal judgment. When all the statistics have been coded and calculated, the columns and data carefully set out on the computer screen, there is still a need to analyze and interpret them – to give them meaning. At the heart of all scientific undertakings there is an element of personal judgment, which cannot be eradicated; nor should it be. The capacity for personal judgment is probably the most sensitive instrument a scientist has.

Scientists depend on, but do not limit themselves to, logical analysis. Logic is one of the methods that scientists use. There are others that are not logical at all. Intuition can be equally important to scientific investigation. Discovery in science often results from unexpected leaps of imagination: the sudden jumping of a logical gap, in which the solution to a problem is illuminated by a new insight, a new association of ideas or a vision of unforeseen possibilities. Many of the great discoveries were made intuitively. Scientists may sense a solution or discovery before an experiment has been done and then design tests to see if the hypothesis can be confirmed or proved wrong. Every attempt is made to be as methodical as possible. Although rational analysis plays the principal part, it is only part of science.

Successive approximations

Objectivity is no guarantee of truth. Scientific arguments may be objective; they are not necessarily true. In the Middle Ages, scientists and the general population believed that the sun moved round the earth. They saw it happen every day. Their conclusion was perfectly objective and completely wrong. Objective meanings are those that are tested using criteria that are agreed by particular communities. This doesn't mean that objective meanings are impersonal; nor can they be. They are *inter*-personal. This doesn't guarantee that they correspond with the way things are. The reason is that "the world of objective knowledge is man-made."[21] Scientific knowledge is subject to revision as new evidence comes to light or new ideas emerge. The essential process of science is argument and debate, of challenging or building on existing knowledge in the light of new ideas or evidence. It is concerned not only with facts but also with what count as facts; not only with observation but also with explanation and meaning. In all of these respects, creativity is at the heart of science.

The work of the arts

The main process of art is *description*. Artists describe and evoke the *qualities* of experience. The artist is not concerned with systematic explanation but with producing unique forms of expression that capture the qualities of his or her personal insights and experience. The poet writing of love or melancholy is trying to articulate a state of personal being: a mood or sensibility. A composer may try to capture a feeling in music and to invoke it in the listener. Artists are concerned with understanding the world in terms of their own perceptions of it: with expressing feelings, with imagining alternatives and with making objects that express those ideas.

At the heart of the arts is the artifact. Artists make objects and events as objects of contemplation. Composers make music, painters make images, dancers make dances, and writers produce books, plays, novels and poems. In its materials, sensuous and aesthetic qualities, the form of the work embodies the meaning.

Artists deal with ideas on any topic that interests them. These may be social or political ideas. They may be interested in formal ideas about their own disciplines. This was one of the driving concerns of modernism in music, theater, literature and in painting. Formalism, conceptualism and cubism, and all the rest, were concerned with exploring the nature and limits of art forms themselves. There is a difference between expressing feelings through the arts and giving vent to them. Artists are not just expressing feelings but ideas about feelings; not just ideas but feelings about ideas. In doing this, they can draw from all areas of their being.

The writer E.M. Forster said that in the creative state, we are taken out of normal ways of thinking: we let down a bucket into our subconscious and may draw up something that is beyond the reach of our conscious minds. An artist, says Forster, "mixes this thing with his normal experiences and out of the mixture he makes a work of art. The creative process employs much technical ingenuity and worldly knowledge; it may profit by critical standards, but mixed up with it is this stuff from the bucket, which is not procurable on demand."[22] The process of the arts is to give shape, coherence and meaning to the life of feeling.

"It is not what interests artists or scientists that distinguishes them from each other, but how it interests them."

Artists do not generally spend their days in states of emotional ferment. Watch a dance company in rehearsal or a musician practicing an instrument. Writing novels and composing poems is as much a diligent craft as a process of inspiration. Creativity in the arts, as in the sciences, requires control of materials and ideas and great discipline in honing exact forms of expression.

Meaning and interpretation

Responding to works of art and trying to make sense of them for ourselves is also creative. In watching a drama, the audience is not faced with something that it can read systematically, like a computer printout or set of instructions. A play is open to interpretation on two levels: what is expressed in the play and what is expressed by the play. We interpret what is being expressed in the play as it unfolds before us, by following piecemeal the actions of the characters. It is only when the play is over that we can make our sense of the play as a whole.

I say our sense because what the play means for us may be different from its meaning for the actors, the dramatist or the director. The world that the dramatist seeks to invoke exists on the page in an abstract form from which it is impossible to derive the performance itself by purely logical means. Giving the world of the drama a living form involves the director and actors in a sustained effort of interpretation, which draws on intuition, skill and cultural knowledge. A written play suggests a performance; it does not determine it. Jerzy Grotowski (1933–99) observed that all great texts represent a sort of deep gulf for us: "Take Hamlet. Professors will tell us that they have each discovered an objective Hamlet. They suggest to us revolutionary Hamlets, rebel and impotent Hamlets, Hamlet the outsider etc. There is no objective Hamlet. The strength of each great work really exists in its catalytic effect. It opens doors."[23] It is for this reason that memorable performances are indelibly stamped not only with the original creative work of the dramatist but with that of the actors who bring it to life: Gielgud's Hamlet, Branagh's Hamlet and so on.

There are often deep disagreements over the judgments people make about works of art, according to personal tastes and cultural values. The significance of a work of art can't be measured with a slide rule. This doesn't mean that it can't be judged at all. There is a difference between unsubstantiated personal opinion and reasoned judgments. Objectivity means that judgments are being made according to criteria that are publicly available and with reference to evidence in the work itself. In this sense, it is as legitimate to talk about the objective processes of making and understanding art as it is about anything. To assume that artistic judgments are simply personal opinion is as mistaken as assuming that all scientific opinion is undisputed fact. Meaning and interpretation are at the heart of all creative work.

Although discoveries are often associated with particular scientists, they're not unique to them in the way that paintings are to the artists who produced them. In 1959, Watson and Crick discovered DNA and described its structure as the building blocks of life. Although they were the first to discover DNA, they were not responsible for it being there in the first place. Any scientist who follows the same route of inquiry as another will reach the same conclusions. If not, there'd be concern about the evidence or procedures. The same is not true of the arts. Two or more artists would almost certainly produce different outcomes from the same starting point. Mathematicians or scientists may be the first to produce particular intellectual work; painters, poets and dancers are the only ones to produce the work. It is always unique to them. Artistic work is personal in a sense that is not true of equations and calculations in mathematics, where the ability to replicate results is inherent in the validity of the work. It is because artists' works are unique to them that biographical enquiries are so interesting to academics.

A work of art can be about anything at all that interests an artist; just as a scientific experiment or theory can be about anything that interests a scientist. Artists and scientists can be interested in the same subject: painters and geographers may share the same passion for the physical landscape; novelists and psychologists for human relationships; poets and biologists for the nature of consciousness. It is not *what* interests artists or scientists that distinguishes them from each other, but *how* it interests them. The difference lies in the types of understanding they are searching for, and in the modes of understanding they employ.

The recognition of commonalities between the arts and the sciences has led to a wide range of collaborative projects and to the early dawning of what may prove, in our own times, to be a new Renaissance. It is a Renaissance based on a more holistic understanding of human consciousness; of the relationships between knowing and feeling; and of how all that we think and feel is part of the creative process of making sense of the world around us and of the worlds within us.

CONCLUSION

A world without feelings would be literally inhuman. Yet our education systems do too little to address this human dimension of our personalities. Louis Arnaud Reid puts it this way: "The neglect of the study of feeling and of its place in the whole economy of the mind has been disastrous, both in philosophy and in education. Sensitiveness plays far more part in understanding of many kinds than is generally understood and acknowledged."[24] Being sensitive to oneself and to others is a vital element in the development of the personal qualities that are now urgently needed, in business, in the community and in personal life. It's through feelings as well as through reason that we find our real creative power. Its through both that we connect with each other and create the complex, shifting worlds of human culture.

"It is through feelings as well as through reason that we find our real creative power. It is through both that we connect with each other and create the complex, shifting worlds of human culture."

YOU ARE NOT ALONE

"Individual creativity is almost always stimulated by the work, ideas and achievements of other people."

THE LONE GENIUS?

A POPULAR IMAGE OF CREATIVITY is of the lone genius swimming heroically against the tides of convention, pursuing ideas that no one has had before. There are numerous examples of iconic figures who've made groundbreaking contributions in their own areas of work. I've mentioned some of them in previous chapters, including Galileo, Isaac Newton, Martha Graham and others. But the image of the lone genius can be misleading. Original ideas may emanate from the inspiration of individual minds, but they don't emerge in a cultural vacuum. Individual creativity is always stimulated by the work, ideas and achievements of other people. As Isaac Newton famously said, if he saw further than others, it was because he stood on the shoulders of giants. Even when working alone, as some people do, there is an unavoidable cultural context to their creative efforts.

In practice, our own ways of seeing the world are deeply influenced by our dealings with other people, not least by using shared forms of representation that we have created together, such as the languages we speak. We each have our own lives, but much of what we create is with each other. What we create together is culture. To use a phrase from the anthropologist Clifford Geertz, all human lives are suspended in "webs of significance" that we ourselves have spun. Creativity is how these threads are formed and woven into the complex fabrics of human culture.

Since the late eighteenth century, culture, in one sense, has meant a general process of intellectual or social refinement. It is in this sense that a person might be described as cultured. Being cultured is associated particularly with an appreciation of the arts. By extension, culture also means the general field of artistic and intellectual activity. A distinction is often made between high art and popular culture. "High art" normally means opera, classical music, ballet, contemporary dance, fine art, serious literature and cinema. "Popular culture" means commercial music, popular cinema, television, fashion, design and popular fiction and other forms that have mass appeal. It is this meaning of culture that economists usually have in mind when they talk about the cultural industries.

The term "culture" is also used in a more general social sense to mean a community's overall way of life; its patterns of work and recreation, morality, intellectual practices, aesthetics, beliefs, economic production, political power and responsibility. It's this broader social definition of culture that I have in mind here: the values and forms of behavior that characterize different social communities. I argued in Chapter 5 that human intelligence is diverse, dynamic and distinct. So too are the cultures we create.

A MATTER OF TIME

I said in Chapter 5 that our physical senses affect what we *can* perceive of the world but there are other factors that influence what we *do* perceive. Many of these factors are cultural.

Different cultures perceive the world in radically different ways. Some cultural differences are obvious, such as the languages people speak, the clothes they wear, the food they eat and the sorts of dwellings they inhabit. Other differences are harder to detect because they are embedded in basic ways of thinking. One example is cultural variations in the sense of time.

In 2001, my family and I moved from Stratford-upon-Avon in England to live in Los Angeles, California. In Europe, a century is not a long time; in Los Angeles it is. Our home in Stratford-upon-Avon was built in 1870 and was one of the newer properties in the area. It was too soon to know if the neighborhood would really catch on. Our house in Los Angeles was built in 1937. In LA terms it is a heritage property. Europeans don't think that ten years is a long time. Americans do and use the word "decade" a lot: I think to convey a sense of instant tradition. Just after we relocated to LA, I was driving on the freeway listening to the radio and heard a commercial for a local car dealership. I missed the name of the company but caught the slogan: it was, "Proudly serving Los Angeles for almost half a decade."

By way of contrast, in Asia, a millennium is not a big deal. On my first visit to Beijing, I had dinner, perhaps unsurprisingly, in a Chinese restaurant. It was a memorable meal. As a starter I chose "black chicken soup." I'd assumed that "black" was a figurative term that referred to the style of cooking, rather than the condition of the chicken. I was wrong. The pieces of chicken were black all through; a color in meat that I usually associate with putrefaction. I was not wrong about that. For my entrée, and to the warm approval of the waiter, I chose a steamed garoupa fish. He took the order to the kitchen and came back a few moments later with a bamboo basket. Inside was the fish in question, alive and flopping around with a look of panic in its eyes. I knew if I approved, I'd be passing a death sentence. I know that animals do need to die if we are to eat them and that being squeamish like this is a feeble hypocrisy. Some cultures, including China, do not indulge in these ambiguities. Even so, I'm not used to meeting my entrée. I nodded weakly and 15 minutes later the fish was back in front of me: steamed, garnished and reproachful. To delay eating it, I said to the waiter how much I like Chinese food. I do, particularly if I've not been socializing with it beforehand. He thanked me but said that this was not really a Chinese dish. The Mongols, he said, had introduced this method of cooking fish into China 900 years ago. That's barely a millennium. In Asian terms, this could be a fad.

Cultural differences in the sense of time affect how people live their lives and their political outlook too. In 1972, President Richard Nixon was preparing for his historic visit to China. Evidently, his Secretary of State, Henry Kissinger, told him that the Chinese Premier and Foreign Minister, Chou En-Lai, was a student of French history. During his trip, Nixon asked Chou what he thought had been the impact of the French Revolution in 1789 on Western civilization. Chou En-Lai thought for a few moments and then said to Nixon, "It's too soon to tell." To an American President concerned about the next day's headlines, this panoramic sense of cause and effect could hardly be more different.

Human cultures are shaped by many factors, including geography, patterns of population, access to natural resources and technology; and by political events, wars, invasions and conquests. They all interact with the ideas and values that communities evolve over time to make sense of their lives. All cultures consist of multiple elements within themselves: systems of government, of justice, education, social class, occupations, economic production and the arts. Complex cultures house innumerable subsets and countercultural groups that hold alternative sensibilities within the dominant culture. Like intelligence, cultures are not only diverse: they are dynamic.

"Human cultures are complex and diverse because human intelligence is, in itself, both rich and creative; like intelligence, cultures are not only diverse: they are dynamic."

DYNAMIC CULTURES

Culture, in the biological sense, implies growth and transformation. This is true of social cultures. The rate of change varies enormously in different cultures and at different times. In our own lifetime we are seeing exponential changes within many cultural communities across the earth, as culture becomes ever more globalized and connected.

Just as individual intelligence is dynamic and interactive, so too is cultural change. There are "hot spots" for certain brain functions: for language, recognition of faces and so on. In any activity, many different areas of the brain work in concert with each other. The same is true of the social culture. We can talk separately about technology, the economy, legal systems, ethics and work, but a culture can only be properly understood in terms of how all of these elements interrelate with each other.[1] One example is the interaction of the arts with technology.

The arts and technology

William Shakespeare was one of the greatest writers to have lived. He was prolific and gifted. But his work was almost entirely in the forms of plays and poetry. He did not write novels. Why not? It would seem the natural form for one of the world's greatest storytellers. Shakespeare didn't write novels because the idea probably didn't occur to him. He was writing in the sixteenth century. The novel developed as an art form in the eighteenth century in the wake of printing and the emergence of a large literate class with an appetite for extended narrative. As literacy spread and methods of printing improved, the novel, as we know it now, began to take shape.

The modern orchestra is a tool kit that makes possible certain types of music. The classical tradition in Western European music evolved with the advance of the orchestra and its constituent instruments of metal or wood. Classical music would not have developed as it did without the string, brass and woodwind instruments, and the sounds that these instruments made possible for composers and musicians alike.

The visual arts have evolved hand in hand with technology. For centuries, painters and sculptors had recorded the likeness of people, places and events. It was one of their main roles, and sources of income. The invention of photography broke their monopoly. It provided a quick, cheap and faithful method of visual record. The new technology caused agonies of debate at the Royal Academy in London about its status. Some worried that photography would be the death of painting. Others asked whether a photograph could ever be a work of art. In fact, photography was breaking the mold in which established ideas of art had been formed. As Walter Benjamin (1892–1940) put it, the issue was not whether a photograph could be a work of art, but what the development of photography meant for the definition of art itself.[2] As photography evolved over the twentieth century into an art form in its own right, it came to be seen not so much as a threat to the visual arts, but as a form of liberation.

Freed from the confines of figurative work, painters explored new possibilities: from the expression of personal feelings to the limits of visual form through abstract and conceptual art. Technological innovations in the production of paints and pigments also opened up new creative horizons in painting. Impressionism was facilitated in part by the invention of flexible metal tubes for transporting paint, which made it easier for painters to work outdoors and capture the fleeting moments of light and landscape. Just as painters feared that photography would be the death of painting, theaters feared that film would be the death of them. Neither proved to be true. In the medium term, theater was released into a new period of invention and innovation, from the 1920s to the 1950s in particular.

Technologies are neutral. What counts is who uses them and what for. Any tool in the hands of an artist can result in a work of art. A felt tip pen or a word processor can be used to compose great literature or a list of groceries. A camera in the hands of an artist may produce art that is as captivating as anything produced with brushes and paints.

"It is an interesting feature of cultural change that, for a period of time, new technologies tend to be used to do the same old thing."

For a time, new technologies tend to be used to do the same old thing. Early photographers arranged their subjects to mimic the portraiture of oil painting. As the technology evolved, photographers found they could capture moments and events that painting could not. The introduction of the portable Brownie camera by George Eastman in 1900 brought photography to the masses and reshaped popular culture. For a while, early moving pictures copied the conventions of theater. Directors pointed a stationary camera at a conventional melodrama and cranked the handle. As cameras became lighter, they realized they could change angles and locations, and the invention of the movable focus made it possible to create more intimate images. As filmmakers experimented with these new technical possibilities, the language of film began to emerge and, as it did, the movies became a distinctive field of artistic creation.

There is a constant synergy between technology and creativity. New technologies present fresh possibilities for creative work: the creative use of technologies leads to technological evolution. Cameras and pigments evolved as artists invented new techniques in using them; instruments and recording techniques evolved with the creative ambitions of musicians and producers. Digital technologies are now providing people everywhere with unprecedented tools for creative work in sound, in design, in sciences and in the arts. As they do, users are generating new networks and applications that are interacting with the design and production of software and hardware at every level. As the digital revolution gathers pace we can expect even more radical modes of creative production to emerge, whose consequences are as hard for us to predict now as those of photography were for the Victorian members of the Royal Academy.

What do you mean?

One of the most vivid examples of the dynamic nature of culture is the rate at which spoken languages evolve. All living languages are in flux. New words and expressions emerge continually in response to new situations, ideas and feelings. *The Oxford English Dictionary* publishes supplements of new words and expressions that have entered the language. Some people deplore this kind of thing and see it as a drift from correct English. But it was only in the eighteenth century that any attempt was made to formalize spelling and punctuation of English at all. The language we speak in the twenty-first century would be virtually unintelligible to Shakespeare, and so would his way of speaking to us. Alvin Toffler estimated that Shakespeare would probably only understand about 250,000 of the 450,000 words in general use in the English language now. In other words, so to speak, if Shakespeare were to materialize in London today he would understand, on average, only five out of every nine words in our vocabulary. As Toffler puts it, if he were to be here now, "the Bard would be semi-literate."[3]

"If Shakespeare were to materialize in London today he would be semi-literate."

Theory and ideology

A third example is the interactions of theory and ideology. I talked in Chapter 4 about the power of generative ideas. Common sense suggests that old theories are replaced as soon as better, new ones come along, which make more sense of the evidence. This is not always what happens. In practice, theories can be as subject to fashion as the length of skirts or the cut of lapels. A good deal of theory stays in relative oblivion. Throughout the world there are scientists, artists and philosophers producing new ideas of every sort. Yet certain ideas can suddenly capture the popular imagination. How do some rise to dominate the others? It's not always because they are better thought out. Other factors are at work.

Theories are taken up not just because they are available but also because they meet a need. Intelligence testing has held the attention of politicians and many educators against all comers from the 1900s to the present day despite the many conceptual and methodological flaws and the high social costs of these systems. Naturalist theories of education were influential in the 1950s and 1960s, not only because they were consistent with the facts of education as they then appeared, but because they expressed a mood among a generation of teachers.

"Theories are taken up not just because they are available but also because they meet a need."

Theories are intended to be explanatory. They are often taken up for other reasons too, and not simply as consequence of progressive development of better ideas. The significance of theory is not only explanatory: it is ideological. In an important sense, theory is expressive. It is part, but only part, of the complex, organic web of human culture.

DISTINCT DIFFERENCES

Culture consists of ideas and beliefs that constitute what philosophers call "Weltanschauung," or worldview. Different worldviews give rise to different forms of behavior. You see examples of Weltanschauung in the discrete worlds that are portrayed in novels, films and theater. Within each play and every genre, only certain sorts of behavior make sense: the same behaviors in another context might be incomprehensible. The playwright, Nicholas Wright, argues that the job of the writer, director and actors is to define the world that the play inhabits and within which the action is plausible. In Middleton and Rowley's Jacobean tragedy *The Changeling*, for example, the only alternative that the heroine Beatrice Joanna sees to marrying her unwelcome suitor is to murder him: "Today young women would see other possibilities. But these possibilities don't have a place in a production of the play. It's the job of the director to present a social world where no other choice is open to her, and it's the job of the actress to present a woman who can't imagine one."[4]

Cultures are systems of permission. They have their own codes of behavior, forms of language, dress and observance. Rewards come for some forms of behavior and sanctions for others. Permission can be formal – enshrined in laws and enforced by judicial punishment; it may be informal – embedded in social attitudes and reinforced in tones of voice and body language. Breaking the conventions of the group can take courage and carry the risk of exclusion. If we look at the codes and conventions of other communities, especially those that are distant from us in place or time, we can easily see how different they are; it is more difficult to grasp how it must feel to be part of them. What strikes us when reading novels and plays written in other times is not only the different circumstances in which people lived but how they saw things, what mattered to them and why they felt as they did. Factual accounts of other cultures cannot capture these nuances. To do that, you must listen to their music, eat their food, absorb the imagery, hear their poetry and move with their dances. They are all manifestations of the sensibilities that make different cultures what they are.

Many people now live within interweaving cultural communities. Adult immigrants to a new country or region often find themselves culturally adrift. The lives of their children often become bicultural or multicultural. They may come to speak two or more languages: one at school or work, another at home. They need to shift their cultural sensibilities as they move between these groups and their different codes and customs.

The socialization of the young arises partly from the need in society "to reach a basis of stable expectation from today. That stability depends upon the same expectations being constantly realized despite changes in personnel." This is not to say that these conventions do not evolve. They do, especially from one generation to another. Although each generation tries to pass on its cultural genes to the next, the new generation may develop its own ways of doing things, in reaction to their parents and in response to the world they inherit: reproducing many aspects of the culture "yet feeling its whole life in certain ways differently and shaping its creative response into a new structure of feeling."[5]

> "Human cultures are constantly evolving through the thoughts, feelings and actions of the people who live in them."

LIFE IS NOT LINEAR

Culture is an organic term that suggests growth and development. Human cultures evolve through the thoughts, feelings and actions of the people who live in them. Like the course of each individual life, the dynamics of cultural change are neither linear nor easy to predict. They are organic and complex: hard to understand in hindsight and almost impossible to anticipate in advance.

In the 1950s and 1960s, rock and roll swept through the Western world like a shock wave. It galvanized a generation of baby boomers and outraged the sensibilities of many of their parents. The stars of rock and roll drew from a huge variety of cultural sources: the blues, country and western, jazz and swing, traditional folk music and many forms of dance. It is impossible to imagine the trajectory of rock and roll being planned by a government committee. No one did or could have predicted the cultural influence of rock and roll. On the contrary, the policy makers who thought about it at all tried to ban it. The phenomenon caught fire as it did because it fed on a highly combustible mixture of creative energy and cultural rebellion. You might say that rock and roll succeeded because it challenged the dominant Weltanschauung and expressed a new Zeitgeist: a new philosophy and spirit of the times. Or words to that effect.

Interestingly, the surge in rock music in Britain in the 1960s and 1970s owed little, if anything, to formal music training. Some of the most notable rock and rollers had gone to college but not to music conservatoires; they went to art colleges. The pedagogic traditions in art schools provided an atmosphere of experimentation, personal creativity and hip culture that was lacking in the more formal atmospheres of the music schools. The art colleges provided an unexpected breeding ground for rock culture: an example of the non-linear nature of cultural trends.

A second example of non-linearity is the explosive growth of social media. When Bill Gates and Paul Allen were developing their fledgling company, Microsoft, in the 1970s; when Steve Jobs and Steve Wozniak were building their alternative personal computer in the 1980s; when Tim Berners-Lee was wondering in Switzerland if he could connect the databases of computers into a world wide web; not one of them had in mind the phenomena they would facilitate in the early twenty-first century. Google, Twitter, Facebook, Flickr and thousands of other forms of social media are now spreading virally throughout global culture. They are fueled by a primal human impulse to connect with each other and share ideas and information. The most sophisticated technologies only change the world when they connect with basic human instincts. When they do, their impact is unstoppable.

A third example is the fate of the phone. In the last decade or so, the cell phone has become the dominant platform for digital communications. Since the advent of the smartphone, millions of applications have converted it into a digital cornucopia. The musical, visual, and gaming capabilities of smartphones leave little time or inclination for phone calls. Young people prefer to text each other. Since the smartphone hit the market, there has been a precipitous drop in voice calls and a corresponding fall in the revenues of the phone companies who were so keen to encourage the sale of the phones in the first place. As with many cultural trends, it was unanticipated and largely impossible to predict.

THE WEB OF KNOWLEDGE

Cultural knowledge is a complex web, about which each of us knows only a relatively small amount. We can all claim to be relatively well informed or even expert in something. In most areas, we are amateur or plainly ignorant. We depend on the knowledge of other people for much of our understanding of the world and it comes in many forms: stories, anecdotes, theories, systems of belief and so on.

"Creativity is about making connections and is usually driven more by collaboration than by solo efforts."

This was always the case, but the store of human knowledge is thought to be doubling every ten years and the rate of expansion is accelerating. One result is increasingly intense specialization: a tendency to know more and more about less and less. As knowledge expands, greater specialization is inevitable. The risk is that we lose sight of how ideas connect and can inform each other. The output of modern science is so fast, for example, that any individual can properly understand only small sections of it. Individual mathematicians can usually deal competently with only a small part of mathematics. It is a rare mathematician who fully understands more than half a dozen out of 50 papers presented to a mathematical congress. According to Michael Polanyi, the very language in which the others are presented "goes clear over the head of the person who follows the six reports nearest to their own specialty. Adding to this my own experience in chemistry and physics, it seems to me that the situation may be similar for all major scientific provinces, so that any single scientist may be competent to judge at first-hand only about a hundredth of the total current output of science."[6]

Creativity is about making connections and, more often than not, as we will see in the next chapter, it is driven by collaboration as much as by solo efforts. Organizations that enforce strict boundaries between specialisms can inhibit innovation. The division of arts and sciences in education is a case in point. Artists and scientists can collaborate and discover common ground. Two examples are new methods in the social sciences and innovative schemes linking the arts and the natural sciences.

"Thick description"

Early psychologists hoped to produce scientific explanations of personality and behavior in the same way that physicists were explaining the behavior of magnets and the forces of gravity. In the physical sciences, these laws are used to predict future events. Magnets do not behave as they do only now and then, or on Tuesdays. They do what they do. Maybe human behavior could be understood and predicted in the same way.

The early pioneers of the social sciences, especially in anthropology, also modeled their work on physics and chemistry. They tried to behave as if they occupied a culture-free zone from which they could draw unbiased, "objective" conclusions about the people they studied. Social scientists have since recognized that this approach is flawed and that in most respects the human world is not much like the world of the natural sciences. An oceanographer charting the movement of tides is not trying to fathom the tide's motives. The inanimate world does not have reasons. It just does what it does. Scientists in these fields try to understand *how*, not *why*. The physical world owes no allegiance to any particular interpretation. Despite the successive reformulations of scientific theory, the physical universe just carries on being itself. What changes is how we make sense of it. This is not true of the social world.

People have reasons for what they do, even if they don't always understand them. The work of social scientists is complicated for that reason. They have their own preconceptions too, which can color what they observe and what they make of it. Early European anthropologists, for example, tended to picture other cultures, and especially little-known ones in Africa, Asia and America, as culturally primitive with relatively childish belief systems. Contemporary studies look deeper into the lived experience of other cultures, aiming to understand them on their own terms. For Clifford Geertz, the task of the social scientist is essentially one of description and interpretation. Understanding human cultures, he says, "is not an experimental science in search of laws but an interpretive one in search of meaning."[7] Alongside conventional methods of statistical analysis, social scientists are increasingly using ethnographic techniques and forms of narrative description, what Geertz calls "thick description," that mirror the skills of travel writers and novelists.

Arts and sciences

Many scientists have a deep interest in the arts, and a growing number of artists take inspiration from scientific ideas. Some are using advanced technologies to produce new forms of artistic expression. Scientists too find inspiration in the arts and in working with artists. One example is an acclaimed collaboration between fashion design and biological sciences.

Primitive Streak
Between fertilization of the egg and the appearance of the recognizable human form, a single cell divides many times to

produce millions of cells. Unchecked, cell proliferation leads
to cancer, the regulation of cell production during the development of the embryo ensures that the right kinds of cells
form in the right place at the right time. How this happens
is a key question in biology. In the Primitive Streak project,
fashion designer Helen Storey and her sister Kate Storey,
a developmental biologist, worked on a fashion collection
chronicling the first 1,000 hours of human life. The collection
and associated research materials were exhibited throughout
Europe, the United States and China, in art houses and science facilities. It attracted tens of thousands of visitors and
challenged a commonly held belief that science and art are
unable to communicate with each other. Helen Storey said
that the most notable feature of the many groups who visited
the exhibition was their sheer diversity: young and old, those
with a love of the arts, those with a life dedicated to science,
and almost anyone in between.[8]

THE POWER OF IDEAS

As Victor Hugo said, "nothing is more powerful than an
idea whose time has come," and there is a powerful relationship between theory and popular culture. Most people do
not have much time for theory, yet their lives are permeated
by it. Ideas that originate in the laboratories of scientists,
the studies of philosophers and the studios of artists can
seep deep into the culture without our realizing it.[9] Contemporary language is peppered with the jargon of psychology, for example. Bar room conversations refer to ego, sex
drives, the Oedipus complex and other Freudian ideas as
if these were simple facts of life rather than nineteenth-
century theoretical propositions. Mothers bring up their
babies according to the fads and fashions of developmental
theories: breast-feeding or not, playing with them or not,
stimulating them with music or pictures, depending on the

seepage rate of theory into culture. Sometimes, the trickle becomes a torrent.

In the 1960s, a disparate group of women, including Gloria Steinem and Germaine Greer, unleashed a tidal wave of change with a series of books on feminism. For very many people, not least men, feminism was a trauma. It tore at the foundations on which people had built their understanding of themselves, their families, their partners and their lives. It overturned cherished ideas about normal life: that men were the dominant sex; that a woman's place was in the home; that sex was a male pleasure and a female duty; that men had great ideas and that women cared and wept. As generative ideas do, these coursed through every field of thought. They helped to recast the history of the arts and sciences, reframing the achievements of celebrated men and women and unearthing the work of others that history had obscured. Feminist ideas challenged the structure of working life that propelled men to the top and kept women at the fringes of corporate success; they affected attitudes to relationships in the community and at home.

Over the next 40 years, that wave of feminism followed the classic track of a great generative idea: initial exhilaration, followed by progressive refinement, to arcane debates about obscure points of interpretation. It gave way in the 1990s to a new phase of post-feminist thought in which some of the basic principles of the early writers were recast too. Along the way, the revolutionary ideas of the first wave had entered the mainstream of cultural thought. The word feminism itself, the need for equal rights and the concept of sexual harassment, are now part of the social and political lexicon. The battles are far from won, but the terms of engagement are much clearer.

New ideas are not always new, and rarely come out of the blue.[10] In earlier times, others had expressed the core ideas of the feminist movement of the 1960s. From the writings of Mary Wollstonecraft in the eighteenth century, through the sacrifices of the suffragettes in the early twentieth, many had shaped the feminist perspective long before it galvanized the 1960s. The work of many women has been lost in the canons of the dominant male culture they set out to criticize. Feminist ideas took hold when they did because of the sensibilities and conditions of the time. They emerged from these conditions and helped to shape them. Feminism developed hand in hand with technological advance. Sexual liberty is a more practical principle when cheap and effective forms of contraception put women in charge of their own fertility. Previously, the advancement of women was held in check by the uncertainties of pregnancy and motherhood. But feminism was part, too, of the general politics of liberation of the 1960s and 1970s and interacted with the civil rights movement in Europe and the United States, with anti-authoritarianism everywhere, the need for self-determination and the emergence of the "me" generation. In presenting a powerful intellectual analysis, feminist theorists helped to articulate a new structure of feeling. What are the implications of 1960s feminism for civilization? Like the French Revolution, it is too soon to say.

A CULTURE OF CREATIVITY?

Culture is the efflorescence of creativity. Creative thinking thrives best in certain cultural conditions. What does this all mean for leading a culture of creativity in communities and organizations, including schools and businesses? What should leaders do to cultivate innovation? There is no single strategy or template, mainly because all creative cultures are unique; but there are principles that apply to the most effective creative organizations. The next chapter looks at the practical implications of the arguments I have presented throughout *Out of Our Minds* and identifies nine principles on which to develop a culture of creativity.

_____

BEING A CREATIVE LEADER

"*Creating a culture of innovation will only work if the initiative is led from the top of the organization. The endorsement and involvement of leaders means everything, if the environment is to change.*"

LEADING A CULTURE OF INNOVATION

ORGANIZATIONS USUALLY TALK MORE about innovation than about creativity and there is a distinction between the two. A culture of innovation depends on cultivating three processes, each of which is related to the others.

- *Imagination* is the ability to bring to mind events and ideas that are not present to our senses.

- *Creativity* is having original ideas that have value.

- *Innovation* is putting original ideas into practice.

Innovation may focus on any aspect of an organization's work: on products, services or systems. Innovation may be the aim, but it has to begin with imagination and creativity. Aiming straight for innovation, without developing the imaginative and creative powers on which it depends, would be like an athlete hoping for gold but with no intention of exercising beforehand. Just as success in athletics depends on building physical fitness, a culture of innovation depends on exercising the powers of imagination and creativity that give rise to it. Even so, as Theresa Amabile puts it, "Creativity by individuals and teams is a starting point for innovation: the first is a necessary but not a sufficient condition for the second."[1] So, what is involved in leading a culture of innovation?

I was once asked to advise a major airline company that needed to improve coordination between the senior management team and the front-line staff who dealt with the clients. The staff had a lot of ideas for improving customer service, which the leadership was not taking seriously. I asked the person who wanted to hire me what the CEO thought of the situation. He said the CEO didn't think there was a problem, but that the company would be appointing a new one in six months. In that case, I said, call me when you have the new CEO. In my experience, if the CEO doesn't think there's a problem that may be the problem. A culture of innovation only thrives if the initiative is supported from the top of the organization.

In fairness, some leaders have well-founded anxieties about promoting innovation. They worry that they'll have to come up with a constant stream of new ideas. The good news is that the role of a creative leader is not to have all the ideas: it's to nurture a culture where everyone can have new ideas. They worry too that unleashing creativity will lead to chaos and loss of control. The good news is that creativity is not a synonym for anarchy. Creativity and innovation work best where there is a balance between the freedom to experiment and proper systems of evaluation. These anxieties about innovation are often born of the command and control mindset of leadership. Creative leadership involves more and less than command and control.

"Organizations are not mechanisms and people are not components. People have values and feelings, perceptions, opinions, motivations and biographies, whereas cogs and sprockets do not."

Mechanisms and organisms

In 1900, Frederick Taylor published *The Principles of Scientific Management*. His premise was that organizations should work like machines and that the main role of leadership is to improve profitability by increasing productivity. Each worker should have clearly differentiated roles and each task should be honed to make the best use of time, effort and company resources. At the heart of Taylor's approach were the principles of standardization, set routines and the division of labor. Taylor's theories had profound effects on how organizations everywhere were run. It was on these principles that Henry Ford developed the hugely successful manufacturing system for the Model T. "Fordism," as it was known, became the template for industrial production for most of the twentieth century and it has infused the cultures of many other types of organization too. Taylorism and Fordism continue, in various guises, to influence corporate cultures to the present day; from the Total Quality Management (TQM) movement of the 1980s to Motorola's Six Sigma strategy.[2]

The management charts of many organizations are patterns of boxes, arranged in hierarchies, with horizontal and vertical lines indicating the directions of power and responsibility. These images add to the impression that organizations really are like machines. Making optimal use of resources and paring away excess capacity in the interests of greater productivity may be good in themselves, but the conception of the organization as a machine is inimical to fostering the culture of innovation upon which the future of most organizations now depends.

Taylorism is not the only game in town. Over the last 40 years, organizational culture has been the focus of intense study. There are myriad alternative schools of thought; many of them challenging the mechanistic metaphor. Peter Drucker, Jim Collins, Warren Bennis, Tom Peters, Charles

Handy, Rosabeth Moss Kanter, Clayton Christensen, Meg Wheatley, Theresa Amabile and many others have shed bright light on the complexities of organizations and different styles of management and leadership. Business schools have generated a trove of research and libraries of journals and books on every aspect of corporate culture. More organizations accept the need for systematic innovation and there are many approaches according to how big they are and what they do. Knowingly or not, many of them are embracing a different metaphor of organizational culture.

However seductive the machine metaphor may be for industrial production, human organizations are not mechanisms and people are not components in them. They consist of people, relationships and energies. They are living communities that exist in the actions and purposes of the people who populate them. They are much more like organisms. Leading a culture of innovation depends on understanding the differences between these two metaphors and on shifting from one to the other.

Two cultural challenges

Organizations face two cultural challenges: external and internal. In the natural world, successful organisms live symbiotically with their environment, drawing nutrients and energy from it and enriching it in return. This is not always true, of course. Some organisms destroy their host environment by sucking the life out of it. They are called parasites. This is famously true of some companies. Let's assume we are talking here of organizations that aim to be ethical, sustainable and beneficial. If they are to flourish, they need a vibrant internal culture, which is synergistic with the changing eternal environment in which they are trying to grow. The task of a creative leader is to facilitate that relationship between the *external* and *internal* cultures.

"The task of a creative leader is to facilitate a resilient relationship between the external and internal cultures."

The challenges of the external culture include technological innovations, population change, new patterns of trade, fluctuation in fiscal and monetary policies, global competition, the strains on natural resources and the effects of all of these on how customers and clients are thinking and feeling.

The internal culture can be thought of as *habits* and *habitats*. By habits, I mean the patterns of everyday work. These include the structures of management and accountability: the horizontal relationships between divisions and the vertical relationships between layers of management. The habits also include all the informal codes of behavior that give each organization its own distinctive feel. By habitats I mean the physical environments in which people work: the structures of the buildings, the design of workspaces, of the equipment and furnishings. The physical habitat can have a profound bearing on the cultural mood of the organization.

THE ROLES AND PRINCIPLES OF CREATIVE LEADERSHIP

Being a creative leader involves strategic roles in three areas: *personal*, *group* and *cultural*. Within each of these there are three core principles of practice. These are not linear phases or steps. They should feed into each other in a continuous cycle of mutual enrichment.

Personal

The first role of the creative leader is: *To facilitate the creative abilities of every member of the organization.*

Principle 1: Everyone has creative potential

I worked for a time as advisor to an international cultural organization, which also has a major art museum. I was having lunch one day with the head of security. He was irritated and I asked him why. He asked if I had heard about the study

"For innovation to flourish, it has to be seen as an integral purpose of the whole organization rather than as a separate function."

that the senior management had commissioned on how to improve the "visitor experience" to the museum. I did know about the study and that a New York firm of consultants had been brought in to conduct it. I asked him what the problem was. He said, "Why doesn't the senior management ask us?"

He led a large team of security staff who spent much of their time in the galleries and corridors, in the car parks and public spaces, interacting with the visitors and answering their questions. They helped visitors to find the restaurants and rest-rooms, directed them to the exhibits and often to particular works of art. He said, "My staff probably know more about the nature of the visitor experience than any other group in this organization, yet the management is spending a small fortune on a firm of outside consultants who've never been here before; and we're not even being consulted. Apparently, the leadership thinks the sole role of security is to slap people's hands if they try to touch the exhibits."

Organizations often associate creativity with specific functions; for example, with marketing, design and advertising. While these can be highly creative fields, creativity and innovation are possible in everything an organization does. For innovation to flourish, it has to be seen as integral to the whole organization rather than as a separate function of part of it. Everyone in an organization has different experiences of how it works and insights on how it might be improved.

In 2001, Gallup published a study that estimated that "actively disengaged employees" were costing the US economy alone between $292 and $355 billion a year.[3] Later studies show that engaged employees, in contrast, are more productive, profitable and create stronger customer relationships. Workplace engagement is a powerful factor in facilitating creative thinking on how to improve business processes and customer service. According to Gallup, 59% of "engaged employees" *strongly agreed* that their job brought out their most creative ideas, while only 3% of "actively disengaged employees" said the same.

I meet many people who don't enjoy the work they do. They endure it. It's not their life's mission: it's just what they do to make a living. I also meet people who love what they do and who couldn't imagine doing anything else. They are in their element. To say that somebody is in their element means firstly that they are doing something for which they have a natural aptitude. It can be for any sort of work: administration, design, teaching, cooking, working alone or with other people. The essence of diversity is that people are good at very different things: what deters one person may have an irresistible attraction for another. Being good at something is not enough. Plenty of people do things they are good at but don't really care for. Being in your element is not only about aptitude, it's about passion: it is about loving what you do. When you're doing something you love, time changes and an hour can feel like five minutes. If you're not in your element, five minutes can feel like an hour. The clock seems to have stopped. Being in your element is about tapping into your natural energy and your most authentic self. When that happens, as Confucius once said, you never work again.

Being a creative leader means ensuring that everyone is playing to their creative strengths and feels valued for their contribution to the overall performance of the organization. In every organization there are all sorts of untapped talents and abilities. People join companies from many different backgrounds and with many different profiles, but they're often perceived only on the basis of their past education and current job descriptions.

Identifying individual talents is not simply a matter of conducting a formal audit. There are some general tests for creative thinking and a growing battery of instruments for assessing personal strengths.[4] Most of these tests give only a rough indication of potential. A better strategy is to put people in situations and give them challenges that reveal their abilities; some of which they may have been unaware of themselves. An advertising company I know in New York has established its own university with classes by members of the company's own staff. The designers run courses on graphics; the copywriters on creative writing; and the accountants on financial management. The program encourages a greater understanding between departments of each other's work and creates a strong sense of common culture. It also develops the skill base of the company and has stirred up the internal talent pool. Several people have moved to other departments because they found that they were good at something other than the job they were hired to do.

"Being in your element is not only about aptitude, it's about passion: it is about loving what you do."

Principle 2: Innovation is the child of imagination

In the early stages of a project, a good deal of creative work is about playing with ideas, riffing, doodling, improvising and exploring new possibilities. The quality of what is done often depends on making fresh connections, breaking with convention and seeing from different perspectives. A creative organization, as Peter Richards puts it, "is first and foremost a place that gives people freedom to take risks; second it is a place that allows people to discover and develop their own natural intelligence; third, it is a place where there are no 'stupid' questions and no 'right' answers; and fourth, it is a place that values irreverence, the lively, the dynamic, the surprising, the playful."5

Pixar is one of the most innovative and acclaimed film studios in the history of the movies. Since launching *Toy Story*, its first animated feature, in 1995, Pixar has produced 17 feature films, a variety of short films and a host of industry-changing technological innovations. The company has won over 210 awards, including 27 Academy Awards, a fistful of Golden Globes, and Grammys and has earned more than $10 billion worldwide. Pixar knows something about corporate creativity.

Pixar has a fascinating culture. It includes the Pixar University, a program of workshops, events, lectures and seminars that takes place on the Pixar campus every day. The university offers the equivalent of an undergraduate education in fine arts and the art of filmmaking and over a hundred courses including filmmaking, painting, drawing, sculpting and creative writing. Every member of the Pixar payroll, including the animators, accountants, catering staff, technicians, production assistants, marketers and security guards, is entitled and encouraged to spend up to four hours of every working week in the Pixar University.

Randy Nelson was Dean of the University for 12 years. Formerly a juggler and co-founder of the Flying Karamazov Brothers, he says that the university is part of everyone's work because everyone on the payroll is a filmmaker. Everyone has access to the same curriculum and people from every level within the company will sit alongside one another in class. At one class on "Lighting and Motion Picture Capture," the students included a post-production software engineer, a set dresser, a marketer and a company chef, Luigi Passalacqua. "I speak the language of food," he said. "Now I'm learning to speak the language of film."

The university has many benefits for Pixar. Since anybody can go to any course, there is a constant flow of new ideas running through the organization. People from different areas of the organization work with each other and are reminded that they are all part of a single effort. The skills that are developed in the university are used everywhere within the organization. A drawing class doesn't just teach people to draw. It teaches them to be more observant, no matter what their usual role. Nelson says, "There's no company on earth that wouldn't benefit from having people become more observant."

"Being creative is not only a matter of inspiration. It requires skill, craft in the control of materials and a reciprocating process of critical evaluation."

The Pixar University crest features the Latin motto, *Alienus Non Diutius*, "Alone No Longer." Nelson says, "It's the heart of our model; giving people opportunities to fail together and to recover from mistakes together." Above all, the Pixar University is a practical way of energizing the imaginations of everyone in the company, of uncovering often-unknown personal talents, and of cross-pollinating the culture of the whole organization.[6]

Principle 3: We can all learn to be more creative

Brainstorming is one of a number of ways to facilitate the first mode of creative thinking: the generation of ideas. Simply being asked to go off and have some new ideas is rarely enough. I was once sent with 40 or so other academics on a training program called "Managing a University Department." In the first session I sat with seven other heads of department including professors of sociology, engineering, physics and social sciences. Just before coffee we were asked to have a brainstorming session on the future of education. We were given large sheets of paper and thick marker pens and five minutes. (If you ever lose consciousness and wake up wondering where you are, check whether you have a thick marker pen in your hand and a large sheet of paper in front of you. If so, there is a good chance you're on a management course.) What followed wasn't quite the monsoon of ideas we'd been led to expect. This wasn't so much a storm, more a light drizzle – a faint condensation on the walls. We ventured a few self-conscious thoughts and then fell into general conversation until the croissants turned up.

Being creative is not only a matter of inspiration. It requires skill and craft. Professional development in the general skills of creative thinking (including how to work in creative teams) is an important feature of creative organizations but, as I noted in Chapter 3, organizations are often reluctant to invest in it.[7] Many take a short-term view of training needs, which can ultimately be counter-productive because it eats away at organizational loyalties and the sense of common purpose on which creative cultures depend.

For McKinsey the moral is straightforward: "You can win the war for talent but first you must elevate talent management to a burning corporate priority. Then, to attract and retain the people you need, you must create and perpetually refine an employee value proposition, senior management's answer to why a smart, energetic, ambitious individual would want to come and work with you rather than with the team next door. That done, you must turn your attention to how you're going to recruit great talent and finally develop, develop, develop!" One solution is "to form smaller, more autonomous units, create the maximum number of P&L jobs each business will bear and use special project teams to provide new challenges and ways of working together."[8] Another, as Pixar and others have shown, is in-house universities that award their own qualifications.

In 1981, Motorola was the first company in the United States to develop a corporate university (CU). Today there are hundreds throughout the world.[9] A corporate university is "an internal structure designed to improve individual and business performance by ensuring that the learning and knowledge of a corporation is directly connected to its business strategy." A corporate university's students are drawn from its employees and it normally accredits the programs it provides. The principal purpose is to offer learning opportunities that advance the organization's goals: by developing a sense of corporate citizenship; enabling staff to understand the context and priorities of the organization's work; and developing the specific skills and aptitudes that give the organization its competitive edge. The benefits are also personal.

I once spoke at the national conference of an international hotel chain, which included awarding degrees to graduates of the company's corporate university. One told me this was her first experience of educational success. She had done well in the company even though she had failed at school. This was the first time she had been on a program that uncovered her real strengths and raised her confidence as a learner. Providing such opportunities is a core role of a creative leader and one of the rewards of a creative culture.

Group

The second role of a great leader is: *To form and facilitate dynamic creative teams.*

Great creative teams model the mind: they are diverse, dynamic and distinct. This leadership role includes *forming* creative teams – deciding which people to bring together for which project; *focusing* the team – setting constraints, boundaries and expectations; and *resourcing* the team – so that it can tackle the brief with adequate time and materials.

Principle 4: Creativity thrives on diversity

IDEO is a leading design and innovation consultancy. Based in Palo Alto, California, it has offices in Chicago, Boston, New York, San Francisco, London, Munich and Shanghai. IDEO has worked with dozens of organizations to develop hundreds of products in industries as diverse as toys, office equipment, furnishings, computers, medical applications and automotives. It has been ranked among the *Business Week* top 25 innovative companies, and has offered consulting advice to the other 24. IDEO's expertise is not in any of the industries it advises: it is in innovation itself. Its work is based on "design thinking." For each project, a team of specialists is brought together from different disciplines, including: engineering, product and industrial, ergonomics, behavioral sciences, marketing and market research. They explore the task from different angles and develop a range of possible solutions. Each idea is prototyped, critiqued and tested until the final version emerges. As Tim Brown, the CEO of IDEO, explains, "a competent designer could always improve upon last year's widget, but an

"Diversity is a powerful resource for creative teams and in the workforce as a whole."

interdisciplinary team of skilled design thinkers is in a position to tackle more complex problems."

From research organizations to commercial companies, the best creative teams bring together people who think differently, who may be of different ages and genders, or with different cultural backgrounds and professional experiences. Diversity is a powerful resource for creative teams and in the workforce as a whole. Not all companies have woken up to this. Leaders and managers tend to hire people who look and seem like themselves. I've worked with a number of organizations on the need for a diversity strategy. One was an international investment bank with offices in Europe, America and Asia. The bank was proud of its diversity strategy though it evidently had some way to go, as I realized when I was briefed by one of the all-male, white, middle-aged senior management team. I asked him how the diversity strategy was coming along. He thought the company was doing pretty well. "In fact," he said, "I'm interviewing a diverse candidate tomorrow." I asked him what he meant by a diverse candidate. He said, "You know, a woman." That evening, I told my wife she was diverse. She had no idea.

Diversity, naturally, takes many forms. One dimension is *innate* characteristics, including gender, age and sexual orientation. A second is *cultural* background, including ethnicity and nationality. A third is *professional* background, including work experience, education and expertise. In a rapidly changing world, there are ethical reasons for promoting diversity in the workplace. There are also strategic reasons. A more diverse workforce helps the organization to be in tune with the changing cultural environment in which it is operating. It also provides a deep resource of different perspectives to sustain a culture of innovation.

Principle 5: Creativity loves collaboration
Bringing people together from different disciplines is no guarantee of creative work. They have to be able to collaborate

so that their differences become assets not obstacles. Collaboration, as Randy Nelson observes, is not the same as cooperation. Cooperation only requires that the efforts of different people be synchronized in some way. They may be doing separate tasks at different times yet still be cooperating, as long as one supports the completion of another one. This is the typical *modus operandi* of industrial assembly lines and the linear processing of many administrative tasks.

"The creative impulses of most people can be suffocated by negative criticism, cynical putdowns or dismissive remarks."

Collaboration means working together in ways that affect the nature of the work and its outcomes. According to Randy Nelson, collaboration has to be based on two key principles. First, everyone has to accept every contribution that's made. The aim is to build on each other's contributions not undermine them. At Pixar, they call this "plussing." Second, always make your work partners look good. The aim is not to judge what they offer but to make something of it and raise everybody's game.[10] The creative ideas of most people can be doused by negative comments, cynical putdowns or dismissive remarks. Effective collaborators "amplify" each other's contributions. Tim Brown from IDEO makes the same point. Design thinking is collaborative, "but in a way that amplifies rather than subdues the creative processes of individuals; focused but at the same time flexible and responsive to unexpected opportunities: focused not just on optimizing the social, the technical and business components of a project but on bringing them a need and a design response."[11] The IDEO slogan is "None of us is smarter than all of us."

VisViva is a teaching and research group of artists and engineers in the United States. A leading member of the group points out a common misconception about interdisciplinary groups: "The notion that we are trying to bring aesthetics to engineers or conversely bring a rigorous empiricism to artists is not the point at all. The point is both of these groups do both of these things in different ways. Our group attempts to foster creativity by creating space for interaction between disciplines and viewpoints."[12]

Creative teams are diverse and dynamic. They are also distinct. They come together for particular tasks and when the job is done they break up. I once worked on a number of creativity events with John Cleese from Monty Python. The six members of Monty Python were very different but they had ways of working which made their differences energizing, highly productive – and very funny. They created many things together that they would almost certainly never have thought of had they not met. A great leader knows who to put in a team, what roles to give each person on the team, and when it's time to move onto something else.

Principle 6: Creativity takes time

Original ideas can take time to evolve. Creative organizations understand that time is an essential resource for innovation. Some offer staff time to work on their own ideas. At Google, engineers are allowed to use 20% of their time for discretionary projects. If they come up with an idea that might interest the company, they can pitch it to the senior management team. Five percent of all products that have been launched by Google were developed in the discretionary time. The 20% allocation is valuable in itself but also because it tells the workforce that the company values their creativity enough to give them the freedom to do what they are most passionate about.

"The processes of creativity can also be stifled by a sense that ideas are unlikely to be taken seriously if they come from the wrong places."

Culture

The third role of a creative leader is: *To promote a general culture of innovation.*

Principle 7: Creative cultures are supple

There is no single strategy for developing a culture of innovation. Some companies set up innovation programs or labs, which can focus on developing new projects without disturbing the rest of the organization. The disadvantage is that they may become detached from the general culture of the organization and rejected by it when they try to reintegrate. Like tissue rejection when organs from one body are transplanted into another, cultural antibodies from the host can attack the alien ideas and neutralize or destroy them. Anyone who has been on an off-site training course might know this feeling when they go back to work on Monday and try to "cascade" what they've learnt over the weekend.

Creativity can be stifled by a sense that ideas are unlikely to travel *up* the organization or not be taken seriously if they come from the wrong places; or by pressure to deliver results too soon; or by the wrong criteria of accountability. The IBM study, *Capitalizing on complexity*, found that CEOs who *are* capitalizing on complexity have focused on three areas:

Embodying creative leadership: Creative leaders consider previously unheard-of ways to engage more actively with customers and partners and employees.

Reinventing customer relationships: With the Internet, new channels and globalizing customers, organizations need to rethink approaches to better understand, interact with and serve their clients.

Building operating dexterity: Successful CEOs refashion their organizations, making them faster, more flexible and capable of using complexity to their advantage.

The report concluded that "creative leaders expect to make deeper business model changes to realize their strategies. To succeed, they take more calculated risks, find new ideas, and keep innovating in how they lead and communicate."

When John Chambers took over at CISCO Systems in 1995, he thought of his leadership role in three main ways:

developing a vision and strategy of the company; building the team to implement that strategy; and communicating the strategy within and beyond the company. After he'd been in the role for four or five years, he began to think differently about his role. He began to focus on the company culture. Great companies, he says, have great cultures. "A huge part of a leadership role is to drive the culture of the company and to reinforce it." He changed his style of leadership from command and control to collaboration and teamwork. "It sounds easy to do, but it is hard, because you are trained that way in MBA school, in law school. Around 80 to 90 percent of the job is how we work together toward common goals, which requires a different skill set."

Engineers, says Chambers, "are part business leaders, part artists, and you've got to know which hat they have on." He now sees the need for a fundamental change in ways of working "that may be really important to the future of business in this country and the world." At Cisco, the emphasis is increasingly on collaborative teams, on cross-sector groups drawn from sales, engineering, finance, legal and other departments. "We're training leaders to think across silos. We now do that with 70 different teams in the company. So we'll have a sales leader go run engineering. A lawyer go and run business development; a business development leader go run our consumer operations. We're going to train a generalist group of leaders who know how to learn and operate in collaborative teamwork. I think that's the future of leadership."[13]

Sir John Harvey Jones, the former leader of ICI, the international chemicals company, made the same point: "Every single person in business," he said "needs to acquire the ability to change, the self-confidence to learn new things and the capacity for helicopter vision. The idea that we can win with brilliant scientists and technologists alone is absolute nonsense. It's breadth of vision, the ability to understand all the influences at work, to flex between them

"In all cases, innovation involves calculating risks."

and not be frightened of different experiences and viewpoints that hold the key. We need every single pressure from business at the moment to make clear that the specialist who cannot take the holistic view of the whole scene is no use at all."[14]

Principle 8: Creative cultures are inquiring
Innovation involves trial and error, being wrong at times and sometimes having to back up and start again. There is a tendency throughout the corporate world towards short-termism. Ironically, these pressures arise in response to the very challenges that call for a long-term view. As organizations compete in increasingly aggressive markets, budgets for experimental research, blue-sky thinking and long-range development are being cut back in the interests of immediate returns and instant results. The effect can be to stifle the very sources of creativity on which long-term success ultimately depends.

Being creative isn't all about chaos and risk. Creativity in any domain is a balance of freedom and control. Innovation involves calculating risks and the organization's tolerance for them. I talked about risk taking and creative leadership with one of the most successful unit trust managers in Europe. Like all financial institutions, his was being borne along on a turbulent current of change. He described how his own style of leadership has changed to meet these new circumstances:

"I have discovered, upon achieving a 'top' position in management, that there is nowhere to hide. One has to make a comprehensive attempt to get things right. This for me at first involved trying to decide everything – I had to know the answers myself, I thought. This led to a series of mistakes and then inertia; indeed I fell flat on my face in the metaphorical mud. I then found that I had to admit my mistakes rather publicly and ask for help from my colleagues to get myself back on two feet. This seems to have been the beginning of some sort of improved understanding of the manager's role.

I began to delegate, realizing that others were more competent than me. I began to listen, rather than compete with others to produce the cleverest answer. I began to do what I knew I could do, which was to offer support and encouragement to my colleagues rather than seek to score points. I found myself gradually beginning to question, and in many instances unlearn, the very lessons I had spent most of my life learning, as I realized that being dogmatic is the fast road to disaster in a changing environment. Yet at the same time I found that I needed a sense of direction; otherwise it seemed that I would be abrogating responsibility rather than delegating it.

I endeavored to balance directness and openness as closely as possible with a willingness to listen and consider positively the viewpoint of other parties. It seems in practice that it is precisely at the point of convergence of these two 'vectors' that the natural way forward always lies. It is hard to find and I'm sure that I never find it precisely as I'm certain that I'm never fully open nor do I fully listen and consider. But it seems to work a whole lot better than my previous approach.

We are now trying to achieve the same balance in the firm as a whole. Admitting what we are not good at has led, for example, to outsourcing of certain functions. Willingness to listen has led to more harmonious senior management discussions, enhanced trust, and speedy decision-taking as colleagues have ceased second guessing each other, particularly in areas where the second guesser has little knowledge. It's also leading to more delegation and to more empowerment of younger members of staff, who often have clearer minds.

This thinking has, in turn, engendered a greater sense of partnership – both within the firm, reflected in the Board's willingness to create stock ownership plans for all staff worldwide who have been with the firm for more than a year – and also with our clients, suppliers and shareholders through better communication. Interestingly, it is also coinciding

"The traditional design of office buildings and spaces is rooted in the nineteenth century." with a greater consciousness that we can contribute to our local community. None of this seems to be at the expense of competitiveness. I believe that our competitiveness is enhanced and I think we are learning once again as an organization and new opportunities are arising continuously.

It has required us to increase training significantly, particularly at senior management levels, including the use of management psychologists, and has led us to introduce 360-degree appraisals for senior managers. In graduate recruitment we are relying much more upon internships. Most of all, it is fun, certainly for me and I hope for my colleagues. Interestingly, being a multinational company with employees from a whole range of cultural backgrounds has been both a spur to re-examine our approaches and a rich source of different perspectives."[15]

Principle 9: Creative cultures need creative spaces

The physical environment is an embodiment of organizational culture. The size and shape of workspaces, the configuration of furnishings and equipment, the quality of lighting, fabrics and colors all create ambiences that may encourage or discourage creativity. Until the 1980s, there was little research into the effects of workspaces on the work done. Since then a number of studies have been published in what is now known as "environmental psychology" and the obscurely named field of "cognitive ergonomics." The traditional design of office buildings and spaces is rooted in the nineteenth-century model of industrial work. When the emphasis is on efficiency, the main considerations in the workspace may be productivity, maximum occupancy and uniformity. These are hardly the right environments for stimulating imagination, creativity and innovation.

More flexible patterns of working mean that there is a blurring of boundaries between the home and office, work, play and personal time. It's often important to allow staff to personalize their workspace in ways that they find most conducive to creative work. Where collaboration matters, there is a need for shared spaces for meetings and workshops.

BORN AGAIN

I said that organizations are like organisms. In some ways, the life cycles of organizations follow those of human lives. They begin as the inkling of an idea. The idea is nurtured and if it's viable it begins to grow. The most creative periods in the lives of organizations are often in the early stages when there's a rush of excitement about possibilities to be explored and everyone lends a hand to do whatever is needed for survival. In its youth, an organization may burn great energy on new ventures and take heady risks in the pursuit of success. As a successful organization matures, it tends to settle into fixed structures and routines and to become more conservative. It enters middle age. Over time, it may suffer from a hardening of the categories and lose its original vitality and suppleness. If the sclerosis continues, it may grow old and die. Many organizations do. But an organization always has the possibility of being revitalized and born again. In a characteristically insightful analysis, Charles Handy, the eminent expert on management and leadership, calls this the "second curve" of growth.[16] A new phase of growth is not inevitable for organizations, and many never reach it. New growth happens first and foremost by investing in the creative powers of the people who are the organization. Organizations that make the most of their people find that their people make the most of them. That is the power of innovation and the constant promise of creative leadership. These principles apply in education too.

"Organizations that make the most of their people find that their people make the most of them. That is the power of innovation and creative leadership."

LEARNING TO BE CREATIVE

"Education is not a linear process of preparation for the future: it is about cultivating the talents and sensibilities through which we can live our best lives in the present and create the future for ourselves."

THERE ARE COUNTLESS CREATIVE TEACHERS who do wonderful work in their own classrooms, studios and laboratories. There are whole institutions that pursue innovative programs within their own districts, and whole districts that are battling to do the same in their regions. For the most part, these innovations are happening not because of the dominant cultures of education but in spite of them. The challenge is to take innovation to scale: to transform education in ways that address the real challenges of living and working in the twenty-first century.

TRANSFORMING EDUCATION

Nowadays, "school" usually refers to particular sorts of formal institution. I'm going to use the term here to mean any learning community, whether for children or adults, public or private, compulsory or voluntary. By "education," I mean all of it from pre-kindergarten to adult education. By "student,"

I mean anyone who is engaged purposefully in learning, whatever their age and whatever the setting. I have two reasons for this approach. First, my arguments are about the qualities of teaching and learning wherever they occur. Second, institutions take many forms. In Chapter 9, I described organizational cultures in terms of *habits* and *habitats*. In schools, the habits include the *curriculum*, the *schedule*, *pedagogy* and *assessment*. The habitat includes the physical fabric of the school, its décor and the surrounding environment. All of these can be transformed with a systematic approach to cultivating imagination, creativity and innovation.

Structures can be changed if there is a will to change them and the purposes are clear. Too often purposes are distorted by institutional habits. As Winston Churchill put it, "We shape our institutions and then they shape us." The challenge is to re-create our institutions by reframing our sense of purpose.

A culture of creativity

In 1997, I was asked by the British Government to develop a national strategy for creative education in elementary and high schools and I formed and chaired a National Commission to do that. There was already a strategy for literacy, part of which involved children in elementary schools spending one hour each day working on approved literacy materials. There was a similar strategy for mathematics. I suspected from my conversations with the Government that they hoped we might recommend something similar: a creativity hour perhaps, maybe on a Friday afternoon. That would have been a tidy strategy, easily accommodated within the existing system. Our recommendations went a lot further. Promoting creativity systematically in schools is about transforming the culture of education as a whole. The best way is to do what policy makers keep asking and get back to basics. They are often thought to be reading and writing and the STEM disciplines. All of these are important. But there are more basic questions to ask about the purpose of education. There's a useful analogy with the theater.

Back to basics

Peter Brook is one of the most accomplished theater directors of our times. Brook's interest is in making theater as transformative an experience as possible. He believes that too often, modern theater is a divertissement. Its purpose has become corrupted by clutter. For Brook, the essence of theater is the relationship between an actor and audience. Nothing should be added to this relationship, he argues, unless it supports or improves it. "I can take any space and call it a bare stage. A man walks across this empty space whilst someone else is watching and this is all that is needed for an act of theater to be engaged." Yet when we talk of theater, says Brook, this is not quite what we mean. "Red curtains, spotlights, blank verse, laughter, darkness, these are all confusedly superimposed in the messy image covered by one all-purpose word. We talk of the cinema killing the theater and in that phrase we refer to the theater as it was when the cinema was born, a theater of box office, foyer, tip-up seats, footlights, scene changes, intervals, music, as though the theater was, by definition, these and little more."[1] Over time the core business of theater has been blurred by every sort of encumbrance, like incremental coats of varnish on an old master.

The analogy with education is direct. At the heart of education is the relationship between teachers and students. If students are not learning, education is not happening. The clarity of that relationship has become obscured by political agendas, terms and conditions of employment, building codes, testing regimes, professional territories, national and state standards and so on. The needs of students are easily forgotten and often are. This is one reason why so many students are pulling out of the system. They feel that the whole baroque system isn't about them at all.

Complex systems like education depend on a multitude of roles: some are front-line and some are supporting. I once visited a leading hotel chain to discuss their approach to staff engagement. Everyone in the company understands that its core business is the comfort and satisfaction of its guests and that every member of staff has a role in that: not only the front-line staff, who interact with the guests, but also the support staff who don't. The dishwashers know that a lipstick mark on a water glass can mar the experience of a guest and that their work affects the quality of service as a whole. This sense of common purpose has driven the company's brand and expansion.

The core purpose of schools is to improve the quality of students' learning. School principals have a particular responsibility to nurture a culture that achieves this purpose. The culture includes everything that goes on in the school and everyone who contributes to it in one way or another, for better or for worse.

"If students are not learning, education is not happening. Clarity of purpose is vital."

PRINCIPLES OF TRANSFORMATION

I suggested in Chapter 3 that education has three core purposes:

Personal: to develop students' individual talents and sensibilities.

Cultural: to deepen their understanding of the world around them.

Economic: to enable them to earn a living and be economically productive.

My arguments about creativity and culture suggest specific principles through which schools can realize these purposes.

Talent is diverse

Human communities depend on a diversity of talents, not a singular conception of ability. The preoccupation in education with academic ability and particular disciplines marginalizes students whose interests and abilities lie in other domains. Cultivating the larger range of students' talents calls for a broader curriculum and a flexible range of teaching styles. I don't mean that students should only study what they like. One of the roles of education is to broaden people's horizons, but it should also develop their personal talents and interests.

When my wife was in high school in England, she had to spend most Wednesday afternoons in the winter outdoors on a frozen hockey field. This was not her favorite part of the week. She was surrounded by people who were taller, faster, stronger and more committed to hockey than she was. For most of the time she felt as if she was standing helplessly in the path of a freight train. She wouldn't have minded so much if the girls who relished knocking her down on the hockey field had had to dance with her in the ballet studio once a week, where her abilities shone and she felt most at home.

Alongside any common curriculum, there have to be opportunities for students to go more deeply into areas that interest them particularly and to pursue different sorts of career options. Not everyone wants to go to university, for example, and not everyone should go immediately after high school. Some want to go to design school or to music school or to a dance academy. Others want to get out in the world and pursue their practical work.

Learning is personal

Dennis Littky and Elliot Washor founded Big Picture Learning in 1995, "to encourage, incite and effect change in the U.S. educational system."[2] With 30 years' experience between them as teachers and principals in public high schools, they started Big Picture with the motto "Education is everyone's business" and a commitment to show that education can and should be changed radically. They wanted to create schools in which students would take responsibility for their own education; would spend considerable time doing real work in the community with volunteer mentors and where they would not be evaluated solely on the basis of standardized tests. Students would be assessed on their performance, on exhibitions and demonstrations of achievement, on motivation, and on the habits of mind, hand, heart and behavior that they displayed, reflecting the real world evaluations and assessments that all of us face in our everyday lives.

The first school opened in South Providence, Rhode Island in 1996 with a freshman class of 50 mostly "at-risk" African American and Latino students who did not fit in conventional schools. That class graduated in 2000 with a 96% graduation rate: 98% of the graduates were admitted to postsecondary institutions. Each subsequent graduating class has matched or bettered its predecessor. Many of these students are the first in their families to earn a high school diploma, and 80% of them are the first in their families to enroll in college.

In 2001, the Bill and Melinda Gates Foundation gave Big Picture Learning a grant to replicate the school design in other areas of the country. In 2003, after the continued success of Big Picture schools, the Gates Foundation gave a second grant to fund the launch of even more schools. The Foundation also gave Big Picture a grant to become lead convener of the newly formed Alternative High School Initiative (AHSI). Today there are 65 Big Picture schools operating in 14 states and schools in Australia, Israel and the Netherlands that use the Big Picture Learning model. All of them, "from Tennessee to Tasmania, from New York City to the Netherlands, embody the fundamental philosophy of Big Picture Learning, educating one student at a time in a community."

Big Picture schools believe "that all students should have the opportunity to learn in a place where people know each other well and treat each other with respect. Schools must be small enough so every student has genuine relationships with adults and other students and no one falls through the cracks. From assessment tools to the design of the school building itself, a truly personalized school approaches each student and situation with a mind to what is best for the individual and for the community." The culture of Big Picture schools is an integral part of their success: "Students are encouraged to be leaders and school leaders are encouraged to be visionaries. Our schools strive to create a respectful, diverse, creative, exciting, and reflective culture."

Littky and Washor say that their mission is to change the way Americans think about the public education system: "Instead of one that judges students and sets limits for achievement, we are building a school system that inspires and awakens the possibilities of an engaged and vital life within our youth ... All of our work is intended to influence the national debate about public education. We want to help convince opinion leaders (policymakers, business leaders, media representatives, and educators) as well as parents and the public, that there are better ways to educate our children."[3]

No one can be made to learn against his or her will. Learning is a personal act. Of course, under conditions of compulsion and penalty even the most reluctant learners will grudgingly commit some things to memory to avoid unpleasant consequences. When students leave high school prematurely, there are all sorts of programs to re-engage them with education. Most are based on personalized learning. If all education were personalized to begin with, far fewer students would pull away from it. Some people argue that personalizing education for every student is an impossible pipe dream: it would be too expensive and teachers simply could not give every student the necessary time and attention. There are two answers to this argument.

First, there is no alternative. Education is personal. Personalized learning is an investment

> "It is possible to personalize learning for every student. One of the ways this can be done is through the creative use of new technologies."

not a cost. I doubt there are many students who leap out of bed in the morning wondering what they can do to raise the reading standards of their local region. The best way to raise standards is to excite the energy and curiosity of the students in the system. We know the cost of not doing that.

Second, it is possible to personalize learning for every student. One way is through the creative use of new technologies. Some countries and states are using web-based technologies to connect students and teachers in personalized learning programs of many sorts. They include Sweden, Finland, New Zealand, Singapore, the United Kingdom and parts of the United States. The changes are happening in universities too. Many institutions are posting their courses online; and every day new resources become available to would-be students. As the market value of university degrees falls and the cost of getting them increases, more people are likely to explore alternative routes to study and qualifications that the Internet is making available. This is not all new.

The Open University is a "distance learning" university that was founded by the British Government in 1969.[4] It awards undergraduate and postgraduate degrees, as well as diplomas, certificates and continuing education units. It has an open entry policy, which means that students' previous academic achievements are not taken into account for entry to most courses. The majority of students are based in the United Kingdom, but its courses can be studied anywhere in the world. The OU has 13 regional centers around the UK and offices throughout Europe, more than 250,000 students enrolled, including over 50,000 students studying overseas. It is the largest academic institution in Europe by student numbers and one of the largest in the world. Since it was founded, more than 1.5 million students have taken its courses. The success of the Open University and other online providers illustrates the widespread hunger for personalized routes into higher education and the growing appetite for innovative ways to provide them.

Life is not an academic exercise

There are many ways to learn other than sitting in a classroom or lecture hall. When education connects with the world beyond school, young people can achieve remarkable things.

"Service-learning" integrates community service with instruction and reflection, to teach civic responsibility and strengthen communities for the common good. The National Youth Leadership Council (NYLC) is one of the worldwide leaders in service education and defines service-learning as "a philosophy, pedagogy, and model for community development that is used as an instructional strategy to meet learning goals and/or content standards." Dr James Kielsmeier founded NYLC in 1983, "to create a more just, sustainable, and peaceful world with young people, their schools, and their communities through service-learning."[5] NYLC now reaches into every state in the US and 35 countries. NYLC programs have included partnerships with schools, colleges, major corporations, government, faith-based organizations and other nonprofits.

Room 13 is a social enterprise organization that includes an international community of artists, educators and other professionals, and a network of studios in Austria, Botswana, Canada, China, Holland, India, Mexico, Nepal, South Africa, Turkey and the United States. Each studio offers professionally run courses and workshops, painting holidays, expeditions, training and all manner of creative development for adults of all ages. The unique feature of Studio 13 is that its management team is aged between 8 and 11.

Studio 13 began in 1994 when a group of elementary school students established their own art studio in Room 13 in Caol Primary School near Fort William, Scotland. The guiding philosophy evolved through artist-in-residence posts held by the project founder, Rob Fairley. He worked with a number of elementary schools and was asked by students at Caol to become artist-in-residence. With his encouragement, they ran the studio as a business, raising funds to buy art materials and to engage other artists to work with them.

"Its stimulus," says Fairley "was exasperation at the lack of interest in teaching visual literacy and in teaching the basic technical skills necessary to express ideas through visual imagery."[6] By approaching children as artists and intellectual equals, Room 13 combines artistic development with the skills to run a successful business. Each Room 13 studio is run by the students. An elected management team is responsible for the day-to-day running of the studio, for keeping track of the finances and for making sure all invoices are paid. No adult is allowed to sign the checks. Room 13 is not age or ability specific and there is no coercion. Students come because they wish to and stay for as long as they want, providing they negotiate the time with their teachers and all class work is up to date. Devised and run by elementary school children, Room 13 has grown from a one-day-a-week voluntary project between Fairley and the children of Caol Primary into an international network of studios, with a reputation for creating high-quality artwork and for pushing the boundaries of creative education.

Success creates success

El Sistema is a national music program that has produced a number of outstanding musicians and has changed the lives of hundreds of thousands of Venezuela's poorest children. The country now has 237 orchestras, 200 youth orchestras and 376 choruses. Among the graduates of El Sistema are internationally renowned musicians such as Edicson Ruiz, Gustavo Dudamel and the acclaimed Simón Bolívar Youth Orchestra. Many children begin attending their local El Sistema center, called a "nucleo," as early as age 2 or 3 and most continue well into their teens. They attend up to six days a week, three to four hours a day, plus retreats and intensive workshops. Participation is free for all students. El Sistema aims "to create a daily haven of safety, joy and fun that builds every child's self-esteem and sense of value." Discipline is relaxed but enforced. Although hard work and achievement are crucial to the success of El Sistema, the feeling of fun is never forgotten.

El Sistema takes time to work with the parents of students. Home visits ensure that the family understand the level of commitment required of them. As the students begin to learn their instruments, teachers instruct parents on how best to support them at home. Teachers and students alike are committed to "creating a place where children feel safe and challenged. El Sistema graduates leave with a sense of capability, endurance and resilience, owning a confidence about taking on enormous challenges in their lives. A deep sense of value, of being loved and appreciated, and a trust for group process and cooperation enables them to feel that excellence is in their own hands."[7]

> "Creativity is possible in every discipline and should be promoted throughout the whole of education."

Creativity is for everyone

The national creativity commission, which I chaired for the British Government, included scientists, economists, business leaders, educators, dancers, musicians, actors and performers. Our report, *All Our Futures*,[8] dealt with the whole curriculum. Yet some members of the Government steadfastly referred to it as "the arts report." Creativity is not only about the arts. Work in the arts can be highly creative but so can anything that involves intelligence. There are many arguments for the arts in education but associating them exclusively with creativity is a mistake. It implies that the arts are mainly opportunities for a break from more rigorous academic work: a chance to get creative for a time; a view that misunderstands both the nature of creativity and the arts. It also implies that other disciplines, including math and science, are not creative, which is untrue. Creativity is possible in every discipline and should be promoted throughout the whole of education.

Creative schedules

The schedule or timetable is the management tool for organizing time and resources. In theory, the purpose of the schedule is to facilitate learning. In practice, it can have the opposite effect. Instead of the timetable flexing to meet the needs of teaching and learning, students and teachers alike are shunted through the day on the fixed rails of the timetable. Lessons take place in set units of time, irrespective of the activity, in patterns that repeat week after week. Practicing a language may be best in short, frequent periods of immersion; working on group projects in science or the arts usually benefits from longer blocks of time. The schedule can and should be sensitive to these differences.

The School of One (SO1) is a middle school mathematics program of the New York City Department of Education.[9] It began in 2009 and is now operating in six schools in Manhattan, The Bronx and Brooklyn. The mission of the school is "to provide personalized, effective and dynamic classroom instruction so that teachers have more time to focus on quality instruction." The school has developed a suite of computer programs, which include *student profiles* based on detailed assessments together with input from parents and teachers, and a *lesson bank* of materials in various formats. At the heart of the system is a computer program known as the *learning algorithm*, which generates unique daily schedules and resources for each student and teacher. These schedules include group work, collaborative projects and individual study time. The teachers are freed from most of the routine tasks of administration and can focus on "providing quality support and instruction to the students." The teachers can override the schedules for themselves or particular students.

The 2010 pilot was evaluated by New York City Department of Education's Research and Policy Study Group, which found that participating students significantly outperformed nonparticipating students. In 2009 it was listed by *Time* magazine as one of the 100 Best Innovations. The School of One promises other innovations using IT, contributing, as the school puts it, to "the mass customization of student learning." Another reason to rethink the schedule is that students' energy levels vary with the rhythms of the day.

Russell Foster is head of Circadian Neuroscience at Brasenose College, Oxford. He has been conducting memory tests with teenaged students at Monkseaton High School in North Tyneside in the UK. His research suggests that teenagers' brains work two hours behind adult time. Young people's body clocks may shift as they begin their teens. Teenagers get up later not because they're lazy, but because they are biologically programmed to do so. Dr Paul Kelley, the principal of Monkseaton and author of *Making Minds*, says that continuous early starts create "teenage zombies" and that allowing them to begin lessons at 11 a.m. has a profound impact on learning.

Dr Kelley argues that depriving teenagers of sleep may affect their mental and physical health as well as their education. We don't need science to tell us that rousing teenagers from their beds early in the morning results in abrupt mood swings and increased irritability. It may also contribute to depression, weight gain and reduced immunity to disease. Dr Kelley said: "This affects all teenagers from about year eleven and stays with them until their university years and beyond. The research shows that we are making teenagers the way they are and that we need to do something about it." One outcome of the research is "spaced learning," in which teachers give short lessons, sometimes of less than ten minutes, before changing to a physical activity and then repeating the lesson. In one trial, the pupils scored up to 90% in a science paper after one session involving three 20-minute bursts, interspersed with ten-minute breaks for physical activity.

The pupils had not covered any part of the science syllabus before the lessons.[10]

The Sudbury Valley School was founded in 1968 in Framingham, Massachusetts, in the United States. It is a private school, attended by children from the ages of 4 to 19 and is organized on two basic principles: educational freedom and democratic governance. It sits in a long tradition of democratic schools that includes Summerhill School founded in 1921 in Suffolk, England by A.S. Neill. In Sudbury Valley as at Summerhill, students are responsible for their own education. The school is run as a democracy in which students and staff are equals.

Students decide for themselves what they will do and when, how and where they will do it. This freedom "is at the heart of the school; it belongs to the students as their right, not to be violated." The premises of the school are that "all people are curious by nature; that the most efficient, long-lasting, and profound learning takes place when started and pursued by the learner; that all people are creative if they are allowed to develop their unique talents; that age-mixing among students promotes growth in all members of the group; and that freedom is essential to the development of personal responsibility."

Students initiate all their own activities and create their own environments.

Adults and students mix freely. "People can be found everywhere talking, reading and playing. Some may be in the digital arts studio, editing a video they have made. There are almost always people making music of one kind or another, usually in several places. You might see someone studying French, biology, or algebra. People may be at computers, doing administrative work in the office, playing chess, rehearsing a show, or participating in role-playing games. In the art room, people will be drawing; they might also be sewing, or painting, or working with clay, either on the wheel or by hand." The physical plant, the staff and the equipment are there for the students to use as the need arises: "The school provides a setting in which students are independent, are trusted, and are treated as responsible people; and a community in which students are exposed to the complexities of life in the framework of a participatory democracy."[11]

Sudbury and Summerhill are not isolated experiments. There are now dozens of schools based on similar principles in more than 30 countries. Although they are mostly private schools, they are part of a growing movement worldwide to engage students directly in the design and management of their own education. They include a remarkable network of democratic schools and of "education cities" which has been cultivated by Yaacov and Sheerly Hecht and their team, and whose work is promulgated through an important and growing global network of related initiatives.[12]

All schools are unique

For several years, I acted as mentor to a statewide program of creativity and innovation in Oklahoma. The state has a nationally recognized program of early years' education. In *The Element*, I describe one school in the Jenks schools district of Tulsa, which has a wonderful relationship with an unusual partner. The Grace Living Center is a retirement home. The supervisor of the Center approached the school district to ask whether they could participate in the district's reading program. As a result, the district established an early years' classroom in the foyer of the retirement home and this is where a group of young children goes to school each day. At the center of the partnership is the Book Buddies program, in which members of the home spend time, one-on-one, listening to the children read and reading to them. The results have been remarkable.

Over 70% of the children leave the program reading at Grade 3 level or higher, outperforming many other children in the district. The reason is that they have had personalized support. Second, they are learning much more than how to read. Through their relationships with the members of the home, they are learning about the rich traditions of life in Oklahoma. Third, medication levels at the home have fallen dramatically. The senior citizens have a new reason to live and a new energy for their days. They have a purpose. But every now and then the children have to be told that one of the book buddies will not be coming back again, because they have passed. So, at this young age the children are learning too about the natural cycles of life and death.

In most education systems, people are segregated by age. This project shows what can happen when the generations are brought back together and re-establish some of their traditional relationships. As with all genuine innovations, the outcomes, as Elliot Eisner once said, are a surprise not a prediction.[13] Small, creative changes in any school can have major benefits. Large changes may have correspondingly dramatic results.

The culture of a school is much more than the curriculum, teaching styles and forms of assessment. Culture is about values, ambience, tone and relationships. In these respects, all schools are different and they should be. Diversity is essential to move the system beyond industrial models of standardization and conformity. The challenge is not to take a single model to scale: it is to propagate the principles of creativity so that every school can develop its own approach as a unique community. As in Tulsa, often the simplest ideas can have large effects.

We're in this together

Transforming education takes partnership and collaboration. Everyone has a stake in the future of education and in many parts of the world there are formal alliances between schools and the business, philanthropic and cultural sectors. In the United States, the Partnership for Twenty First Century Learning is a national organization that "advocates for 21st century readiness for every student."[14] The partnership and its members provide tools and resources to help the US education system keep up, "by fusing the three Rs and four Cs (critical thinking and problem solving, communication, collaboration, and creativity and innovation)." The partnership advocates for local, state and federal policies that support this approach for every school.

The Partnership for Next Generation Learning is a collaboration between The Council of Chief State School Officers (CCSSO) and a consortium of states and foundations. The partnership is establishing a network of "innovation laboratories" in education. CCSSO has called for a new education system, "one that is designed around the fundamental premise that we will provide each and every child with personalized learning experiences leading to success." The aim of the strategy is to change the national conversation about how to improve educational outcomes. The CCSSO notes that there are many examples, in the US and internationally, in both formal education and other sectors, of what transformative learning looks like: "Unfortunately, these examples remain exceptions rather than the norm. We are still falling short of wholly systemic transformation because existing federal, state, and local systems are not conducive to fostering innovation and making transformative shifts to new policy." Although many are working to improve various elements of the current system, the Partnership for Next Generation Learning "is ready to engage those who are prepared to shift energy, time, and investment away from fixing what we have toward creating the public education system that we need ... and making this transformation a reality for all students."[15]

In the United Kingdom, The RSA (Royal Society of Arts, Manufactures and Commerce) has been a leading campaigner for educational transformation. It coordinated the drafting of an "Education Charter" with multiple partner organizations, committed to a more holistic education. The Charter led to the development of the national Whole Education movement, which "knits together academic, practical and vocational learning calibrated to the potential of each individual." The basis of Whole Education is the conviction that education should "invest in the intellectual development of the young person as well as the development of social and emotional competencies. These competencies are a major part of the foundations that allow every young person to learn effectively and contribute positively to their own development and attainment and to the development of a good society." Whole Education partners with over 5,000 schools and colleges and numerous youth organizations and charities that work directly with young people. The aim is "to ensure that all young people have access to an education that equips them with the skills, knowledge, attitudes and resources necessary to cope and thrive in life beyond school and make a positive contribution to their societies."[16]

National, state and local policies for education have profound effects on the climate in schools. It is important to persuade policy makers to change the policy climate in the best way possible. But schools cannot wait for policy changes before they do anything themselves and students can't postpone their lives in the meantime. Schools often have more freedom to innovate than they commonly think. Creativity is not about a lack of constraints; it is about working within them and overcoming them.

CREATIVE TEACHING

No school is better than its teachers. National reform movements in education often focus on curriculum and assessment. The element that is most often overlooked is the only one that really makes a difference to student achievement: the quality of teaching. When you think of your own time at school it is the people you remember, and especially the teachers who turned you on and the ones who turned you off; who built you up or knocked you down. A casual remark by a teacher, or even a raised eyebrow, can set you on a lifelong journey of discovery or put you off taking the first step. Mastery in teaching is like mastery in any other profession. Expert practitioners in any field – doctors, lawyers, chefs, artists, scientists – have a wide repertory of techniques and deep knowledge and practical experiences to draw from. Knowing which to draw from to meet the needs of the present situation is the connoisseurship that expert teachers also share. A creative culture in schools depends on re-energizing the creative abilities of teachers.

"There are three related tasks in teaching for creativity: encouraging, identifying and fostering."

In Chapter 7, I distinguished between the two traditions of individualism: the *rational* and the *natural*. To some extent these have been associated with different styles of teaching. So-called traditional methods are usually associated with formal instruction to the whole class and with rote learning; progressive methods with inquiry-based learning, and with students working individually or in groups to explore their own interests and express their own ideas. Both have an important place in creative education. Sometimes it is appropriate for the teacher to give formal instruction in skills and techniques, or to convey specific ideas and information; at others it is more appropriate for the students to explore ideas for themselves. Some of these methods do put a strong emphasis on creativity; some do not. Some of this work is excellent; some is not.

There is a difference between teaching *through* creativity and teaching *for* creativity. Good teachers know that their role is to engage and inspire their students. This is a creative task in itself. Teaching *for* creativity is about facilitating other people's creative work. It involves asking open-ended questions where there may be multiple solutions; working in groups on collaborative projects, using imagination to explore possibilities; making connections between different ways of seeing; and exploring the ambiguities and tensions that may lie between them. Teaching for creativity involves teaching creatively. There are three related tasks in teaching for creativity: *encouraging*, *identifying* and *developing*.

Encouraging

The first task in teaching for creativity in any field is to encourage people to believe in their creative potential and to nurture the confidence to try. Other important attitudes for creative learning are high motivation and independence of judgment; a willingness to take risks and be enterprising; to be persistent and to be resilient in the face of false starts, wrong turns and dead ends.

Identifying

Everyone can learn the general skills of creative thinking. In addition, we all have personal creative capacities. A creative musician is not necessarily a creative scientist; a creative writer is not necessarily a creative mathematician. Creative achievement is often driven by a person's love of a particular instrument, for the feel of the material, for the excitement of a style of work that catches the imagination. Identifying people's creative abilities includes helping them to find their creative strengths: to be in their element.

Developing

In teaching for creativity, teachers aim to:

- promote experiment and inquiry and a willingness to make mistakes;
- encourage new ideas, free from immediate criticism;
- encourage the expression of personal feelings;
- convey an understanding of phases in creative work;
- develop an awareness of the roles of intuition and of aesthetic judgment;
- facilitate critical evaluation of ideas.

CURRICULUM

The curriculum is the knowledge, ideas, skills and values that students are expected to learn. There is a difference between the formal curriculum, which all students have to follow, and the informal curriculum, which is optional, including after-school programs. The whole curriculum is all the learning opportunities that a school provides *including* the formal and informal curriculum.

One obvious purpose of the curriculum is *cultural*. One of the roles of education is to put a stamp of approval on certain sorts of knowledge and experience and to suggest, by implication, that others are not so worthwhile. As the French sociologist Pierre Bourdieu puts it, education distinguishes between the spheres of "orthodox and heretical culture."[17] Many things are not taught in schools. Witchcraft and necromancy are not, at least not usually. A curriculum has a second function, which is *managerial*. Schools need curricula so that they can organize themselves, know how many teachers to hire, what resources are needed, how to arrange the day, whom to put where, at what time and for how long. A balanced curriculum should give equal status and resources to literacy and numeracy, the sciences, the humanities, the arts and to physical education.

High standards in literacy and numeracy are essential in themselves and they are the gateways to learning in many other disciplines. Languages and mathematics offer much more than basic literacy and numeracy. The study of languages should include literature, and the skills of speaking and listening. Mathematics also leads into rich fields of abstraction and the conceptual languages of science and technology.

Science education encourages an understanding of evidence and the skills of "objective" analysis; gives access to existing scientific understanding of the processes of the natural world and the laws that govern them; and provides opportunities for practical and theoretical inquiry, by which existing knowledge can be verified or challenged. Science education also promotes understanding of the scientific concepts and achievements that have shaped the modern world and of their significance and limitations.

The humanities are concerned with understanding human culture. These include history, the study of languages, religious education and aspects of geography and social studies. Humanities education deepens students' understanding of the world around us: its diversity, complexity and traditions. It enlarges our knowledge of what we share with other human beings, including those removed in time and culture, and develops a critical awareness of our own times and cultures.

The arts are concerned with the qualities of human experiences. Through music, dance, visual arts, drama and the rest, we give form to the currents of feeling and perception that constitute the lived experience of ourselves and of other people. The arts illustrate the diversity of intelligence and provide practical ways of promoting it. They provide the most natural processes for giving form to personal feelings and emotions and how they connect with our ways of thinking about the world; they are among the most vivid manifestations of human culture.

Physical education contributes directly to the health and well-being of students. We are embodied beings and there are intimate relations between mental, emotional and physical processes. Physical education enhances creative work by quickening concentration and mental agility.[18] Physical education and sport are entwined in all cultural traditions and practices and evoke powerful feelings and values, both in relation to the games themselves and through the sense of collective belonging they can generate. They provide important opportunities to develop individual and team skills and to share success and failure in controlled environments. In these and other ways, physical education has essential and equal roles with other curriculum areas in a balanced approach to creative and cultural education.

There should be equal balance between all these areas of the curriculum because each reflects major areas of cultural knowledge and experience. Each addresses different modes of intelligence and creative development and the strengths of any individual may be in one or more of them.

ASSESSMENT

Assessment is the process of making judgments about students' progress and attainment. Assessment has several roles. The first is *diagnostic*. Students may be given tests and assignments of various sorts to help teachers to understand their aptitudes and levels of development in various areas. The second is *formative*, the purpose of which is to gather evidence on students' progress to inform teaching methods and priorities for further work. The third role is *summative*, which is about making judgments on overall performance at the conclusion of a program of work. Methods of assessment can take many forms: from informal judgments in the classroom, to formal assignments and public examinations. They can draw on many forms of evidence: from student participation in class, to portfolios of work, to written essays and assignments in other media. Summative and formative assessment both have essential roles in teaching and learning; in improving the quality of achievement; and in ensuring a healthy balance between factual knowledge and more open-ended styles of learning, all of which are necessary to creative education. The problem for creative education is not the need for assessment, but the nature of it. There are three related problems: the emphasis on summative assessment and testing; the emphasis on measurable outcomes and league tables; the pressures of national assessment on teachers and schools.

National assessment systems tend to emphasize summative assessment. They are used to judge how well the school itself is doing when compared to other schools. The outcomes of these assessments are linked to the public status of schools, to their funding and sometimes to their survival. Generally, national assessments emphasize "measurable outcomes" and focus on testing students' recall of factual knowledge and skills that can be measured comparatively. They generally take little account of experimentation, original thinking and innovation. The focus of teaching narrows, and so does students' learning and achievement. Some areas of the curriculum, especially arts and humanities; some forms of teaching and learning, including questioning, exploring and debating; and some aspects of particular subjects, are neglected.

An assessment has two components: a description and a comparison. If you say that someone can run a mile in four minutes or can speak French, these are neutral descriptions of what someone can do. If you say that "she is the best athlete in the district" or that "he speaks French like a native," these are assessments. Assessments compare performances with others and rate them against particular criteria. Assessments that use letters and grades are light on description and heavy on comparison. Students are given grades without always knowing what they mean, and teachers sometimes give grades without being sure why. I once talked with a high school student who had just completed a three-year program in dance. I asked her what she had got out of the course and she said, "I got a B."

A single letter or number does not convey the complexities it is meant to summarize. Some outcomes can't be expressed in this way anyway. As Eliott Eisner put it, "not everything important is measurable and not everything measurable is important."[19] One way to improve assessment is to separate description and comparison. Portfolios allow for detailed descriptions of the work that students have done, with examples and comments by themselves and others. Providing clear criteria improves the transparency of assessments. In peer group assessment, students judge each other's work and agree on the criteria by which it is assessed. These approaches can be especially valuable in assessing creative work.

Assessing creative development is more nuanced than testing factual knowledge. Creative work has to be original and of value. There are degrees of originality. Judging value depends on clear and relevant criteria. Teachers are often unclear about the criteria to apply to students' creative work and may lack confidence in their own judgment. Creative work usually passes through various phases. It may involve false starts, trial and error and a series of successive approximations along the way to the finished work. The educational value of creative work can lie as much in the process as in the final product. Assessment has to take this into account and teachers often need advice on how this should be done. Insensitive assessment can damage students' creativity and may encourage them to take a safe option, avoiding experimentation and never learning how to find and correct their mistakes. There are also issues of comparability. How should people's creative work be compared between schools or regions?

The difficulties of assessing creative development can be overcome and there is much research, experience and expertise to draw from. Tackling these issues is not a priority in many education systems. The net effect is to increase the emphasis on some forms of learning and to lower the status of others.

LOOKING TO THE FUTURE

In many parts of the world, people are coming together to develop their own alternatives to standardized schooling. Many of them are in the public sector; some are independent schools and some are hybrids, like the charter schools in the USA.[20] A small but growing number of people are opting for more radical alternatives including home schooling and "un-schooling."[21] The new pioneers of alternative education come from many different backgrounds and often are driven by dissatisfaction with their own experiences in school and a determination to do better for their own and other people's children.

Blue Man Group is a world-renowned creative organization based in Lower Manhattan, New York City. The group was founded in 1988 by Phil Stanton, Chris Wink and Matt Goldman. Blue Man Group produces unique performances that combine music, elaborate improvised instruments, comedy and multimedia theatrics. The group has recorded scores for film and television and appears regularly on television. The Blue Men wear black, utilitarian clothes, blue make-up on their hands, faces and bald heads and never speak. They meet everything around them with a childlike innocence and curiosity. Since it was founded the group has grown into an international creative phenomenon, with theaters in New York, Las Vegas, Orlando, Boston, Chicago, Berlin and Tokyo. Now they have started their own elementary school. None of the group's founders had any of this in mind when they first set out on their journey together.

As Chris Wink says,[22] "When Blue Man first started we weren't a business, we weren't a company, we weren't a show. We were just a community of friends looking for something interesting to do. All we had was a character and a few principles that we shared. We had no idea what we were going to do: we just knew that we were going to explore these ideas using this character." None of the group remembers which of them first thought of becoming bald and blue. And as Matt Goldman says, it was not a very bankable idea. A trio of bald, blue, silent performers did not have obvious investment potential. They loved the character though, partly because it was as neutral as they could imagine in terms of culture, age and gender.

Being bald and blue was hardly a long-term, linear plan; the evolution of the group was simply carried forward on the excitement of its own creative collaboration. Together they generated lives and careers that none of them could have foreseen. As Chris Wink puts it: "Some people are lucky and want to be rocket scientists or cellists. These are existing media. For others we wanted to be post-modern multimedia vaudevillians who create instruments and explore popular culture in a sort of shamanic primal atmosphere. Where's that job exist? Because if we could have found it we would have signed up for it."

The group's work was guided by some clear principles. One of them was that everyone could be creative. "We needed that idea," said Chris Wink, "because we had gone through our educational experiences thinking maybe we weren't creative. And then we got together and said maybe that's not true. What if that isn't true?" For Phil Stanton, this was a vital principle from the outset, "and it influenced everything throughout our career." Although they are a performance-based group, they aim to be creative in everything they do. As Matt Goldman put it: "Being creative wasn't confined to if you could mold clay or paint on canvas or write music. In the business setting you could be creative in anything in any discipline."

Matt Goldman and Chris Wink have been friends since they were in elementary school together. Phil Stanton met them later when he moved to New York City in his early 20s. They had an instant rapport. One of the things that drew the group together initially, he says, "even before there was a Blue Man was that we were in our own ways disappointed with our educational experience. It seems like when we're all kids everybody paints and has fun. But somehow we throw away that kind of inspiration and get rid of a bunch of other things too."

When they had their own children, they and their wives faced the dilemma of where and how to educate them. After long reflection, they decided they should start their own school: The Blue School. As Matt Goldman explains it:

"We wanted to create the kind of school that either we wished we had gone to or that we fantasized would be the school for our children: a school that emphasizes creativity as much as anything else, that teaches kids a special way to treat one another through social and emotional learning. A place where you don't lose your childlike exuberance, where you have such a zest for learning, a love of life all the way through, and not have it educated out of you."

The educational model of the Blue School consists of two main elements: the core curriculum, which represents the basic disciplines of the program: language arts, science, fine arts, lively arts, social studies, technology and media literacy, math, physical arts and fitness. The second element is the school's values: creativity and expression, family and community connections, playfulness, exuberance and fun, self-awareness and well-being, global and environmental exploration, multiple perspectives and differentiated learning styles. Each of the Blue School's values relates in some way to the idea of connection, "whether it be the connection to a community, to one's emotions, to one's artistic voice, to one's body, to the world, to one's interests, or to one's sense of joy and wonder." The model reflects the work of and principles of The Blue Man Group itself and emerged from the school's commitment to achieve a new kind of balance between "rigor and enchantment" and a belief that both are essential in education.

According to Chris Wink, "on a metaphorical level, the traditional model of education is that children are freight cars and the school is a grain silo. It fills each of the kids up and then moves them down the track. We're creating a launch pad where kids are the rockets and we're just trying to find the fuse." The Blue School's approach, he says, "involves having the entire brain alive and exhilarated and tingling with life force. That needs to be part of our educational model. That seems like a crazy revolutionary idea but it really actually seems to us to make sense, to make actual academic sense."

The work and ambience of the school also reflects the Blue Man Group's original commitment to trusting in our natural creative powers. As Chris Wink puts it, "People tend to think that the part of ourselves that feels different should be hidden or covered up. The Blue Man message is that you should not hide that part of you because it is the key to your individuality. Letting it out lets all this creativity out. You should have the courage to expose that part of yourself." There is a point in the Blue Man show when brightly colored paint pours from tubes around the performers' chests onto drums that they are pounding in a shared, primal beat. "When we drum on paint during our show," says Wink, "the vibrant colors are a way of expressing what happens when you let your outsider come out."

Whether in the public or the independent sector, in schools or at home, being creative in providing education and promoting creativity are not dispensable luxuries. They are essential to enable us all to make lives that are worth living and to sustain a world that is worth living in. The cultural and economic circumstances in which we and our children have to make our way are utterly different from those of the past. We cannot meet the challenges of the twenty-first century with the educational ideologies of the nineteenth. We need a new Renaissance that values different modes of intelligence and that cultivates creative relationships between disciplines and between education, commerce and the wider community. Transforming education is not easy. The price of failure is more than we can afford and the benefits of success may be more than we imagine.

AFTERWORD

"Education and training are the keys to the future. A key can be turned in two directions. Turn it one way and you lock resources away; turn it the other way and you release resources and give people back to themselves."

ALL OF THE IDEAS about imagination, creativity and innovation in this book point to the need for a different conception of ability, in education, in business and in our communities. I see these issues in terms of ecology. Since the Industrial Revolution we have squandered and damaged much of what the earth has to offer because we have not seen the value of it. We have jeopardized the balance of nature by misunderstanding how its many different elements nourish and sustain each other. Although the dangers persist, they are at least more widely understood.

I believe there's a similar calamity in our use of human resources. In the interests of the industrial economies, we have subjected generations of people to narrow forms of education that have marginalized some of their most important talents and qualities. In pursuit of higher levels of productivity, we have overlooked the essential human factors on which creativity and innovation naturally depend. We have wasted much of what people have to offer because we have not seen the value of it. Along the way, we have jeopardized the balance of communities by not recognizing how our different talents and passions sustain and enrich each other. The dangers persist, and they are not yet widely understood.

These are not trivial matters. Our own times are being swept along on an avalanche of changes. To keep pace with these changes, we will need all our wits about us. It is often said that education and training are the keys to the future. They are, but a key can be turned in two directions. Turn it one way and you lock resources away, even from those they belong to. Turn it the other way and you release resources and give people back to themselves. To realize our true creative potential – in our organizations, in our schools and in our communities – we need to think differently about ourselves and to act differently towards each other. We must learn to be creative.

ENDNOTES

CHAPTER 1: OUT OF OUR MINDS

1 Life never stands still. Compared to other species, the rate of change in human societies has always been frenetic. Even so, the pace of change has been picking up considerably for the past 300 years. The eighteenth century saw political revolutions in Europe and in America. In the eighteenth and nineteenth centuries much of the world was convulsed by the rise of science and by the Industrial Revolution. The twentieth century was the bloodiest on record. It saw two World Wars, numerous regional conflicts and tumultuous revolutions in Russia and China. Overall, the twentieth century was the most murderous in human history: it's estimated that more than 100 million people died at the hands of other human beings. It also saw extraordinary advances in science and technology and massive cultural changes, especially in the old industrial economies.

2 "No country has moved up the human development ladder without steady investment in education," Mrs Irina Bokova, the Director-General of UNESCO, is quoted as saying at the launch of the Education for All Global Monitoring Report,

Reaching the Marginalized, in January 2010. "The failure to stay competitive in the international playing field is a direct result of our failure to stay competitive in the education field," says Jeff Beard, the Director-General of the International Baccalaureate in Geneva, Switzerland.

3 In 2010, IBM published *Capitalizing on Complexity*, the fourth edition of its biennial global CEO study series led by the IBM Institute for Business Value. The study was based on personal interviews with 1,541 CEOs, general managers and senior public sector leaders representing different sizes of organizations in 60 countries and 33 industries. In addition, the study surveyed the views of 3,619 students from more than 100 major universities around the world including students on undergraduate and graduate programs, including MBA and doctoral students. Introducing the report, Samuel J. Palmisano, Chairman, President and Chief Executive Officer of IBM said, "We occupy a world that is connected on multiple dimensions and at a deeper level – a global system of systems."

4 Diamond, J. (2006).

5 Friedman, T. L. (2007).

6 Abraham Lincoln, Second Annual Message to Congress, December 1, 1862.

CHAPTER 2: FACING THE REVOLUTION

1 Ian Pearson, British Telecom, interviewed in *The Sunday Times*, 4 June 2000.

2 For a brief account of the origins of the Center see Lehrer, J. (2007).

3 Kurzweil, R. (1999). Reproduced with permission.

4 Ostman, C. (1998). Reproduced with the kind permission of Charles Ostman.

5 Kurzweil, R. op.cit

6 During the past two decades, most of the world's fastest-growing countries were in the Middle East and Africa. Kuwait's population

grew from 1.9 to 2.3 million between 1998 and 2008 and at the current rate the population will have doubled in less than 20 years. The population of the African continent is growing at 2.4%, yielding a doubling time of only 27 years (though the infant mortality remains the highest of any continent at 76 per 1,000 live births). "Between 2005 and 2050, the populations of Afghanistan, Burundi, the Democratic Republic of the Congo, Guinea-Bissau, Liberia, Niger, Timor-Leste and Uganda are projected to increase at least threefold." World Population Prospects: 2006 summary, United Nations (ST/ESA/SER.A/261/ES).

7 "Between 2005 and 2050, half of the increase in the world's population will be accounted for by a rise in the population aged 60 or over; whereas the number of children (aged under 15) will decline slightly." Ibid.

8 For a detailed analysis of this sector, see Florida, R. (2002).

9 MacRae, H. (2010). Another effect of these changes in the workforce is that more people are now working flexibly and from home. In the United States, the numbers have grown from 1.9 million in 1991 to 3.6 million in 1997. In 2010, the Trades Union Congress (TUC) in the UK estimated that as many as one in eight people earned a living from home, an increase of 600,000 in three years. www.workwiseuk.org/events/tucwork-fromhomeday.html

10 For an outline history of the evolution of BBC radio news, see https://goo.gl/ZR3Fms

CHAPTER 3: THE TROUBLE WITH EDUCATION

1 Formal education for all was introduced in Britain in 1870. The government provided for all children to have a basic grounding in literacy and numeracy to the age of 12. In the closing years of World War II, the government set about planning the post-war reconstruction of the country. Its plans for education were set out in the Education Act of 1944. One of the main aims was to provide post-elementary education for all young people.

2 Gutek, G.L. (1972).

3 Ibid.

4 New civic universities were opened in Birmingham (1900), Liverpool and Wales (1903), Leeds (1904), Sheffield (1905), and Bristol (1909). Between 1954 and 1966, the numbers of school leavers qualifying for university entrance rose from 24,000 to 66,000. During the 1960s, 23 new universities were established in the UK to meet the demands of the baby boomers, culminating in the creation of the Open University, which provided university-level education for all via distance learning. Two-thirds of current British universities were founded after 1960 when the polytechnics became eligible for university status.

5 Robinson, K. (1992).

6 According to one study, after NCLB was passed into law, almost half of the school districts eliminated or seriously reduced their arts programs, and the associated teaching posts. McMurrer, J. (2007).

7 See: "China pushes to ease grim Chinese unemployment", Reuters, 7 January 2009. https://goo.gl/arFZkj.

8 Chambers, E. *et al.* (1998).

9 Michaels, E. and Handfield-Jones, H. (2001).

10 Guthridge, M., *et al.* (2008).

11 Only 23% of the 6,000 executives surveyed strongly agree that their company attracts highly talented people and 10% that they retain almost all the high performers. Only 16% think their company knows who their high performers are and only 3% said their company develops high performers effectively and moves low performers on quickly.

12 Guthridge, M., *et al.* op cit (2008).

13 See: Farrell, D. and Grant, A.J. (2008).

14 Alliance for Excellent Education, (2009).

15 Department for Education and Employment (2000).

16 International Labour Organisation (2010).

17 In the United Kingdom, in 2009, 17,000 pupils were excluded from schools for physical attacks on adults. Haydn, T. (2010).

18 These figures and accounts are taken from a survey by the National Union of Teachers of members at all the city's secondary schools. Response to the survey was comparatively small – 116 useable replies – but the union is convinced they are typical. Seventy percent of teachers who had been assaulted had more than five years' teaching experience.

19 Hilty, L. (2009).

20 Alliance of Artists' Communities (1996). The report concluded that the result of the misplaced emphasis on the punitive rather than on the educational roles of government is that upward mobility, a staple principle of American life, is under assault and with it "the possibility of creative reinvention of the individual … a fundamental aspect of the American imagination." As the symposium concluded, if this comparison between investment in education and in prisons shocks us, "it should also spur us into action because it reflects a change in the nation's priorities away from building the future and toward short-term solutions for the complex social and cultural problems we face."

21 Prensky, M. (2001).

22 O'Connor, R. and Sheey, N. (2000).

23 Hemming, J. (1980).

CHAPTER 4: THE ACADEMIC ILLUSION

1 These tests are from the official Mensa website: www.mensa.org.uk. The answers are:
Question 1: "O."
The letters are the first and last letters of Mercury, Venus, Earth, Mars, Jupiter, Saturn, Uranus, Neptune and Pluto.
Question 2: "140."
The alphabetical positions of all the letters are added to give the amount.

Question 3: "South."

The series is: south, east, north, south, west, east spirals clockwise from the top left-hand corner.

2 Galton built upon Darwin's ideas and considered that natural selection was potentially disrupted by human civilization. Because society sought to protect the underprivileged and weak, it was contrary to the natural selection process that generally forfeits the weakest.

3 Richardson, K. (1999).

4 Hernstein, R. and Murray, C. (1996).

5 Langer, S. (1951).

6 Kuhn, T.S. (1970).

7 Langer, S. op cit.

8 Rada, J.F. (1994). Reproduced with the kind permission of Dr J.F. Rada.

9 The term "grammar school" first appeared in English in 1387 in the form *gramer scole* but its Latin form *schola grammatica* was in use at least 200 years before that. Grammar, with its alternative form *gramarye* and *glomerye*, was highly revered by the uneducated who regarded it as a form of magic, a meaning that survives in our modern word "glamour." For more on this, see Davis, R. (1967).

10 St Paul's school, founded in 1518, was funded by the Mercers Company and was independent of the Church. During the reign of the Tudors there was a huge increase in the foundation of grammar schools. Many schools that had been closed during Henry's dissolution of the monasteries were reopened. Schools were established by successful individuals and by the city livery companies including the Merchant Tailors. King Edward VI also promoted and lent his name to the foundation of grammar schools in many cities throughout the land. The growth of grammar schools continued under the Stuarts. There were 155 founded between 1501 and 1601; and 186 between 1601 and 1651.

In England the term public school, *schola publica*, appeared in the twelfth century. The term distinguished them from private or home-based schools. It meant that they were open for those who could afford to send their children to them: literally public in that sense. These days, public schools are a particularly prestigious and self-appointed group of independent grammar schools.

11 The first three – grammar, rhetoric and dialectic – were known as the trivium and formed the basis of the grammar school curriculum. The remaining four, the quadrivium, were the foundation of the university curriculum.

12 Quoted in Davis, R. op cit.

13 It was also seen as vital to address the manifest and, to many social reformers, offensive problems of social deprivation among the laboring classes.

14 By 1908 there were 663 grammar schools and by 1963 there were 1,295. This massive expansion was directly related to the development of the industrial economy and the need for a better-educated workforce. From the outset, the grammar schools had been seen as a means of social advancement and as superior to the secondary moderns. One of their main purposes was to provide a route to the universities.

15 Where the private system had been based on ability to pay, the state system was founded on the idea of ability and intelligence quotient. Selection for different types of school was by a national test taken at the age of 11, the eleven-plus, which was based on theories of IQ. Less than a quarter of children were accepted for a grammar school education. The rest, having failed the eleven-plus, went to secondary modern schools. Understandably, many thought of themselves as educational failures and decades later many still do. When children failed the eleven-plus they weren't told it was for economic reasons. They assumed they just weren't as clever as those who passed. It was a myth that only 20% of children were capable of passing the test. Only 20% of children were required to pass it. The numbers of grammar school places were planned on that basis. It was harder to pass the eleven-plus in some parts of the country than others because of local variations in the numbers of grammar schools.

It was harder in some years to pass the eleven-plus. If there was a particularly good year and 30% or more performed well, the authorities raised the pass level. This is a system known as "norm-referencing." It means that the assessment of individual students is based not on absolute but on relative achievement. If all candidates were to be given "A" there would be complaints about falling standards. A pupil's placing does not depend solely on personal performance. He or she may improve performance by 100% over a year, but if everyone else improves similarly, personal grades will be no higher than before.

The bar was set higher for girls. Because not so many were expected to go into professional or managerial jobs there were fewer grammar school places for them and the competition was tougher. The prospects of passing the eleven-plus were greatly increased by coaching. Success relied as much on knowing the techniques involved as on natural aptitude. Many who failed the eleven-plus might have passed with training and many of those who did pass had had it.

16 Simon, B. (1978).

17 Britton, J. (1972).

18 As Peter Scott (Scott, 1997) puts it, the university system has become a mass system in structure but remains elite in its private instincts. In universities, business schools are valued for their contribution to the balance sheet but have relatively low academic status. Philosophy and mathematics departments may generate little income but their intellectual capital is very much higher. In some ways these are typical problems for new disciplines. New fields of study are commonly disparaged by established ones.

CHAPTER 5: KNOWING YOUR MIND

1 Laing, R.D. (1975).

2 This is the term used by the German philosopher Alfred Schutz.

See Schutz, A. (1972).

3 Russell, B. (1970).

4 The American psychologist Edward Thorndyke (1874–1949) showed that learning poetry or Latin vocabulary did not improve the memory in general; only the skill of learning poetry or Latin vocabulary.

5 Gardner, H. (1993).

6 Sagan, C. (1978).

7 See also Hall, A. (1999). Deutsch, D. (ed.) (1999).

8 Ellis, P. (1989).

9 See: The Soundbeam website press release: "New sounds from Sunderland" www.soundbeam.co.uk/news/news-sunderland.html. Dr Ellis's research led to an award for his work and to the establishment of a Sound Therapy Centre in Sunderland.

10 With acknowledgement to "Derek Paravincini's extrordinary gift" 60 Minutes. A profile by Lesley Stahl. See https://goo.gl/sBrG. See also: Ockelford, A. (2007).

11 Savants' abilities, though exceptional, seem highly localized. How does this square with my argument about the interactive nature of intelligence? There is still a dynamic process between different capacities in the mind of the savants. But in these cases it is between very high and often very low abilities in different areas of intelligence.

12 Lichtman, J. (2009). Reproduced with the kind permission of J.W. Lichtman, MD, PhD.

13 Half the problem is the way they are taught, of course. The best way to learn French is to go to France and have to speak it all day with French people. The worst way is to speak it for a few minutes a week with an English person who doesn't speak it properly. This is exactly how I tried to do it. Learning a language in 30-minute periods at school is something like trying to learn to swim on dry land. It would be like balancing children on desks for 30 minutes a week miming the breast stroke and promising them that if they get the hang of it in three years' time they will be put into water. We know how they would get on.

14 Greenfield, S. (1997).

15 Referrals to The Academy were made by a range of agencies, including the Bradford Youth Offending Team (YOT) and Nacro (National Association for the Care and Resettlement of Offenders), who referred young people on Intensive Surveillance and Supervision Programmes (ISSPs) or other community orders. Some referrals also came from school exclusion units. The participants who completed the program successfully received a Certificate in Practical Performance Skills (Dance), accredited by Trinity College, London. Each individual built their own portfolio and gained module credits as they progressed through the program. They could also work towards a Young People's Arts Award at Bronze level. The Academy, with its partners, was committed to finding routes back into education and employment for its participants. It set out to help young people acquire the kinds of transferable skills that would help them in the world of work. Those who wanted to continue their dance training and their links with Dance United could join the weekly youth dance group or the emergent graduate performing dance company. All graduates were offered regular contact and tutorials with Academy staff to support them in whichever path they chose to follow.

16 The quotations in this section are from *The Academy*, a film by Dan Williams and Andrew Coggins. Further details on www.dance-united.com.

CHAPTER 6: BEING CREATIVE

1 Langer, S. (1951).

2 Our sense of reality is not only a function of social convention. There is a difference between saying that social factors influence knowledge and that social factors determine knowledge. The fact that we distinguish in our culture between

cats and dogs may be due to certain social conditions. The fact that we can distinguish between them "has something to do with cats and dogs." Lawton, D (1975). Any person's mental model will contain some images that approximate closely to reality, along with others that are distorted or inaccurate. But for the person to function, the model must bear some overall resemblance to reality: "Every reproduction of the external world, constructed and used as a guide to action must, in some degree, correspond to that reality. Otherwise the society could not have maintained itself; its members, if acting in accordance with totally untrue propositions, would not have succeeded in making even the simplest tools and in securing therewith food and shelter from the outside world."

3 See Miller, D.L. (1973).

4 In developing this example, I am grateful for the advice of Barrie Wiggham, formerly of the Hong Kong Government and Hong Kong's Representative in Washington.

5 Polanyi, M. (1969).

6 From a filmed interview with Richard Feynman, reprinted with permission of Melanie Jackson Agency, LLC. Available in the Masters of Science series from the Vega Trust: www.vega.org.uk. The Vega Trust was established to promote and deepen public understanding of the processes and excitement of science. One of its leading figures was the distinguished chemist and Nobel laureate, Professor Sir Harry Kroto.

7 Kelly, G. (1963).

8 This is the case even when the actual outcomes are unexpected or unintentional.

9 Polanyi, M. op cit.

10 A notorious example is Carl André, the sculptor who displayed a pile of bricks in London's Tate Gallery and drew the outrage of every popular journalist.

11 Koestler, A. (1975).

12 www.edwarddebono.com

13 William J.J. Gordon and George M. Prince were the co-founders of Synecticsworld (www.synecticsworld.com). Synectics theory is based on three assumptions:

- Creative output increases when creative people become aware of the psychological processes that control their behavior.
- The emotional component of creative behavior is more important than the intellectual component; the irrational is more important than the intellectual component.
- The emotional and irrational components must be understood and used as precision tools in order to increase creative output.

14 I'm grateful to John Haycraft, the distinguished English auctioneer and valuer, for helpful background information and advice.

CHAPTER 7: FEELING BETTER

1 Actually it isn't. I invented Dombey to save the blushes of the student and of the real town.
2 The exile of feeling is obvious in everyday language. Arguments are often dismissed for being only "value judgments" or "merely subjective." It is hard to imagine any argument being dismissed as "merely objective."
3 Quoted in Abbs, P. (1979).
4 Siroka, R.W. *et al.* (1971).
5 Marx and Maslow would argue that the economic prosperity of the times provided the material comfort for this sort of introspection. Herbert Read would have seen it as a response to the dehumanization of society brought on by industrialism. Certainly people finding themselves removed from the products of their own labor, exposed to ever-widening horizons through the new media, and whose roots in community life are loosened by massive social upheaval, are more likely than their

parents or grandparents to feel a loss of identity and personal significance.

6 Frankl, V. (1970).

7 Jung, C.G. (1933).

8 Goleman, D. (1996).

9 Ibid.

10 In Hemming, J. (1980).

11 It is commonly said that the literal meaning of education is to draw out, from the Latin word *educo*. The more common Latin word for drawing out is *educere*, a third conjugation verb, which gives us the English words "educe" and "eduction." But education derives from *educare*, a first conjugation verb meaning to bring up or educate. So this doesn't really help.

12 Board of Education, (1932).

13 In the early 1970s, Robert Witkin, a British sociologist, published a book looking at the creative processes of the arts. He called it *The Intelligence of Feeling* (Witkin, R., 1974). He develops, in a different way, some of the themes that are elaborated in Goleman, D. (1996).

14 In certain cases, emotional states have physical causes, as in some forms of depression or through the metabolic changes associated with illness.

15 Goleman, D. op cit.

16 In the modern world, science came to be seen as the largely unquestioned source of authoritative knowledge. Scientific methods enjoy the claim of being factually true "... even if they are in no way demonstrable, even if they must be taken on faith, even if they tend to answer what are, after all unanswerable questions. Scientific methods have the great advantage in this self-conscious society of not appearing as myths at all but as truth, verified by the inscrutable methods of the scientist." – Carey, J.W. (1967).

17 Simon, B. (1978).

18 Polanyi, M. (1969).

19 Descartes, R. (1968).
20 Pivcevic, E. (1970).
21 Popper, K. (1969).
22 Forster, E.M. (1974).
23 Grotowski, J. (1975).
24 Reid, L.A. (1980).

CHAPTER 8: YOU ARE NOT ALONE

1 The complexities of cultural identity are explored in many fields: in social history, sociology, culture, anthropology and in cultural studies. The long revolutions, as Raymond Williams (1966) has called them, in industry and democracy are also enmeshed in a broader revolution in social values, which is, in turn, being interpreted and "indeed fought out in very complex ways in the world of art and ideas."

2 Benjamin, W. (1980).

3 Toffler, A. (1970).

4 He continues: "The pleasure lies not in watching the play develop in a straight line but in the parodies, the lifelike contradictions, the surprises possible within the worldview of the play … When the rules are broken audaciously we are delighted as when (a tennis player) throws his racket at the umpire. But the success of these effects rests on our pleasure in seeing conventions smashed." – Robinson, K. (ed.) (1980).

5 Williams, R. op cit.

6 Polanyi, M. op cit.

7 Geertz, C. (1975).

8 Department for Education and Employment (1999). For a fascinating discussion of the growing links between the arts and sciences, see Ede, S. (2000).

9 The idea of modernism fired intellectual energies to the late 1960s. They were gradually replaced by new ways of thinking that came to be grouped under a general heading of postmodernism.

10 The ideas that underpinned the growth of the scientific method were not invented in the fifteenth century. They date back
to the ancient Greeks and beyond. They found a new reso-
nance in the fifteenth century and later because of contemporary cultural conditions. The applications of these ideas interacted with the development of new technologies, which they
had also helped to make possible. In turn, these created new
opportunities for the development and application of scientific ideas.

CHAPTER 9: BEING A CREATIVE LEADER

1 Amabile, T.M., *et al.* (1996).
2 Both Total Quality Management and Six Sigma strategy are
systems of quality control devised to reduce errors that occur
during the manufacturing and supply chain process.
3 "What Your Disaffected Workers Cost," *Gallup Management
Journal*, 15 March 2001.
4 For a comprehensive survey of the development of creativity
testing, see Sternberg, R.J. (1999).
5 Quoted in Alliance of Artists' Communities (1996).
6 Taylor, W.C. and La Barre, P. (2006).
7 For some people, one of the most powerful forms of development can be taking on new roles that stretch their existing expertise into different areas of responsibility. Yet, according to
one study, only 10% of 200 executives surveyed said that their
company uses new job assignments as a lever for professional
development, whilst 42% have never made cross-functional
moves, 40% have never worked in an unfamiliar business unit,
34% have never held positions with responsibility and 66%
say they have never had a leadership role in starting a new
business.
8 Chambers, E. *et al.* (1998).
9 Department of Trade and Industry (2000).
10 https://goo.gl/gLpq

11 Brown, T. (2009).
12 Quoted in Alliance of Artists' Communities (1996).
13 Newsweek, 04.06.10.
14 Harvey-Jones, J. (2003).
15 These comments are from a personal interview.
16 Handy, C. (2016).

CHAPTER 10: LEARNING TO BE CREATIVE

1 Brook, P. (1995) *The Empty Space*, Touchstone, p. 9.
2 Washor, E. and Mojowski, C. (2013). See also www.bigpicture.org
3 Ibid.
4 The Open University: www.open.ac.uk
5 www.nylc.org
6 www.room13scotland.com. See also Adams, J. (2005).
7 www.elsistemausa.org
8 Department for Education and Employment (1999).
9 www.izonenyc.org/initiatives/school-of-one
10 Kelley, P. (2007).
11 www.sudval.org
12 For a powerful exposition of the principles and practice of democratic schools, see Hecht, Y. (2011).
13 Eisner, E. (1996).
14 www.p21.org
15 www.ccsso.org
16 www.wholeeducation.org
17 Bourdieu, P. (1971).
18 Kelley, P. (2007).
19 Eisner, E. op cit.
20 Charter schools receive public money but are not subject to some of the rules, regulations and statutes that apply to other public schools. They do have to meet agreed terms of accountability, which are made explicit in each school's charter. Charter schools provide an alternative to other public schools, but

legally they are part of the public education system and are not allowed to charge tuition.

21 Un-schooling is a range of philosophies and practices centered on allowing children to learn through self-directed play, household responsibilities and work experience rather than through a formal school curriculum.

22 The Blue Man quotes are all from a short video that they recorded and made for my use. Reproduced with permission.

REFERENCES

Abbs, P. (1979) "Education and the Expressive Disciplines," *Tract* 25, The Gryphon Press.

Adams, J. (2005) "Room 13 and the Contemporary Practice of Artist-Learners," *Studies in Art Education* 47 (1), 23–33.

Alliance for Excellent Education (2009) "High School Dropouts in America," Fact Sheet, updated February.

Alliance of Artists' Communities (1996) *American Creativity at Risk: Restoring Creativity as a Priority in Public Policy, Cultural Philanthropy and Education*, Report on Symposium, November 8–10. Available from 225 South Main St, Providence, Rhode Island, RI 02903.

Amabile, T.M., Conti, R., Coon, H. *et al.* (1996) "Assessing the Work Environment for Creativity," *Academy of Management Review* 39 (5), 1154–1184.

Bajer, J. (1999) "The Paradox of the Talents," in *People Management Magazine*, December.

Barber, M. and Mourshed, M. (2007) *How the World's Best Education Systems Come Out On Top*, McKinsey Education, London.

Benjamin, W. (1980) *Illuminations*, Fontana, London.

Board of Education (1932) *Report on Primary Schools*, HMSO, London.

Boden, M. (1994) *The Creative Mind*, Abacus, London.

Bourdieu, P. (1971) "Systems of Education and Systems of Thought," in Young, M.F.D. (ed.) *Knowledge and Control*, Collier MacMillan, London.

Britton, J. (1972) *Language and Learning*, Penguin Books, Harmondsworth.

Britton, J. *et al.* (1975) *The Development of Writing Abilities: 11–18*, Macmillan Education, London.

Brook, P. (1995) *The Empty Space*, Touchstone, New York.

Brown, T. (2009) *Change by Design*, Harper Business, New York.

Carey, J.W. (1967) *The Antioch Review*, XXXVII, Yellow Springs, Ohio.

Chambers, E. *et al.* (1998) "The War for Talent," *McKinsey Quarterly* 3, 44–57.

Davis, R. (1967) *The Grammar School*, Penguin Books, Harmondsworth.

Department for Culture, Media and Sport (1998) *Creative Industries Mapping Exercise*, DCMS, London.

Department for Education and Employment (1999) *All Our Futures: Creativity, Culture and Education*, HMSO, London.

Department for Education and Employment (2000) *Skills for All: Proposals for a National Skills Agenda*, DfEE Publications, London.

Department of Trade and Industry (2000) *The Future of Corporate Learning*, HMSO, London.

Descartes, R. (1968) *A Discourse on Method*, transl. Sutcliffe, F.E., Penguin Books, Harmondsworth.

Deutsch, D. (ed.) (1999) *The Psychology of Music*, 2nd Edition, Academic Press, San Diego.

Diamond, J. (2006) *Collapse*, Penguin Books, London.

Ede, S. (2000) *Strange and Charmed*, Calouste Gulbenkian Foundation, London.

Editorial (2001) "What Your Disaffected Workers Cost," *Gallup Management Journal*, 15 March 2001.

Education for All (2010) *Reaching the Marginalized*, January.

Eisner, E. (1996) *Cognition and Curriculum Reconsidered*, Paul Chapman Publishing, London.

Ellis, P. (1989) *Touching Sound – Connections on a Creative Spiral*, in *Education and Computing* 5, Issues 1–2, 127–132, Elsevier B.V., Oxford.

Farrell, D. and Grant, A. J. (2008) "China's Looming Talent Shortage," *The McKinsey Quarterly* **1**.

Feynman, R. filmed interview in the 'Masters of Science series', The Vega Trust, CPES, University of Sussex, BN1 9QJ. www .vega.org.uk

Florida, R. (2002) *The Rise of the Creative Class*, Basic Books, New York.

Forster, E.M. (1974) *Two Cheers for Democracy*, Penguin Books, Harmondsworth.

Frankl, V. (1970) *Psychotherapy and Existentialism*, Souvenir Press, London.

Friedman, T.L. (2007) *The World is Flat 3.0: A Brief History of the Twenty First Century*, Picador, London.

Friedman, T.L. (2009) "The New Untouchables," *New York Times*, October 21.

Gardner, H. (1993) *Frames of Mind: The Theory of Multiple Intelligences*, Fontana, London.

Geertz, C. (1975) *The Interpretation of Cultures*, Chicago University Press, Chicago.

Goleman, D. (1996) *Emotional Intelligence*, Bloomsbury, London.

Gould, S.J. (1996) *The Mismeasure of Man*, W.W. Norton & Co., New York.

Greenfield, S. (1997) *The Human Brain: A Guided Tour*, Weidenfeld & Nicolson, London.

Grotowski, J. (1975) *Towards a Poor Theatre*, Methuen, London.

Gutek, G.L. (1972) *A History of the Western Educational Experience*, 2nd Edition, Waveland Press, Prospect Heights.

Guthridge, M., Lawson, E. and Komm, A. (2008) "Making Talent a Strategic Priority," *McKinsey Quarterly* **1**.

Hall, A. (1999) "Speaking in Tones," *Scientific American*, November 1.

Handy, C. (2016) *The Second Curve: Thoughts on Reinventing Society*, Random House Business, London.

Harvey-Jones, J. (2003) *Make it Happen: Reflections on Leadership*, Profile Books, London.

Haydn, T. (2010) "Behaviour Now – The Classroom – How Good is Discipline Today?" Analysis, *TES Connect*, June 18.

Hecht, Y. (2011) *Democratic Education: A Beginning of a Story*, Alternative Education Resource Organization, Israel.

Hemming, J. (1980) *The Betrayal of Youth*, Marion Boyars, London.

Hernstein, R. and Murray, C. (1996) *The Bell Curve: Intelligence and Class Structure in American Life*, Simon & Schuster, New York.

Hilty, L. (2009) "What Does it Cost to Educate a Child," *Journal-News*, October 5, Ohio, USA.

Husserl, E. (1970) *Logical Investigations*, Routledge and Kegan Paul, London.

International Labour Organisation (2010) *ILO Global Employment Trends for Youth 2010*, ILO, Geneva.

Jay, R. (2000) *The Ultimate Book of Business Creativity*, Capstone Publishing, Oxford.

Joint Council for Education Through Art (1957) *A Consideration of Humanity, Technology and Education in Our Time*, Report of the Conference at the Royal Festival Hall, London, April 22–27, 1957.

Jung, C.G. (1933) *Modern Man in Search of a Soul*, Routledge and Kegan Paul, London.

Kelley, P. (2007) *Making Minds: What's Wrong with Education and What Should We Do About It?* Routledge, London.

Kelly, G.A. (1963) *A Theory of Personality: The Psychology of Personal Constructs*, W. W. Norton & Co., New York.

Koestler, A. (1975) *The Act of Creation*, Picador, London.

Kuhn, T.S. (1970) *The Structure of Scientific Revolutions*, Chicago University Press, Chicago.

Kurzweil, R. (1999) "The Coming Merging of Mind and Machine," *Scientific American* **10** (3), 56–61.

Kurzweil, R. (2006) *The Singularity is Near: When Humans Transcend Biology*, Penguin, New York.

Laing, R.D. (1975) *The Divided Self*, Penguin Books, Harmondsworth.

Langer, S. (1951) *Philosophy in a New Key*, New American Library, New York.

Lawton, D. (1975) *Class, Culture and Curriculum*, Routledge and Kegan Paul, London.

Lehrer, J. (2007) Hearts and Minds, *The Boston Globe* 29 April. https://goo.gl/YS22WR

Levitas, M. (1974) *Marxist Perspectives in the Sociology of Education*, Routledge and Kegan Paul, London.

Lichtman, J. (2009) "Neuroscience: Making Connections," *Nature-News*, January, *Nature* 457, 524–527.

MacKenzie, D.A. (1981) *Statistics in Britain, 1865–1930: The Social Construction of Scientific Knowledge*, Edinburgh University Press, Edinburgh.

MacRae, H. "The World in 2010," unpublished seminar paper.

McKinsey Education (2009) *Shaping the Future: How Good Education Systems Can Become Great in the Decade Ahead*, Report of The International Education Roundtable, July 7, 2009, Singapore.

McMurrer, J. (2007) *Choices, Changes, and Challenges: Curriculum and Instruction in the NCLB Era*. A report published by the Center on Education Policy, Washington, DC.

Mental Health Foundation (1999) *The Big Picture*, The Mental Health Foundation, London.

Michaels, E. and Handfield-Jones, H. (2001) *The War for Talent*, Harvard Business Review Press, Cambridge.

Miller, A.I. (1996) *Insights of Genius: Imagery and Creativity in Art and Science*, Springer-Verlag, New York.

Miller, D.L. (1973) *George Herbert Mead: Mind, Self, Language and the World*, Texas University Press, Texas.

O'Connor, R. and Sheehy, N. (2000) *Understanding Suicidal Behaviour*, Wiley-Blackwell, London.

Ockelford, A. (2007) *In The Key of Genius*, Hutchinson, London.

Ostman, C. (1998) "Techno Marvels in the Making," *Magical Blend* magazine 47, October.

Peters, T. and Waterman, R.H. (1982) *In Search of Excellence*, Harper & Row, New York.

Pivcevic, E. (1970) *Husserl and Phenomenology*, Hutchinson University Library, London.

Polanyi, M. (1969) *Personal Knowledge*, Routledge and Kegan Paul, London.

Popper, K. (1969) *Conjectures and Refutations: The Growth of Scientific Knowledge*, Routledge and Kegan Paul, London.

Prensky, M. (2001) "Digital Natives, Digital Immigrants," *On the Horizon* **9**, No. 5, NCB University Press, October.

Rada, J.F. (1994) "The Metamorphosis of the Word: Libraries With a Future," Fifth Mortenson Memorial Lecture, University of Illinois, Urbana Champaign, October 7. Unpublished.

Reid, L.A. (1980) *Yesterday's Today: A Journey into Philosophy*, unpublished autobiography.

Richardson, K. (1999) *The Making of Intelligence*, Phoenix, London.

Robinson, K. (ed.) (1980) *Exploring Theatre and Education*, Heinemann, London.

Robinson, K. (1992) *Arts Education in Europe: A Survey*, Council of Europe, Strasbourg.

Robinson, K. (2009) *The Element: How Finding your Passion Changes Everything*, Viking Penguin, New York.

Robinson, K. (2013) *Finding Your Element: How to Discover Your Talents and Passions and Transform Your Life*, Viking Penguin, New York.

Robinson, K. (2015) *Creative Schools: Revolutionising Education from the Ground Up*, Allen Lane, London.

Rogers, C. (1969) *Freedom to Learn*, Merrill, New York.

Russell, B. (1970) *The Problems of Philosophy*, Oxford University Press, Oxford.

Sagan, C. (1978) *The Dragons of Eden*, Coronet, London.

Schutz, A. (1972) *The Phenomenology of the Social World*, Heinemann, London.

Scott, P. (1997) *The Meanings of Mass Higher Education*, Open University Press, Bristol.

Simon, B. (1978) *Intelligence, Psychology, Education*, Lawrence Wishart, London.

Siroka, R.W. *et al.* (eds) (1971) *Sensitivity Training and Group Encounter*, Grosset & Dunlop, New York.

Sternberg, R.J. (1999) *The Handbook of Creativity*, Cambridge University Press, Cambridge.

Taylor, W.C. and LaBarre, P. (2006) "How Pixar Adds a New School of Thought to Disney," *New York Times*, January 29.

Tiner, J.H. (1975) *Isaac Newton: Inventor, Scientist and Teacher*. Mott Media, Milford, Michigan.

Toffler, A. (1970) *Future Shock*, Random House, New York.

United Nations (2006) *World Population Prospects: 2006 Summary*, United Nations.

Washor, E. and Mojowski, C. (2013) *Leaving to Learn: How Out-of-School Learning Increases Student Engagement and Reduces Dropout Rates*, Heinemann, Portsmouth.

Williams, R. (1966) *The Long Revolution*, Penguin Books, Harmondsworth.

Witkin, R. (1974) *The Intelligence of Feeling*, Heinemann, London.

Yeats, W.B. (1978) *Collected Poems*, Macmillan, London.

INDEX